The Letter to the Romans

McMaster Divinity College Press
McMaster New Testament Studies Series, Volume 7

Patterns of Discipleship in the New Testament (1996)

The Road from Damascus: The Impact of Paul's Conversion on His Life, Thought and Ministry (1997)

Life in the Face of Death: The Resurrection Message of the New Testament (1998)

The Challenge of Jesus' Parables (2000)

Into God's Presence: Prayer in the New Testament (2001)

Reading the Gospels Today (2004)

Contours of Christology in the New Testament (2005)

Hearing the Old Testament in the New Testament (2006)

The Messiah in the Old and New Testaments (2007)

Translating the New Testament: Text, Translation, Theology (2009)

Christian Mission: Old Testament Foundations and New Testament Developments (2010)

Empire in the New Testament (2011)

The Church, Then and Now (2012)

Rejection: God's Refugees in Biblical and Contemporary Perspective (2015)

Rediscovering Worship: Past, Present, and Future (2015)

The Bible and Social Justice: Old Testament and New Testament Foundations for the Church's Urgent Call (2015)

The Letter to the Romans

Exegesis and Application

edited by

STANLEY E. PORTER

and

FRANCIS G. H. PANG

◆PICKWICK *Publications* • Eugene, Oregon

THE LETTER TO THE ROMANS
Exegesis and Application

McMaster New Testament Studies Series, Volume 7
McMaster Divinity College Press

Copyright © 2018 Wipf and Stock Publishers. All rights reserved. Except for brief quotations in critical publications or reviews, no part of this book may be reproduced in any manner without prior written permission from the publisher. Write: Permissions. Wipf and Stock Publishers, 199 W. 8th Ave., Suite 3, Eugene, OR 97401.

Pickwick Publications
An Imprint of Wipf and Stock Publishers
199 W. 8th Ave., Suite 3
Eugene, OR 97401

McMaster Divinity College Press
1280 Main St. W.
Hamilton, ON, Canada
L8S 4K1

www.wipfandstock.com

PAPERBACK ISBN: 978-1-4982-3856-4
HARDCOVER ISBN: 978-1-4982-3858-8
EBOOK ISBN: 978-1-4982-3857-1

Cataloguing-in-Publication data:

Names: Porter, Stanley E., 1956-, editor. | Pang, Francis G. H., editor.

Title: Book title : The letter to the Romans : exegesis and application / edited by Stanley E. Porter and Francis G. H. Pang.

Description: Eugene, OR: Pickwick Publications, 2018. | McMaster New Testament Studies Series 7. | Includes bibliographical references and indexes.

Identifiers: ISBN 978-1-4982-3856-4 (paperback). | ISBN 978-1-4982-3858-8 (hardcover). | ISBN 978-1-4982-3857-1 (epub).

Subjects: LCSH: Bible. Romans—Criticism, interpretation, etc.

Classification: BS2665.52 L 2018 (print). | BS2665.52 (epub).

Manufactured in the U.S.A.   05/18/18

Contents

Preface / vii

Contributors / xi

Abbreviations / xii

The Letter to the Romans: An Introduction / 1
—*Stanley E. Porter and Francis G. H. Pang*

1   There Is No Longer Any Place for Me in These Regions: The Historical Setting of Romans / 7
—*Christopher D. Land*

2   "I Have Written You Quite Boldly on Some Points": The Register and Structure of Romans / 45
—*Stanley E. Porter*

3   Deliverance and Demographics: The Pastoral Riches of "Romans Righteousness" (Romans 1–4) / 65
—*Robert W. Yarbrough*

4   Changing Allegiance: Set Free and Spirit-led (Romans 5–8) / 80
—*Cynthia Long Westfall*

5   What Is the Future of Israel in Romans 9–11? / 115
—*August H. Konkel*

6   How Then Shall We Live? (Romans 12:1—15:6) / 128
    —L. L. Belleville

7   The Old Testament and Romans: Interpreting the Scriptures
    Which Instruct and Encourage / 148
    —Mark J. Boda

Index of Modern Authors / 163

Index of Ancient Sources / 167

Preface

THE 2014 H. H. Bingham Colloquium in the New Testament at McMaster Divinity College in Hamilton, Ontario, Canada, held on June 7, was entitled "Romans: A Conference." We realize that Paul's letter to the Romans is not a conference but is the magisterial letter written by the Apostle to the Gentiles that still inspires much deep reflection, but we wished to highlight the fact that this continuously provocative and challenging book was the clear and singular focus of our annual conference. For this publication, we have indicated a shift in emphasis by changing the sub-title to the appropriate areas that we are covering: exegesis and application of Romans. This Colloquium was the eighteenth in a continuing series held here at MDC. This conference continued the format that we use for such conferences, although we continue to innovate in various ways. We were able to invite two scholarly guests to participate in the conference as plenary speakers. They provided a range of helpful perspectives in our examination of Romans. Rather than having a respondent to all or each of the speakers, we had a formal concluding theological chapter that drew together the various theological threads of the conference as they focused on Romans. The bulk of the content of this volume, as at the conference itself, is provided by two sets of papers, followed by the concluding paper.

The first set of papers provides useful background material for understanding Romans. Christopher Land, assistant professor of New Testament and linguistics at MDC, places Romans within the historical context of its significance in critical biblical scholarship. Stanley Porter, president of MDC and professor of New Testament, provides a linguistic introduction to Romans, by describing the kind of language that is used in the book. These two papers comprise the first section of the book, and they lay a necessary foundation for the exegetical essays of the second part.

Preface

The second and largest part of the volume comprises four papers on the exegesis and application of Romans itself. These four papers are designed to introduce the major interpretive contours of the book, set these theological and historical contents in context, and, especially important for this conference, indicate some of the lines of application of the New Testament material. We found it convenient to divide the book of Romans itself into four useful interpretive sections, corresponding with major structural and thematic divisions within the book. The first of these exegetical sections, Rom 1–4, is discussed by Robert Yarbrough, professor of New Testament at Covenant Theological Seminary near St. Louis, Missouri. Bob is a well-known theological interpreter of the Bible who has spent much of his academic career educating biblical exegetes. Bob examines these important four chapters in light of recent discussion of what it means to be united with Christ. He is followed by Cynthia Long Westfall, associate professor of New Testament at MDC, who handles Rom 5–8. Cindy consciously offers comments on the background, content, and application of the major sections of this interpretive unit, arguably forming the theological heart of Paul's letter. The third paper in this section focuses upon Rom 9–11, a highly contentious set of chapters in recent debate, because of the issues of Jewish and Gentile relations. This chapter is appropriately presented by Gus Konkel, professor of Old Testament at MDC, who considers the relationship of Israel, the Jews, and the Gentiles, and provides a nuanced understanding of how these terms are used and understood by Paul. The fourth and final section, Rom 12–15, is treated by L. L. Belleville. Linda Belleville, adjunct associate professor of New Testament at Cornerstone University in Grand Rapids, Michigan, has focused her career upon Pauline interpretation, and so brings much considered thought to her exposition. She notes how this important ethical material is mistakenly underrepresented in the Pauline literature. She attempts to redress this wrong in her treatment of the section.

The third and final part of the volume concludes the previous discussion by examining the use of the Old Testament in Romans and introducing a new set of considerations of the role of Romans in biblical theology. Mark Boda, professor of Old Testament at MDC, offers theological insights into Romans that trace various strands of the book back to their Old Testament origins, and formulates a Pauline biblical theology that provides a coherent and unified picture of Paul's theology, at least in Romans.

Preface

The Bingham Colloquium is named after Dr. Herbert Henry Bingham, who was a noted Baptist leader in Ontario, Canada. His leadership abilities were recognized by Baptists across Canada and around the world. His qualities included his genuine friendship, dedicated leadership, unswerving Christian faith, tireless devotion to duty, insightful service as a preacher and pastor, and visionary direction for congregation and denomination alike. These qualities endeared him both to his own church members and to believers in other denominations. The Colloquium has been endowed by his daughter as an act of appreciation for her father. We are pleased to be able to continue this tradition.

The first volumes of the Bingham Colloquium were published by Eerdmans Publishing, but since 2010 all of the volumes in this series have been published by McMaster Divinity College Press, in conjunction with Wipf & Stock Publishers of Eugene, Oregon. We appreciate this active and continuing publishing relationship.

I finally would like to thank the individual contributors for accepting their assignments and for all their efforts in the preparation and presentation of papers that make a significant contribution of benefit to New Testament scholars, students of the Bible, and believers who wish to understand Paul's letter to the Romans more fully. I would especially like to thank my New Testament colleague, Francis Pang, for working together with me to edit this volume for publication. We would like to thank the staff and student helpers and volunteers at McMaster Divinity College, all of whom were integral in creating a pleasant environment and a supportive atmosphere for the colloquium.

Stanley E. Porter

Contributors

L. L. Belleville, Adjunct Professor of New Testament, Cornerstone University, Grand Rapids, Michigan

Mark J. Boda, Professor of Old Testament, McMaster Divinity College, Hamilton, Ontario

August H. Konkel, Professor of Old Testament, McMaster Divinity College, Hamilton, Ontario

Christopher D. Land, Assistant Professor of New Testament and Linguistics, McMaster Divinity College, Hamilton, Ontario

Francis G. H. Pang, Assistant Professor of New Testament, McMaster Divinity College, Hamilton, Ontario

Stanley E. Porter, President and Dean, Professor of New Testament, Roy A. Hope Chair in Christian Worldview, McMaster Divinity College, Hamilton, Ontario

Cynthia Long Westfall, Associate Professor of New Testament, McMaster Divinity College, Hamilton, Ontario

Robert W. Yarbrough, Professor of New Testament, Covenant Theological Seminary, St. Louis, Missouri

Abbreviations

AB	Anchor Bible
ACCS	Ancient Christian Commentary on Scripture
BECNT	Baker Exegetical Commentary on the New Testament
Bib	*Biblica*
BibInt	*Biblical Interpretation*
CSEL	Corpus Scriptorum Ecclesiasticorum Latinorum
CTL	Cambridge Textbooks in Linguistics
CurBR	*Currents in Biblical Research*
DJD	Discoveries in the Judaean Desert
HHBS	History of Biblical Studies
ICC	International Critical Commentary
Int	*Interpretation*
IVPCS	IVP Commentary Series
JBL	*Journal of Biblical Literature*
JECS	*Journal of Early Christian Studies*
JETS	*Journal of the Evangelical Theological Society*
JGRChJ	*Journal of Greco-Roman Christianity and Judaism*
JSNT	*Journal for the Study of the New Testament*
JSNTSup	Journal for the Study of the New Testament Supplement
LBS	Linguistic Biblical Studies

Abbreviations

NAC	New American Commentary
NICNT	The New International Commentary on the New Testament
NIVAC	The NIV Application Commentary
NovT	*Novum Testamentum*
NovTSup	Supplements to Novum Testamentum
NTS	*New Testament Studies*
PAST	Pauline Studies
PNTC	Pillar New Testament Commentary
PTS	Patristische Texte und Studien
SBG	Studies in Biblical Greek
SBLDS	Society of Biblical Literature Dissertation Series
SP	Sacra Pagina
ST	*Studia Theologica*
SymS	Symposium Series
TDNT	*Theological Dictionary of the New Testament*
WBC	Word Biblical Commentary
WUNT	Wissenschaftliche Untersuchungen zum Neuen Testament
ZNW	*Zeitschrift für die neutestamentliche Wissenschaft und die Kinde der älteren Kirche*

The Letter to the Romans
An Introduction

STANLEY E. PORTER AND FRANCIS G. H. PANG

MANY PEOPLE REGARD PAUL'S letter to the Romans as the most theologically significant book of the Bible. It is certainly the Apostle Paul's most enduring contribution to the New Testament. Written at a time when Paul's ideas and practices were provoking opposition even from fellow Christians, the letter articulates Paul's understanding of God's plan for humanity and discusses the implications of this plan for different groups of people. It stresses that a new way of life should characterize anyone who has placed his or her trust in the Lord Jesus, and it issues an impassioned plea for greater Christian unity and for a more effective and widespread dissemination of the good news about Jesus.

Paul's letter to the Romans was the topic of discussion for the 2014 Bingham Colloquium, an annual conference organized by McMaster Divinity College. We invited two scholars from the United States to join together with members of the biblical studies department of McMaster Divinity College to exchange ideas on the life and theology of the apostle Paul and his letter to the Romans. Most of our Bingham conferences, while designed for broad appeal and lay audiences, are focused upon particular scholarly subjects and often technical matters of discussion and even dispute. For this conference, we tried to do something different. We designed this conference so that all of the papers—but especially those devoted to the content of Romans—were written with both exegesis and application in mind. As a result, readers will notice that there are varying types and degrees of comments throughout especially chapters 3 to 6, as well as in chapter 7, that are addressed in various ways to preachers, teachers, and lay readers (chapters 1 and 2 should also help to answer the kinds of questions that such readers are asking, and be of help to them). We hope that the focus of our comments on the kinds of issues that those studying Romans are confronting will help to bridge the gap between study of Romans as an academic enterprise and the question of how Romans can speak today in the life of the church. All of the contributors to this volume strongly believe that Romans, as does all of Scripture, has a crucial voice within the church and that those who preach, teach, and study the book need to be attentive to its witness and to proclaim it appropriately so that it is usefully applied within the church.

This volume is the testimony of our fruitful and stimulating discussion at the colloquium. There were seven presentations in total and they are arranged into three sections. The first section focuses on the book of Romans as an example of ancient epistolary literature, covering the historical setting, purpose of writing, structure, and register of the letter. The middle section deals with the content of the letter, dividing the letter into four major sections. The last section covers the theology of Romans by putting the letter in biblical theological perspective, providing a fitting conclusion to the volume.

The volume starts with a contribution by Christopher Land regarding the historical setting of Romans. He revisits the influential nineteenth-century German scholar F. C. Baur's well-worn hypothesis regarding the development of the early church. Baur insisted that the expansion of early Christianity involved ongoing tensions between the Apostles Paul and Peter. Acknowledging the many problems with Baur's historical reconstruction, Land argues that Baur's hypothesis nevertheless remains, in its most basic form, "a simple and compelling explanation of the tension and conflict" (10) in Paul's letters. Land goes on to argue, however, that the conflict was not so much theological, but sociological. After examining a few key incidents between Paul and other Christian Jews (in Jerusalem, Antioch, Galatia, and Corinth), Land argues that the disagreements chiefly pertained to purity and to the visible segregation of Jews and non-Jews. Paul's concerns in writing Romans thus include his strong and abiding desire to produce unity within and among both Jewish and non-Jewish Christians. As a result of this reconstruction of the historical setting, he suggests that Romans should not be read simply as a manifesto of Paul's view of salvation, but as a call to broaden the definition of God's people so as to include both Jews and Gentiles.

Stanley Porter's chapter opens with a brief introduction to the understanding of linguistic register found in Systemic Functional Linguistics. He contends that by exploring the register of Paul's letter, we can come closer to the organization and structure of the work, and thus come closer to understanding its purpose. The analysis of the register of Romans consists of three major elements: field, tenor, and mode of discourse. An adequate examination of the field of discourse of Romans shows that it is not a letter simply about justification, but about how various "agents, especially divine agents, are involved in actions in relation to humanity" (60), in other words, more than simply justification. Porter also contends that the analysis of tenor can move scholarly discussions regarding the audience of Romans in a more productive and fruitful direction. And finally, in terms of the mode of discourse, Porter argues that the letter form is used, not as a substitute for the personal presence of Paul, but to accomplish his purpose in ways not as easily accomplished by another written form. In conclusion, Porter summarizes Paul's argument as one that progressively moves from the human sinful condition to justification to reconciliation to sanctification and salvation. It does this by means of a dialogical interaction that frames the discussion between the authorial voice and the audience, even though it often involves others. This is conveyed in written form meant to be read out, and even to be read again by others, whether aloud or not.

The second section of this volume consists of four chapters that each focus on a specific section of Romans, concentrating upon their exegesis and application. The book of Romans is divided into four exegetical sections. The first is concerned with Rom 1–4, the second with Rom 5–8, the third with Rom 9–11, and the fourth with Rom 12–15. The reasons for this division will be obvious from the chapters themselves.

Robert Yarbrough's chapter opens the group of four exegesis and application chapters with a discussion of Rom 1–4. He starts off by questioning whether salvation is at the core of the message of the opening chapters of Romans. Surveying some work on Romans, Yarbrough observes three trends in recent discussion of salvation in Rom 1–4. First, whereas modern interpreters question whether Romans is about personal salvation, salvation is front and center in discussions of patristic interpreters. Second, a recent trend in Pauline studies is the rise of the "union with Christ" discussion. Yarbrough considers the recent upsurge of attention to this topic as a possible signal of the end of scholarly obsession with the discussion of justification and righteousness in Paul. Finally, recent Romans commentaries suggest that the scholarly community has finally chosen to turn away from the seemingly never-ending argument regarding the so-called New Perspective on Paul and justification and begun to rediscover the comprehensiveness of theological riches in Romans. Yarbrough concludes his chapter by including important comments on pastoral implications for the church at both local and global levels.

Cynthia Long Westfall opens her chapter with a lament that Rom 5–8 has often been treated as a theological treatise rather than as what it really is, part of a letter written by Paul to a particular first-century church. Westfall's chapter is a call for exegetes, preachers, and teachers to interpret Rom 5–8 in its original literary, historical, and cultural context, that is, to understand "its words and phrases through how Paul uses them in the text of Romans and through the context of the language and culture" (96 n. 1). For each biblical chapter, Westfall offers a brief but careful examination of the background of the text. This is followed by a discussion of the core message of the section and by useful homiletic and pedagogical insights. Westfall argues that the change Paul attempts to persuade his Romans addressees to make is not only in thought but in behavior and commitment. She further argues that the vision Paul has for his readers in Rom 5–8 is a radical change in allegiance "from sin and death to righteousness with the appropriate life and service that it entails" in response to God's gracious work and free gift in Christ (97).

August Konkel considers Paul's rhetorical strategy in Rom 9–11 as something similar to the Latin *argumentum*. According to him, what Paul tries to do in Rom 9–11 is to provide a defense of the mystery of the gospel, that the gospel was for the nations. This understanding of the gospel, however, creates a tension with the promises of God to Israel: a tension between the good news to the nations and the promises of God to Israel, and a tension between Jewish unbelief and Gentile belief. Konkel distinguishes three interrelated references of the term *Israel* in Rom 9–11: Israel as an ethnic group, Israel as the faithful remnant, and Israel as Abraham's spiritual descendants. Other terms, such as *Jew* or *Israelite*, refer to an ethnic identity and a particular relationship with the law. Konkel argues that by clearly distinguishing Paul's uses of the terms, one can answer the three questions posed concerning Israel in Rom 9–11: Has the word of God failed (9:6–29)? How did the Gentiles attain righteousness while Israel failed (9:30—10:21)?

Can God reject his people (11:1–24)? Konkel concludes by arguing that, for Paul, the salvation of Israel is not a political act but an act of redemption. The final saving act of Israel as a nation collectively is an eschatological event, associated with the coming of Christ, "in which Israel will receive mercy by the mercy that has been shown to the Gentiles" (150). This is the great mystery of Rom 9–11.

Linda Belleville's chapter on Rom 12–15 rounds off the second group of papers of this volume. Belleville expresses her surprise at the lack of attention paid to Rom 12–15 in recent scholarly works on New Testament and Pauline ethics. She laments that "Paul's ethical teachings in Romans do not appear to be a high priority in scholarly circles" (154). After offering a few possible explanations for this lack of attention, she sets out to fill this scholarly lacuna by offering a detailed study of Rom 12–15. She contends that the opening verses of the section (12:1–2) can be seen as a transitional statement from matters of "the mind" to matters of "the life." She argues that the focus of the rest of the letter pertains to what this opening moral imperative of a renewed mind looks like in everyday life.

In the final section and final chapter of the volume, Mark Boda examines the use of the Old Testament in Romans and offers a reflection on its theological and hermeneutical implications for modern interpreters of Romans. He starts off by highlighting the written as well as the oral characters of the Old Testament quotations and allusions in Romans. Examining the Old Testament text in Romans, Boda emphasizes the diversity displayed in every aspect of the analysis. One can find diversity in the material used (canonical units, text-types, and sources), the methods of connection (citation, allusion, typology, etc.), and the ways Paul relates the Old Testament to his letter (continuity, discontinuity, re-actualization, etc.). Boda also points out that there are certain core theological values that function as binding agents between the Old Testament and Romans. He concludes his chapter by commenting on the biblical theological implications for our own reading of Romans and the Old Testament. He argues that an examination of Paul's use of Scripture in Romans, on the one hand, provides insights for modern readers into the use of the Old Testament for their own exegesis of Romans, and, on the other, guides us in our own biblical theological reflection on the Old Testament.

In this volume, we examine Romans through the eyes of a group of scholars, each of whom has attempted to shed some new light on the letter of Romans itself, the controversies that surround its interpretation, and some possible practical understandings for further interpretation and application. Whatever one's current perspective on Paul, we are confident that this volume will offer a clearer sense of his theology and mission as well as a greater confidence when dealing with his letter to the Romans.

1

There Is No Longer Any Place for Me in These Regions
The Historical Setting of Romans

CHRISTOPHER D. LAND

INTRODUCTION

IT IS AN AXIOM of New Testament scholarship (and a principle of common sense) that context matters for interpretation. While the definition of relevant context and the nature of context's relevance can vary significantly between different text types, most contemporary interpreters of the New Testament perceive the occasional character of Paul's letters and hence appreciate the importance of investigating their social and historical settings. Increasingly, this is even true of the Epistle to the Romans, which has traditionally been treated in ways that ignore or underestimate the extent to which Paul's remarks in the letter are historically situated and hence functional first and foremost in relation to a specific social and historical setting.[1]

In general terms, the Apostle Paul wrote his letter to the Romans within the context of a long-term effort that can be helpfully called a *mission*, provided we scrupulously avoid anachronism and seek to discern how Paul himself regarded his missionary labors. These labors had already

---

1. Since much of this essay is devoted to the Baur hypothesis (the proposal made by the German scholar Ferdinand Christian Baur regarding Christian origins, and in particular the origins of the Pauline letters; see below), it is fitting to note his remarks on this issue: "The origin and aim of the Epistle are generally determined from the purely dogmatic point of view. Scholars have failed to inquire carefully into the historical occasion and the circumstances in the Roman Church on which the Epistle proceeds, and to make these the starting point of their discussions" (Baur, *Paul*, 310).

extended, at the time Romans was written, all the way to what is now modern Greece.² Furthermore, Paul writes in Rom 15:23–24 that, following the delivery of a financial gift to Judea, he intends to make his way, at long last, to Rome—and from there, he hopes, onward to Spain. The Epistle to the Romans must, therefore, be understood within the context of Paul's mission, as a letter sent in advance to readers whom he expects to visit in the course of an increasingly expansive missionary effort.

A great deal of current scholarship is fruitfully exploring the social conditions of Roman society and consequently illuminating our understanding of Paul's earliest readers and the manner in which his letter addresses their specific situation. And indeed, we will fail to understand Romans if we fail to understand the social dynamics that held between Jewish and non-Jewish followers of Jesus within that specific city (and, I hasten to add, between these Christians and various non-Christians, both Jewish and non-Jewish).³ Yet Romans is also conditioned by Paul's own historical circumstances, and these are not at all unrelated to circumstances affecting the Christian communities in Rome. In this essay, therefore, I will focus less on the immediate setting of Rome itself and more on Paul's missionary work in the years leading up to the composition of his Roman letter, drawing primarily from his earlier correspondence.

As the title of my essay suggests, I wish to take as my point of departure Paul's sentiment that there was "no longer any place" for him to work in the regions extending from Jerusalem to Illyricum (Rom 15:23).⁴ This state of affairs is framed quite positively by Paul as the natural consequence of his

---

2. Relative to most New Testament documents, the date and provenance of Romans are uncontroversial. It is agreed that Paul wrote to Rome from Achaia just prior to his arrest in the Jerusalem temple and hence sometime in the late 50s, perhaps c. 56–57 CE. At this point in his life, the Apostle was perhaps around 60 years old (e.g. "He would have been born about the same time as Christ" [Murphy-O'Connor, *Paul*, 9]) and he had been working on the mission field for around two decades.

3. In this essay, I will routinely alternate between the English terms *Jew* and *Judean*, recognizing that the Greek *Ioudaios* is not fully equivalent to either of these terms. See Miller, "Meaning of *Ioudaios*"; Miller, "Ethnicity." Against some recent objections, however (e.g. Eisenbaum, *Not a Christian*), I will persist in using the term *Christian* alongside phrases like *Christ-follower* and *follower of Jesus*. Although we must studiously avoid anachronistic notions about the status of "Christianity" in the first century, the terms *Jew* and *Christian* continue to serve a useful function.

4. Whereas I take this passage as an indication that Paul, amidst ongoing controversy, is setting his sights on further frontier mission work, Baur denies the authenticity of the final two chapter of Romans, viewing them as the work of a later Paulinist. See Baur, *Paul*, 352–65.

pride-worthy service in proclaiming the good news of Christ (15:17–22). The impression we are given as readers is that Paul and his colleagues are on the vanguard of early Christian missionary expansion, pressing into new territories and by implication leaving behind areas already evangelized. We are also left with the strong impression that Paul likes it this way and derives no little satisfaction from being the first to proclaim Christ. In his own words, he aspires to proclaim Christ, but "not where Christ is named," because he has no desire "to build on someone else's foundation" (15:20). Paul, in other words, prefers to work in places where his mission constitutes the first and only manifestation of the good news of Christ—a preference that, however much it may derive from Paul's sense of calling, can hardly be unrelated to his repeated conflicts with other Christian leaders who, arriving after him all around the eastern Mediterranean, sought "to build on someone else's foundation." Contemplating an increasingly crowded Mediterranean mission field within which he has experienced both invigorating success and frustrating controversy, Paul sets his sights on Spain, deciding that the proliferation of other Christian leaders has made it both undesirable and unnecessary for him to continue working where "there is no longer any place for him."

Significantly, within this plan to evangelize Spain, the city of Rome is a mere stop-over. Indeed, there are already non-Jewish people naming Christ in Rome (as is evident from the way that Paul directly addresses them at points) and even Paul himself is already known to people in the city (as is evident from his concluding greetings). All is not well in Rome, however. At least some of the non-Jewish followers of Jesus are manifesting inappropriate attitudes towards Jews (Rom 11) and the community is becoming inhospitable towards Jews with a particular understanding of Jewish table regulations (Rom 14–15).[5] It is also significant that Paul is choosing to go east before heading west. The delivery of a financial gift is the ostensible reason, but there is also evidence that people in Judea are outraged at Paul's mission to the nations (Rom 15:31; cf. Acts 21:17–21). In both Judea and Rome, therefore, Paul is confronting issues that have arisen with respect to matters of Jewish identity. He is anticipating controversy in the east because

---

5. Although alternative interpretations of Rom 14–15 persist in the literature, Barclay rightly observes that "there is also now almost universal consensus that the topics addressed in these chapters concern the practice of the Jewish Torah, especially the rules of *kashrut* concerning 'clean' and 'unclean' food (14:1–2, 14, 20), the honoring of the Sabbath (and Jewish feasts/fasts?; 14:5–6), and (perhaps) Jewish anxieties concerning idol-dedicated wine (14:21)" (Barclay, "Faith and Self-Detachment," 192).

his mission among the nations is allegedly eroding Jewish identity, and he feels it necessary to write to the west that people should not be made to feel unwelcome because of the way they observe Jewish traditions. Within this historical setting, I suggest, Romans functions as an exposition of Paul's views on topics especially pertinent to Jewish identity, with the upshot (according to Paul, at least) being that his gospel does not efface Jewish identity.

At this point, questions immediately arise with regard to Paul's teachings in Romans and how exactly they address the topic of Jewish identity. My assigned task, however, is to sketch the letter's historical setting, and so I will stay away from these pressing questions and focus instead on the mutual suspicion and hostility that arose when other Christian leaders moved into Paul's already-evangelized territories, "proclaiming Christ where he was already named." Perhaps surprisingly, given the way that I have just framed Paul's argument in Romans, I will insist in the remainder of this essay that Baur and his followers got a few key things right and that we would do well not to forget Baur's positive contributions in our zeal to avoid his many errors.[6] Paul's footsteps really were dogged by another mission (of sorts) that originated in Jerusalem and that operated primarily under the oversight of Peter (Gal 2:9), and Paul really was quite hostile towards some of the people associated with this mission. Granted, we cannot fully understand the contours of this missionary debate by framing it as *Judaism vs. something else*—i.e. Baur's "Paulinism" does violence to the historical and sociological realities under consideration. Yet the question "Judaism or something else?" captures something significant about the anxieties and allegations directed at Paul's gospel in Judea. Moreover, it captures something significant about the problematic attitudes emerging among non-Jews in Rome. So even though we cannot summarize Paul's theological message in Romans as "Judaism or something else," neither can we read it in context without noting that this very question hangs over the entire epistle, with the epistle itself being Paul's answer to it.

A CONTROVERSIAL HYPOTHESIS

As a starting point for discussing Paul's having "no longer any place" in the Eastern Mediterranean, I have brought up an old idea, namely, the

---

6. For a recent treatment of Ferdinand Christian Baur and his ongoing influence on the study of early Christianity, see Bauspieß et al., eds., *Baur*. An English alternative is Harris, *Tübingen School*.

Baur hypothesis. Readers well-acquainted with biblical scholarship will know that Ferdinand Christian Baur proposed, back in the nineteenth century, that we must chart the early expansion of Christianity with reference to ongoing tensions within the Jesus movement. In his own words, Baur proposed "that the harmonious relation which is commonly assumed to have existed between the Apostle Paul and the Jewish Christians with the older Apostles at their head, is unhistorical, and that the conflict of the two parties whom we have to recognize upon this field entered more deeply into the life of the early Church than has been hitherto supposed."[7] In simple terms, Baur insisted that there was a sustained conflict between Paul (together with other like-minded individuals) and the rest of the early Jesus movement. Or, taking Gal 2:7 as a point of reference, he envisaged the expansion of early Christianity as involving two expanding missionary efforts, one "to the nations" headed by the Apostle Paul and another "to the circumcision" headed by the Apostle Peter, with the former—although recognized in some sense by the Jerusalem leadership—being a controversial phenomenon with which the Jerusalem leaders and their various representatives had to cope.[8]

Perhaps inevitably, Baur's hypothesis has not continued to enjoy widespread acceptance. It is now frequently cited as an important detail in the history of scholarship, but many authors invoke it simply to critique or dismiss it. This is understandable, given that the hypothesis entailed, for Baur, far more than the simple proposition quoted above. To the extent that Baur tied his hypothesis to some erroneous—or even, by today's standards, reprehensible—ideas, biblical scholars have rightly taken issue with his work.

For starters, Baur advanced his hypothesis not simply as a reconstruction of some key historical events or social developments, but as a description of the emergence of newer and higher forms of religion. In this, his work depends upon Hegel,[9] such that the "Judaism" (or occasionally, "Jewish Christianity") of Jesus' disciples is treated as a *thesis* with respect to

---

7. Baur, *Paul*, v. The basic thesis, albeit with some differences, is first articulated in Baur, "Die Christuspartei."

8. There is no need to discuss here the precise nature of the relationship between the Jerusalem "pillars" and the "Judaizers" in Baur's writings. It should be noted, however, that there are complexities in this regard.

9. In saying this, I do not mean to depict Baur's reconstruction as the mere imposition of Hegelianism onto early Christianity, as this would be an unfair critique and an unhelpful oversimplification. For some discussion, see the sources cited in Lincicum, "Baur's Place," 151 n. 47.

which "Paulinism" constituted an *antithesis*.[10] The former is deemed "particularistic," whereas the latter is deemed a higher form of religion moving in a more "universalistic" direction.[11] Baur's perspective here is perhaps understandable in view of his own particular context, but it is not faithful to Paul's self-perceptions or to the manner in which the Apostle wanted others to perceive his missionary efforts. Indeed, one cannot help but see a latent anti-Semitism in Baur's work, such that even the most sympathetic reader must constantly wince and wish that Baur had expressed his historical reconstruction rather differently. With good reason, few authors today would be willing to speak of Paul's gospel as "the principles of true Christianity as freed from Judaism," and fewer still would endeavor to advance this description of Paul's gospel as one that the Apostle himself might have voiced in the first person![12] Romans 9–11 as a whole, but especially the olive tree image in chapter 11, shows that Paul was not prepared to construe "Christianity" as something separate from (let alone opposed to) "Judaism."[13] Insofar as our aim is to situate Paul within his own historical setting, therefore, we must studiously avoid Baur's way of framing things.

10. It is vital to appreciate that Baur uses the phrases *Judaism* and *Jewish Christian* in such a way that a Jewish Christian is a representative of Judaism, since Baur regards the religion of Jesus' disciples, even in the post-Easter period, as "a mere form of Judaism" (Baur, *Paul*, 3). Thus Paul's gospel stands in opposition to "Judaism," and *on this basis* (according to Baur) Paul opposes "Judeo-Christian opponents" who comprise the "Jewish-Christian party" (ibid., 12). This terminological system enables Baur to make bold assertions, such as: "That Christianity...was the work of the Apostle Paul is undeniably a matter of historical fact" (ibid., 3). The assertion is true in a certain sense—but only because Baur has defined Christianity as Paulinism and then defined Paulinism solely with reference to matters of controversy between Paul and other early followers of Jesus.

11. "In the Epistle to the Romans his task is to remove the last remnants of Jewish particularism, by showing that it is not but a stage, a stepping-stone to the universalism of Christianity" (ibid., 309). For a recent response to the well-worn dichotomy between particularistic and universalistic forms of religion, and for a proposal that is more nuanced, see Runesson, "Particularistic Judaism."

12. See Baur, *Paul*, 122.

13. In fairness, Baur does not view Paul as fully abandoning his Jewish roots in any absolute sense, notwithstanding statements like "what is most characteristic of the Apostle is just his opposition to Judaism" (ibid., 363 n. 1). Rather, we must recall how Baur uses his terms. His Paulinism is most assuredly a development *of* Judaism (a controversial development that was generally opposed and that eventually "took its stand as a new form of religious life and thought, essentially differing from Judaism" [p. 3], but a development out of Judaism nonetheless), with "the great point on which the controversy between Judaism and Paulinism turned" being "the claim of primacy with which the Jewish Christians, as born Jews, confronted the Gentiles and Gentile Christians" (ibid.,

Unfortunately, the problems do not stop here. So strong was Baur's "Judaism vs. Paulinism" framework that he employed it as the filter with which he sifted for reliable evidence. Passages or letters attributed to Paul were rejected as spurious if they failed to conform to Baur's reconstruction of Paulinism. Conversely, the Clementine literature was made to play a crucial role, despite its questionable usefulness as a source for the first century, no doubt because its portrayals could be made to support Baur's claim that there was an entrenched and uncompromising opposition in the first century between Jewish-Christians and Paulinists. In essence, Baur oversimplified the story of early Christianity and then handled the relevant evidence in such a way that it was not permitted to complicate the story.[14] If we are to re-examine his basic hypothesis, we will need to be more subtle in our handling of the key texts.

Alongside these very widely known problems, I note a third way in which Baur failed to adequately work out his hypothesis. Despite his strong criticisms of other scholars who sought to interpret the Pauline corpus in a purely dogmatic fashion, Baur himself persisted in seeking a dogmatic basis for the tensions and conflicts he observed in the historical data.[15] Indeed, Baur tends to treat all points of disagreement as delineating competing forms of religion, with philosophical or dogmatic categories providing

---

319). To say that Paul abandoned Judaism would thus imply that Judaism quite simply *is* the assertion of Jewish primacy within the context of debate over non-Jewish followers of Jesus. But Judaism can hardly be reduced to this, and so Baur's use of terms is not only anachronistic but also unhelpful and counter to Paul's own aims.

14. As Zetterholm notes, "Baur's hypothesis of the evolution of the early church is impressive—but not correct. As in the case of all historic reconstructions, the outcome is entirely dependent on the fundamental assumptions upon which it is based . . . Using the conflict between Judaism and Christianity as the only criterion for dating the texts simply does not work, and Baur's analysis is a fine example of reasoning in a circle: the books of the New Testament are used for reconstructing history, while the historical development at the same time constitutes the basis for forming a judgment for dating the respective text" (Zetterholm, *Approaches*, 40).

15. In one place, Baur writes scathingly of his fellow scholars, observing in their work that "the dogmatic view is not to yield one step to the historical, lest the position of an Epistle such as that to the Romans should be impaired, and the Lutheran forensic process of justification, which it is of such moment to maintain in its integrity, suffer from the shaking of its great buttress" (Baur, *Paul*, 313). Notwithstanding such remarks, scholars continue to point out the striking resemblance between Baur's early catholic "synthesis" (he himself does not characteristically employ this term) and German Lutheranism (e.g. Zetterholm, *Approaches*, 40).

the appropriate means by which to describe these different forms.[16] This suits Baur's idealistic project, but if our goal is a rich and textured historical description, then we must give more consideration to how the historical actors in a conflict understood their own disagreements. Is it not the case that people who are at odds with one another routinely regard themselves as members of a single community with (for the most part) shared ideas and shared goals? And is it not the case that even the most passionate in-group opponents can, given sufficient time and opportunity, allow their shared sense of identity and purpose to motivate innovative compromises? Baur quite rightly insists that Paul is resolute and uncompromising on certain points articulated in his letters, but Baur's idealistic program with its two opposed forms of religion prevents his Paul from pursuing *any* kind of compromise with his so-called "opponents." Thus when signs of compromise appear in the extant evidence, whether in Acts or in portions of the Pauline corpus, Baur consistently attributes them to later Paulinists "who ... had no scruples in letting [their] Apostle make all possible concessions to the Jewish Christians."[17]

Ultimately, then, Baur's presentation of his hypothesis must be rejected as idealistic and over-simplistic, and, at the end of the day, he is just flat-out wrong on a number of things, including his dating of certain key documents, his views on the authorship and integrity of several Pauline texts, and his interpretation of several key passages, to say nothing of his latent anti-Semitism. Without question, no responsible person today could uphold the Baur hypothesis as Baur himself advanced it.

What I am suggesting in this essay—notwithstanding all these valid criticisms—is that Baur's hypothesis remains, in its most basic form, a simple and compelling explanation of the tension and conflict we see in Paul's letters. According to Baur's reconstruction of the first century, "the conflict of the two parties whom we have to recognize upon this field entered more deeply into the life of the early Church than has been hitherto supposed."[18] As a post-Tübingen school scholar, I can no longer preserve Baur's "hitherto," nor can I assert quite as nakedly that the idea of a harmonious relation

---

16. Here again, although a detailed consideration of Baur's writings would reveal the diversity and complexity of his thought, my purposes here are served by an observation of his general tendency.

17. Baur, *Paul*, 356. For Baur, the synthesis of Judaism and Paulinism comes with the writing of the book of Acts, which Baur thought represented a resolution of the great tension by means of a concession on the part of Paulinism.

18. Ibid., v.

between Paul and the other apostles is simply "unhistorical." Still, it does seem to me that there was a significant conflict between Paul and Peter, and even more so between their respective missionary enterprises, with Peter's mission more consistently aligning with the interests of James and the elders in Jerusalem. It also seems to me that the depth and duration of this conflict is still underestimated and under-appreciated in certain ecclesial and academic circles. This is unfortunate for readers of Paul's letter to the Romans, because we cannot fully appreciate what Paul is doing in this letter—or perhaps more importantly, how he goes about doing what he is doing—unless we appreciate that his mission work was both recognized *and* criticized by other leading figures in the Jesus movement, with the criticisms relating mostly to unexpected and undesired consequences for Jewish followers of Jesus resulting from the Pauline mission's successes among non-Jews.

THE HYPOTHESIS RECONSIDERED

A full scholarly re-assessment of the Baur hypothesis is well beyond the scope of the present forum, so my strategy here needs to be more modest: I will examine some key texts that pertain to Paul's interactions with other leaders and missionaries in order to show just how well they cohere with Baur's claim that the story of the early Jesus movement's expansion is essentially a tale of two missions, a front-running mission headed by Paul and a slower but no less expansive mission headed by Peter.[19] Given the scope of this re-assessment and the goals of this volume, I will be somewhat cursory in my handling of scholarly debates and will make no effort to provide full scholarly documentation. I will not presuppose that my readers know Greek. Readers who are interested in a more thorough scholarly treatment will need to look elsewhere.[20]

Although scholars continue to debate the sequence and timing of certain things that are purported to have occurred in Jerusalem and Antioch, interpreters agree in broad terms that Paul's written objections to other Christian leaders, not only in Galatians but also in 1–2 Corinthians, were composed after the meeting recounted in Gal 2:1–10 and after the face-to-face conflict recounted in Gal 2:11–14. In its broadest strokes, therefore, the basic chronology is more or less undisputed: after at least two

---

19. For a fairly recent articulation of something similar to Baur's hypothesis, see Goulder, *St. Paul*.

20. As regards the Corinthian correspondence in particular, see Land, *Integrity*.

meetings involving the so-called "pillars" in Jerusalem (as reported in Gal 1:11—2:10), Paul publicly confronted Peter in Antioch (as reported in Gal 2:11–14),[21] and he later wrote to oppose newly arrived Christian leaders both in Galatia (as evidenced by Galatians) and in Corinth (as evidenced by 1–2 Corinthians). Accordingly, in my reconsideration of Baur's hypothesis, I will follow a trajectory from Jerusalem, to Antioch, to Galatia, and then to Corinth.

Jerusalem

For evidence regarding Paul's interactions with Christian leaders in Jerusalem, we must begin by looking at his remarks in Gal 1–2. These remarks, it should be noted, are hardly a detached and objective historical recounting, and so everything Paul says must be treated as a conscious effort to win over his readers. In its basic form, Gal 1–2 raises questions about deviations from a received gospel (1:6–9) and then jumps immediately (1:10) into questions about people-pleasing (i.e. does Paul obediently serve Christ, or does he desire to please people?). The narrative then reveals that Paul's knowledge of the gospel and his calling to mission work originated with Jesus Christ independently of Jesus' disciples (1:11–17). It vehemently insists that Paul is in fact personally acquainted with Peter, despite Paul's being personally unknown to most Christians in Judea (1:18–24).[22] It reports that he and Barnabas stood firm together with Peter, James, and John in the face of an internal controversy over the circumcision of non-Jews that erupted on account of some "false brothers" (2:1–10). Finally, it reports that Paul publicly rebuked Peter in Antioch because his behavior was (according to Paul's view of things) no longer what one would expect from a "pillar" but rather the fearful behavior of a man seeking not to upset "the circumcision people" (2:11–14).

---

21. See, e.g., Manson, *Studies in the Gospels and Epistles*, 171: "Any reconstruction of events which involves tampering with the order in Gal. i, ii is to be regarded with suspicion. And, on the other hand, a reconstruction which allows us to preserve the Galatian order should have that fact accounted to it for righteousness."

22. Although other explanations have been given, this seems to me the most plausible explanation for Paul's oath of truthfulness and his remarks about being known only by reputation in Jerusalem. Paul is not, at this point, concerned with some kind of ongoing independence from Jerusalem. Quite to the contrary, he has *already* established his independent call to mission; he is *now* establishing, seemingly against popular opinion, that he did *not* persist in isolation from Jerusalem but rather met with the leaders there on multiple occasions.

LAND—*There Is No Longer Any Place for Me in These Regions*

This way of recounting things, I suggest, makes the most sense if Paul is seeking to reframe his readers' perception of early Christian leaders and of himself and Peter in particular. We can debate history and we can debate the relationship these stories have to the similar (but not identical) ones told in Acts, but the function of the overall narrative given to us in Gal 1:11—2:14 (or perhaps 1:11—2:21) hangs on an evaluative contrast between Paul and Peter. Before he starts, Paul provides the relevant criteria by giving his readers the twin lenses of "preservation of received tradition" and "obedience to Christ vs. people-pleasing" (1:6–10). And then, in the end, he climaxes his narrative with the Antioch incident, which shows that Peter, in his efforts to avoid upsetting the circumcision people, has fallen away from the truth of the gospel with which he was entrusted, whereas Paul has continued to stand for the truth of the received gospel even to the point of opposing his co-worker Barnabas and all the leaders of Antioch. Apparently, for some reason, Paul wants his Galatian readers to know that *he* is the one holding fast to the truth, whereas *Peter* is a compromised people-pleaser.

Later, I will discuss the Galatian crisis and whether or not Peter played any role in it, a question raised very pointedly by Paul's depiction of Peter, at the very end of his narrative, as someone who "compels the nations to Judaize" (Gal 2:14). Here, my claim is only that the earlier scenes recounted in Gal 1:11—2:10 serve to present Peter and Paul as fellow missionaries with much in common, and that their commonality sets up the climactic dispute in Antioch. Most importantly, the two men both received a call to mission work directly from Jesus himself, as demonstrated by Paul's testimony regarding his "conversion."[23] Moreover, unbeknownst to most people, Paul and Peter spent fifteen days together in Jerusalem three years after the former's "conversion"—yet significantly, *after* Paul had already engaged in some Arabian mission work, so that these conversations were between fellow missionaries.[24] Furthermore, Paul was endorsed as a mis-

---

23. Given Paul's wording in Gal 2:7 (i.e. "just as Peter had been entrusted with the gospel"), we can safely assume that Peter's commissioning by Jesus was well known.

24. Although it is routinely observed that Paul's remark about Arabia serves to distance his apostleship from the Jerusalem leaders and demonstrate his obedience to Christ's call (e.g. Hunn, "Pleasing God," 37), the remark also serves the function of pointing out that, when he and Peter did become personally acquainted with one another by means of some extensive conversations spanning more than two weeks—hardly a brief or insignificant encounter—they became acquainted *as fellow missionaries*. Thus the talks were not between an established leader and a total newcomer, but between two leaders actively engaged in mission work.

sionary by Peter, James, and John upon the occasion of a much later visit to Jerusalem with Barnabas.[25] Indeed, the Jerusalem leaders agreed, Paul tells us, that they themselves would go to the circumcised, whereas Paul and Barnabas would go to non-Jews, and this agreement was predicated on their perception of the fact that Paul and Peter had each, independently, been personally appointed by Jesus to these respective tasks. The reader is thus, by the narrative in Gal 1:11—2:10, prepared to understand the crucial narrative in Gal 2:11–14 as Paul wants it to be understood, as a tale of two well-acquainted foreign missionaries, each commanded by Jesus to go with good news and each recognized in this role by the wider Jerusalem leadership.[26]

If Gal 1:11—2:10 begins a tale of twin missionaries, then 2:11–14 finishes the tale by showing that, as regards the integrity of their behavior

---

25. It is fascinating to consider the various ways that James, John, and Barnabas repeatedly fade from view throughout Gal 2:1–10 as Paul vacillates back and forth between singular and plural references in both the first and third person. While this is not the place to present a full discourse analysis, I suggest that Paul's primary agenda in Gal 2:1–10 is to inform his readers about a private meeting specifically concerned with his and Peter's twin callings, a meeting at which the twin callings became the basis of a partnership in which 'we' (i.e. Paul along with Barnabas) go to the nations while 'they' (i.e. Peter along with James and John) go to the circumcision. Within this story, the remark about Titus in v. 3 gives way to further remarks about the false brothers and the rejection of their demands in vv. 4–5, such that Paul shifts his use of the first person plural and consequently needs to re-orient his reader by re-invoking the pillars and himself at the beginning of v. 6. This suggests to me that the resistance to the false brothers did not take place within the private meeting but was somehow peripheral to it. It would seem, then, that Paul's main goals in Gal 2:1–10 are: (1) to establish his and Peter's recognized status as key leaders in the Christian movement's missionary expansion; and (2) to establish that the Jerusalem and Antiochene leadership stood united with regard to circumcision, with both missions represented in this united stand. The first point is accomplished by the story of a private meeting; the second is accomplished by the interrupting remarks about opposition to the false brothers and about Titus not being pressured to circumcise. But while both the private meeting and the stand against false brothers seem to have taken place during a single visit with Barnabas and Titus, the form of the narrative suggests that we are not being directed to envisage both as a single narrative scene. Probably, I suggest, the Galatians already know about the Jerusalem decision regarding circumcision, such that they will not confuse the mention of this well-known event with the unknown private meeting about which they are hearing for the first time.

26. It is not possible here to discuss at length the way Paul initially contrasts "the good news of [the] uncircumcision" with "the good news of [the] circumcision" but then rebukes Peter simply for not acting consistently with "the good news." Likely, the qualifiers in Gal 2:7 acknowledge that the good news entailed somewhat different things for the two distinct groups (e.g. a long-awaited Messiah vs. an opportunity to turn from paganism).

on the mission field, one of these missionaries is not like the other. Or, to frame things using the categories that Paul lays out in 1:6–10, if 1:11—2:10 shows that Peter and Paul were both entrusted by Jesus with the truth of the gospel, 2:11–14 shows that one of them is a faithful servant who still stands for the truth with which they were entrusted, while the other is a people-pleaser whose behavior is not in line with that truth. We should not be surprised, then, to observe details in the earlier stories that anticipate the climactic dispute between Peter and Paul in Antioch and the negative assessment entailed by it.

For example, Paul recounts his "conversion" as a forsaking of social advancement through Judaism, a framing that picks up the criterion of people-pleasing given immediately prior to the narrative and that resonates very strongly later on when Peter is said to fear the circumcision people.[27] Along similar lines, the Jerusalem controversy regarding circumcision is presented in Gal 2:1–10 as a story about peer pressure, as is evident from the way that Paul reframes his narrative in v. 4. After v. 3, the reader might legitimately infer that the Jerusalem leaders *themselves* posed a potential risk to Titus's persistence as a non-Jew, with the point of the story being that the pillars, based on their understanding of the gospel, did not pressure Titus to Judaize.[28] Yet Paul's story, quite unlike Luke's story in Acts 15, is *not* about what Peter, James, and John ultimately decided with regard to non-Jews. From Paul's perspective, these leaders knew in advance that Jesus' gospel does not require non-Jews to undergo circumcision, and the uncertain factor surrounding Titus was *social power* rather than theological principle: "Even Titus, who was with me, was not compelled to be circumcised—not compelled, that is, on account of false believers who slipped in . . . We did not submit to them even for a moment."[29] By abruptly introducing the false

---

27. Here it is important to note the "still" in Gal 1:10 and the subsequent "for" in 1:11. By means of these details, Paul frames his decision to heed Christ's call as the end of a former way of life in which he sought to advance his social status by pleasing people. Whether this also entailed the end of a life within Judaism is a point of debate, with the wording of the text being amenable to alternative interpretations.

28. This would be a natural inference regarding the source of the pressure, given the third person references to the Jerusalem leaders in Gal 2:2. Indeed, the naturalness of this (wrong) inference best explains the abruptness of v. 4 (i.e. v. 4 is a clarification prompted by Paul's belated awareness of a likely misunderstanding).

29. The syntax of this section in Galatians in notoriously difficult, and various proposals have been made with regard to it. Personally, I do not find the existing proposals about ellipsis convincing (e.g. Betz, *Galatians*, 89–92; Orchard, "Ellipsis"; Blommerde, "Ellipsis"; Orchard, "Once Again"), preferring instead the linguistically more natural

brothers as the instigating factor in the uncertainty that surrounded Titus in Jerusalem, and by restating the ultimate outcome in the first person (i.e. "we" did not give in), Paul keeps his key characters consistently aligned with one another and helps his reader stay focused on his main idea: the *preservation* of truth by means of the avoidance of people-pleasing (Gal 2:5; cf. 1:6–10; 2:12–14).

So then, once upon a time, Paul and Peter were like twin missionaries, and in Jerusalem the two of them stood together with James, John, and Barnabas at a time when the leadership of the Christian movement was pressured to forsake the truth of the gospel. But then one day, on another occasion in another place . . .

Antioch

It is difficult to underestimate the role that the Antioch incident plays in historical reconstructions of Paul's life and mission. As I have already observed, the Antioch incident is recounted as the conclusion of a narrative in which Peter and Paul are twin missionaries. The two men are acquainted with one another as fellow travelling missionaries commissioned directly by Jesus, and each is attempting—in the face of various social pressures—to faithfully preserve the truth of the gospel with which they have been entrusted. Yet in the end Peter falls into people-pleasing and loses sight of Jesus' gospel, whereas Paul risks even his closest relationships for the truth of the gospel. Without a doubt, the way we understand Peter's actions in Antioch is highly significant for our understanding of the Pauline mission's place in the social matrix of early Christianity.

Routinely, in today's socially-conscious scholarship, interpreters assume that Peter's actions must be interpreted against a historical or sociological backdrop comprising special interest groups. Thus Peter is said to worry about violent non-Christian zealots, or he is said to be seeking revenge for the way the "pillars" were shamed by Paul in Jerusalem, or he is said to be fearful of a Jewish interest group that has taken issue with the community's acceptance of non-proselytes as full members.[30] Such

---

reading in which the content elided in Gal 2:4 comprises the last two words of v. 3 ("pressured to circumcise"). Moreover, I see v. 6 as a rather jumbled resumption of the private-meeting story and the contrastive point in vv. 7–9 comprising a single sentence with an enclosed supporting statement in v. 8.

30. See, e.g., Jewett, "Agitators"; Esler, "Breaking an Agreement"; Nanos, "What Was at Stake."

reconstructions are interesting, and they remind us of potentially relevant historical and sociological conditions at the time of the Antioch incident. They are constructed largely from generalizations, however, and they tend to think that Paul's wording has been adequately handled provided that it can be made to cohere with whatever reconstruction is being advanced. By way of contrast, I think that we ought to explore the choices that have gone into Paul's wording in Gal 2:11–13 and then ask what best accounts for what Paul does and does not say at each particular point in his unfolding discourse. As it turns out, despite numerous reconstructions that give a prominent role to special interest groups, Paul's language manifests little interest in delimiting such groups and his overall narrative gives no clear indication that competing special interest groups played any immediate role in the Antioch incident. To the contrary, in contrast with the earlier scene in Gal 2:1–10, *Paul recounts the Antioch incident in such a way that there is no opposition between Judean groups, Peter has become a foreign representative of Judean interests, and Jewish leaders outside of Judea willingly conform to Judean policies*. I will highlight two linguistic features to support this claim: (1) Paul's non-specific language about various groups of people; and (2) the vague and offline nature of Paul's remarks about Peter's changed table practices.

Beginning with the Jerusalem-based events discussed in the preceding section of this essay, I note that Paul initially uses the Greek article in Gal 2:4 to present "the infiltrating false brothers" as a specific and recognizable group,[31] but then elaborates using an indefinite relative ("which people infiltrated us in order to scrutinize the freedom we have in Christ").[32] This may indicate that the infiltrators and their actions were generally well-known in Judea (such that Paul's natural impulse is to present them as a specific and recognizable group) but not necessarily in Galatia (such that with the indefinite relative he clarifies things for his readers, sketching in very general terms their behavior and motives). Alternatively, Paul may be taking it for granted that the Galatians know about the infiltrators, with the

---

31. By specific and recognizable, I do not mean that Paul's readers are already familiar with every member of the group or even familiar with the group as such. Rather, what the Greek article indicates is that, given the wording "infiltrating false brothers," Paul's readers should be able to recognize instances of the group, so that the group as a whole is by implication both specific and recognizable.

32. The Greek verb here does not by itself convey the pejorative meaning of the English *infiltrate*, but *the entering false brothers* is hardly colloquial English. In any case, the phrase as a whole is pejorative because of the Greek term meaning "false brother."

indefinite relative clause ensuring a discourse-appropriate assessment of their conduct.[33] Either way, a second relative clause ("to whom we did not yield even for a moment") reveals that the false brothers were not merely an uninvolved factor "on account of" whom Titus might have been forced to circumcise (v. 4); rather, they in some way exerted pressure on Paul and the other leaders (v. 5).

With "the infiltrating false brothers," then, we have a clear invocation of particular people with a particular agenda putting pressure on the leaders of the Christian movement. We have, in other words, a special interest group. Possibly, the people in question were known by many within the Judean Christian community as "the infiltrating false brothers," in which case Paul may be invoking a well-known group of non-Christians who for some reason sought to investigate the newly emerging Christian movement, with their intrusion causing a controversy in which the leaders of the movement were put under pressure to Judaize non-Jews (e.g. Titus).[34] Alternatively, Paul himself may be branding the people "infiltrating false brothers," in which case he is anathematizing a group of Judean Christians by depicting them as illegitimate members of the Christian community. But most interestingly, and most unfortunately for modern historical reconstructions, Paul does not seem to view such details as important to the Galatians or to the story he is telling them. As far as his narrative is concerned, *what matters is that the demands of a specific Judean special interest group were unanimously rejected in Jerusalem by a united leadership, with the result that the truth of the gospel was preserved.*

Proceeding to the subsequent narrative and hence to the Antioch incident, we find that Paul mentions the arrival of 'some people' from James (2:12), indicating by the indefinite pronoun that the specific identity of these individuals is either unknown to his readers or irrelevant (or both). Also in v. 12, Paul refers to "the circumcision people" (2:12) as a specific and recognizable group. With regard to the people from James, Paul's use of the indefinite pronoun completely precludes their precise identification.[35]

---

33. See the similar construction in Rom 16:3-4, where an indefinite relative clause is used to construe certain people as risking their lives for Paul even though the people in question (i.e. Priscilla and Aquila) are already specific and recognizable within the discourse.

34. See esp. Nanos, "Intruding 'Spies.'"

35. One could propose that it makes little sense to use the indefinite pronoun if these people are the special interest group invoked earlier in connection with Titus (i.e. "the infiltrating false brothers"). All the indefinite pronoun really shows, however, is that Paul

LAND—*There Is No Longer Any Place for Me in These Regions*

Positively, however, this lack of specificity reveals that, at least as regards the story he is now telling about events in Antioch, *Paul is interested solely in the Judean and Jacobean origin of these people*. So irrespective of whether Gal 2:12 describes the aforementioned false brothers infiltrating Antioch (see below) or whether it introduces previously unmentioned people, the focus of Paul's narrative has shifted in such a way that Paul is no longer interested in talking about a special interest group within Judea but is instead interested in talking about the influence of *Judean Christians in general* outside of Jerusalem (i.e. Judeans from the community led by James the Just). Indeed, the whole question of who will dictate Judean policy has given way to a new question: how will Judean influences shape foreign policy? As regards this new question, the identity of the people from James is apparently unimportant, as is their social positioning within the Judean community. What matters is simply that they are from James, because being from James means that they—ostensibly, at least—represent his interests and James is—ostensibly, at least—responsible for their behavior. The people from James, in other words, are not *presented as* a special interest group (although they may well have been one); rather, they are presented as evidence that Peter's missionary practices have come to represent Jacobean and hence Judean interests.[36]

With regard to "the circumcision people," we once again face some interpretive uncertainty. The Greek article presents the group as specific and recognizable, but the wording that Paul supplies (lit. "people of the circumcision") would seem to delimit the entire Jewish community, broadly speaking. So, in context, are we to infer that Paul has a more precise group in view, perhaps the special interest group that earlier put pressure on the Jerusalem leaders to Judaize non-Jewish Christians like Titus, or perhaps the people from James? One could argue that it is incumbent on Paul to clarify if, by "the circumcision people" in v. 12, he does *not* mean those who put pressure on the Jerusalem leadership in vv. 3–5, given that no other mention has been made of circumcision since those earlier verses and given

---

does not, at this point in his narrative, wish to identify these people as the same ones mentioned earlier (e.g. because the battle lines have shifted with the scene shifting to Antioch and it is no longer helpful to draw attention to distinct groups within the Judean community).

36. See below for some remarks about the timing of this visit. Personally, I see no reason to deny that the "false brothers" and "people from James" are the same people, namely, certain Judean Christians who pressured the Christian movement to make a decision regarding the mandatory Judaizing of all Christians (as reported in Acts 15).

that the circumcision people, like the earlier false brothers, influence Peter to ignore the truth of the gospel (cf. vv. 5, 14) and to Judaize non-Jews (cf. vv. 3, 14). Also, Paul's use of the phrase "the rest of the Jews/Judeans" in 2:13 could be cited, since the application of this very *general* phrase *specifically* to members of the Antiochene community potentially licenses the inference that the similarly general phrase "the circumcision people" refers to some similarly specific group recognizable in context.[37] On the other hand, one could infer from Paul's failure to deploy an unambiguous wording that he is making no real effort to delineate a special interest group. Probably, as with the people from James, his agenda in telling the story makes it unnecessary to be precise, with the point being once again that Christian practices in Antioch are being dictated by Jewish/Judean interests, broadly speaking, with "the rest of the Jews/Judeans" in the Antiochene community following Peter's lead in this. On this reading, neither the people from James nor the circumcision people are presented by Paul as a special interest group; rather, within the setting of the Antioch incident, it is Judaism as a whole that constitutes a special interest group, with Peter being so fearful of displeasing "the circumcision people" that he ceases to have any real regard for non-Jews.

Overall, therefore, what do we learn from Paul's use of non-specific language to describe groups of people important to the Antioch incident? We learn, I suggest, that his point is not to show Judean special interest groups jostling for power. At least one such group existed, as we know from Gal 2:1–10, but the wording of Gal 2:11–14 does not clearly identify any such group. Rather, the vague references to "some people from James" and "the circumcision people" paint Judeans with a deliberately broad brush. The best explanation for this, I suggest, is that Paul wants to accentuate the contrast between his former unity with the Judean Christians and his current status as an external critic. What is significant for the Galatians as regards the Antioch incident is that, whereas Paul once stood firm with the

37. Linguistically speaking, the most immediate candidates are the people from James and the infiltrating false brothers. Moving outside of the text itself, one could also infer the wider Jewish community of which the Jews/Judeans of Gal 2:13 remain a part, or perhaps even a violent, militant group of so-called Jewish zealots. To support any particular hypothesis, however, one needs to provide a compelling case not just for the plausibility of the group's historical existence but also for the plausibility of their status *among the Galatians* as a specific, contextually-relevant group that would be immediately called to mind by Paul's rather vague and imprecise wording. This is difficult to accomplish, making it simpler to treat Paul's point as the prioritization of Judean/Jewish interests over the interests of those non-Jews who are entering the Christian community.

Jerusalem leadership in the face of social pressure from a Judean special interest group (which may or may not have been internal to the Christian movement), Paul now stands alone, because the others are allowing their fear of negative reactions from other Jews (perhaps the earlier special interest group, but perhaps nobody in particular) to legitimize behaviors that constitute a betrayal of the gospel.

Turning to Paul's remarks about Peter's table practices and their adjustment, I will next explore what exactly Paul does and does not say about the coming of "certain people" from James and in particular about the timing of their movements. Specifically, I will argue that the wording of Gal 2:11–12 does not explicitly involve the people from James in the Antioch incident, but rather locates their influence at some vague time prior to the incident and potentially as early as the events recounted in Gal 2:1–10. This contributes to our understanding of Peter's missionary practices by further eroding the notion that the Antioch incident was prompted by immediate actions on the part of a special interest group.

I begin by noting that, notwithstanding the usual reconstructions, the text of Galatians does not necessarily present Peter's failure in Antioch as an immediate reaction to the coming of the people from James. Galatians 2:11 merely indicates that Peter stopped having table fellowship with non-Jewish Christians sometime after people came to Antioch from James. It does not say how promptly Peter withdrew after the people's arrival, nor does it in any way relate the duration of their visit to the duration of Peter's own visit. Similarly, interpretive caution must be exercised with v. 12. Given that the singular reading "but when *he* came" has very strong support in early manuscripts, we should presume it unless there is good reason to prefer the plural.[38] Yet if we adopt the singular "*he* came" in v. 12, *we have no evidence that Peter and the people from James were ever in Antioch at the same time.* We have a temporal sequence: Peter eats with non-Jews; people come (to Antioch) from James; in Antioch, Peter eats apart from non-Jews.[39] But although Paul is surely insinuating with this sequence that

---

38. See esp. Carlson, *Text of Galatians*, 121–23. Commentators on Galatians routinely assume that the singular leads to nonsense, but this merely shows how deeply certain presuppositions have been entrenched in Pauline scholarship. In actual fact, the singular makes very good sense, provided one appreciates that the conjunction "for" in Gal 2:12 introduces an off-line comment that interrupts the sequential flow of the narrative.

39. The initial reference to Antioch is parenthetical here, because it derives from an inference rather than from the explicit wording in the text. Specifically, we infer from the preceding clause's mention of movements to Antioch that the coming of the people

Peter's change of behavior was prompted in some way by the movements of people from James, the fact remains that *a sequence is not a chronology*. We cannot, on the basis of what Paul says in Galatians, conclude that people from James arrived while Peter was in Antioch, because the possibility exists that their arrival *preceded* Peter's. Moreover, whatever sequence we imagine, we cannot conclude anything with regard to the amount of time that *separated* the two arrivals, nor can we say much about the *duration* of the respective stays in Antioch. Supposing that Peter arrived first, we can infer that the people from James arrived while he was still there. But supposing the alternative, the people from James may have departed long before Peter arrived in Antioch.[40]

Let me try to articulate this same point in somewhat different terms. In essence, if we adopt the better-attested singular reading "when *he* came," Gal 2:12b is best regarded as a resumption of sorts. Verse 11 reports Peter's visit to Antioch and an ensuing confrontation with Paul. Verse 12a steps off the narrative mainline sequence in order to discuss Peter's table habits, providing relevant (but potentially out-of-sequence) background information.[41] Finally, v. 12b restates the earlier words "when *he* [i.e. Peter] came" and then commences a much elaborated recounting of the visit and confrontation first reported in v. 11. When we read the text this way, however, it follows that Peter is not necessarily understood to have eaten with

---

from James is also being depicted from an Antiochene perspective (i.e. they came "to Antioch"). Notably, the fact that an Antiochene perspective is adopted for both of the arrivals does not entail that they were concurrent or even temporally proximate relative to one another, given that Paul spent considerable time in Antioch and will have observed (or heard about) numerous people coming to the city.

40. Notably, this last reading of Galatians coheres entirely with Luke's sequence in Acts: (1) Peter eats with non-Jews (i.e. Cornelius and his household) and then stands firm when his behavior is challenged in Jerusalem (Acts 10:1—11:18; Gal 2:12); (2) people go out from James to Antioch and insist on the circumcision of all Christian men (Acts 15:1; Gal 2:12); (3) Peter and James, with Paul present, reject the circumcision requirement at a gathering in Jerusalem (Acts 15:2–29; Gal 2:1–10); (4) Peter travels to Antioch, but he abandons his earlier practice of eating with non-Jews and convinces everyone but Paul that this is for the best (Gal 2:11–14). If anything, Paul's depiction of Peter as a hypocrite makes even better sense if Peter himself rebuffed criticisms of his eating with Cornelius prior to the Acts 15 meeting, but then began advocating segregated meals in the aftermath of Acts 15.

41. As regards the people from James, it is possible that Peter drew no direct inspiration from them. Or at least, he may have disclaimed any connection between his behavior and the people from James just as he will have denied that his policy was a compromise motivated by fear.

non-Jews in Antioch, because the withdrawal and separation recounted in v. 12b are not necessarily part of a narrative sequence begun with the description of Peter's eating in v. 12a. And indeed, Paul's aspectual choices in vv. 12b–13 would seem to confirm this view, since the two main verbs in v. 12b do not in fact advance the mainline of the narrative, contrary to what is indicated by translations like the NRSV (i.e. "after they came, he drew back and kept himself separate"). Instead, the two imperfective verbs open up expansive and ongoing processes within which other events in Antioch are then situated.[42] Peter, when he travelled to Antioch, "was retreating and was separating himself," and it was within this *setting* that the *real* Antioch incident took place: (1) the rest of the Jews/Judeans followed Peter in allowing Jewish/Judean interests to dictate their practices; and (2) Paul confronted Peter in front of everyone.[43]

Given the above considerations, I conclude that the Antioch incident recounted in Gal 2:11–14 is not one in which Peter suddenly becomes fearful because of some special interest group, changes his mealtime practices, and then leads others to do the same. Instead, Gal 2:11–14 recounts *an incident in which all the Antiochene Jews defer to Peter's leadership as regards mealtime practices, with Peter having already deferred in this respect to the interests of the Jewish/Judean community* (broadly represented as 'the circumcision people,' but also by 'some people from James' and ultimately by James himself). In short, everyone defers to Judea except for Paul, who opposes Peter in front of everyone, and thus by implication opposes Peter's missionary policy and the Judean community that stands behind it.

---

42. So even if we adopt the inferior textual reading here (i.e. "when they came"), the imperfective verbs in v. 12b ("he was withdrawing and separating himself") still constitute a problem, inasmuch as they do not seem to depict Peter's withdrawal as a reaction to an arrival (for which we would expect "he withdrew and separated himself," using perfective verbs) but as an established behavior that was Peter's practice *already at the time of the arrival*, with the reaction belonging to Barnabas and the others (i.e. "the rest of the Jews/Judeans joined him in his hypocrisy"). See Carlson, *Text of Galatians*, 122.

43. Notably, the text does not say that Peter physically withdrew from non-Jews sometime during his stay in Antioch, first eating with them but then later not eating with them. In fact, the text never conveys that Peter ate with non-Jews *in Antioch* at all, because it is possible to understand Peter's "separating himself" as something he practiced as a general rule at the time of his arrival in Antioch. Similarly, the text never conveys that Peter became fearful in Antioch or that his fear was a direct reaction to the presence of people from James. It conveys only that Paul somehow knew about Peter's earlier willingness to eat with non-Jews and that Paul regarded an Antioch visit on the part of people from James as playing some role in Peter's subsequent change of practice.

The Letter to the Romans

What is the upshot of these observations for the Baur hypothesis and for our understanding of Peter and Paul's respective roles in the missionary activities of the early Christian movement outside of Judea? Negatively, we cannot with confidence treat Peter's adoption of segregated meals as an impulsive decision made at the time of the Antioch incident, nor can we confidently involve people from James in the Antioch incident itself. Positively, we learn that segregated eating became the almost universal practice of "Christian Judaism" for at least a brief period around the time of the Antioch incident, and that the dissemination of this practice across the Mediterranean produced a clear and public divide between Paul and all of the other key leaders in the movement, because Paul saw the segregated tables as a practice that 'pressures non-Jews to Judaize' (Gal 2:14) and hence as both a forsaking of the gospel and a betrayal of the united stand made earlier in Jerusalem.[44] It would seem, then, that Baur was correct in proposing that Peter's leadership brought Judean interests to bear on the early Christian mission field, whereas Paul stood more-or-less alone in opposing certain practices within Peter's Jerusalem-based mission as a betrayal of the gospel. Indeed, it is the delineation of these two groups that is the major accomplishment of Gal 1–2, with all other special interest groups—including 'the infiltrating false brothers,' 'certain people from James,' and 'the circumcision people'—entering into the narrative only to support Paul's thesis that the majority of the Christian movement, despite previously standing firm against social pressures by rejecting mandatory circumcision, has collapsed under social pressures so as to endorse segregated eating.[45]

---

44. In this essay, I am not directly concerned with the concrete details of the segregated meals, and so I will not discuss whether or not the segregation had anything to do with the food that was served. I note in passing, however, that the text of Gal 1–2 draws the dividing line in terms of Jews vs. non-Jews, with there being no indication that one could cross the line simply by agreeing to accommodate Jewish dietary practices. At the time of the Antioch incident, therefore, it would seem that no flexibility existed in Peter's policy with regard to the voluntary accommodation of non-Jews to Jewish dietary regulations. Whether or not such an accommodation was subsequently successful in eliminating the segregation at meals is a matter beyond the present essay (but certainly, a matter of great importance for our understanding of Rom 14–15).

45. As I will clarify below, there is actually a somewhat blurry distinction between these two requirements, inasmuch as the practice of social segregation along Jewish/non-Jewish lines entails that circumcision is indeed an obligatory pre-requisite—albeit for unrestricted community participation rather than for eschatological salvation.

Galatia

So far, my re-assessment of Gal 1–2 has identified two distinct but closely related fault lines. The first fault line involves the Judaizing of non-Jews seeking to follow Jesus, with 'the infiltrating false brothers' advocating a pro-Judaizing position. This fault line may or may not have fallen within the early Christian movement, depending on how one understands the special interest group represented by false brothers. A second fault line involves the integration of Jews and non-Jews at meals, with Peter initially embracing integration but then subsequently advocating segregation in deference to Judean interests. This second fault line very clearly runs through the Christian movement, but there is no clear evidence that it was the accomplishment of a special interest group. To the contrary, although the vague insinuation in Gal 2:12a *might* implicate a special interest group in the emergence of this second fault line (to my mind, it does), Paul chooses not to present any of these historical details but instead to paint with a broad brush.[46] Thus the narrative concludes with Paul standing firm against a united front consisting of all his former allies, and it construes this united front as advancing a pro-Judaizing position, inasmuch as segregated meals "compel the nations to Judaize" (v. 14).[47] In this section, I will consider the relevance of this opening narrative for Paul's Galatian readers. Who was troubling them, how were they being troubled, and why were they being troubled?

One common historical reconstruction (among church-goers, at least) proposes that Christian Judaizers travelled to Galatia and there proclaimed, in the words of Acts 15:1, "Unless you are circumcised according to the

---

46. While the text does not explicitly state anything about James and John, we know that Peter and Barnabas changed their practice and adopted segregated meals, and it is a reasonable inference—particularly in view of the insinuating remark about 'certain people' coming from James—that James and John either never endorsed the common table or else similarly changed their position.

47. Much more could be said about Paul's passionate remarks in Gal 2:14–21, particularly with respect to the way they continue the twin themes of Gal 1–2. The importance of preserving the good news received from Jesus is evident in Paul's observation that he and Peter both know how a person is justified (v. 16) and in his remark about ignoring the grace of God (v. 21). The issue of social acceptance/rejection (i.e. the temptation towards people-pleasing) is evident in the question about Peter and Paul being found sinners (v. 17), in the question about Jesus potentially being regarded as a servant of sin (v. 17), and especially in Paul's being co-crucified with Christ (19). As a whole, the speech urges Jewish people to accept the negative social consequences that go along with affirming the Christian gospel.

custom of Moses, you cannot be saved." This reconstruction is purportedly compatible with the narrative of Acts. Unfortunately, problems arise when we consider Paul's passionate response to the Galatian crisis in Gal 1–2. If Christian Judaizers are insisting upon the circumcision of all male Christians in Galatia without the explicit endorsement of the Judean leadership (along the lines of Acts 15:24, although Acts 15:1 mentions only Antioch), why does Paul's narrative begin with a long preamble about himself and Peter as fellow missionaries and then end with a resounding condemnation of Peter's adoption of segregated meals? Why does Paul make so little of the critical scene in which the leaders in Jerusalem accept Titus as a non-Jewish Christian, sandwiching it between other material and drawing no direct conclusions from it? And why does Paul invest more words within that seemingly critical scene on the pillars' recognition of his and Peter's parallel mission work than on Titus not being forced to undergo circumcision? In short, if Christian Judaizers are demanding the circumcision of all male Christians in Galatia at a time subsequent to the events described in Gal 2:1–10, then why does Paul produce a long and meandering narrative when he could have bluntly dismissed the pro-Judaizing position as inconsistent with the views of the movement's most significant leaders, including Jesus' brother James, Jesus' closest disciples Peter and John, and Paul himself?

A possible retort at this point is that Paul fails to invoke the other leaders because there has emerged an apparent (and temporary?) change of attitude among them. Perhaps Paul has come to see that their failure to pressure Titus entailed less than he initially thought, or perhaps they have experienced a change of mind regarding the necessity of circumcision. Or maybe Paul simply lacks confidence in the Jerusalem leadership because of Peter's segregated eating in Antioch. Any of these scenarios, if true, might explain Paul's preoccupation with establishing his independent authority. But do they explain his decision to climax his opening narrative with the emergence of a dramatic division in the Christian movement with regard to segregated meals?[48] If we want to regard the mandatory Judaizing of non-Jewish Christians as an overt policy of the agitators in Galatia, I suggest, we must conclude one of two things: either Peter now supports the mandatory

---

48. Consider the facts as Paul himself presents them: (1) Peter separates himself from non-Jews when eating; (2) all the other Jews in Antioch embrace this as a good idea; (3) Paul stands alone in rejecting the practice. These facts, taken by themselves, do not indicate a resurgence in the claim that non-Jews must Judaize in order to become Christians. They establish only that Peter and the others have come to endorse the practice of segregated meals.

Judaizing of all non-Jewish Christians, but Paul has for some inexplicable reason failed to say so (at a point when saying so would greatly strengthen the point he is making about Peter's failure to stand firm), or Peter does not fully and wholeheartedly support the mandatory Judaizing of all non-Jewish Christians, but Paul is so angry at his cowardice in adopting segregated meals that he condemns him anyway (instead of citing him as an ally in his campaign to oppose the Judaizers in Galatia).

Some interpreters have followed the first of these alternatives, others the second. There is, however, a third option. A third interpretive possibility is that Paul ends his narrative as he does because *his Galatian readers will see their immediate circumstances enter the narrative with the implementation of segregated meals in Antioch under the oversight of Peter*. On this reading, Paul knows full well that nobody in Galatia is openly demanding the mandatory Judaizing of all non-Jewish Christians (i.e. telling non-Jews they must be circumcised in order to be saved). What is happening is that Christian missionaries are imposing the now widespread practice of segregated meals, producing a two-tier social reality in which Judaizing is the only way to overcome the social barrier that has separated the non-Jews as "others."[49] Paul quite rightly sees that this imposition of segregated tables will implicitly, if not explicitly, put pressure on his non-Jewish converts to undergo proselyte conversion, inasmuch as they will not want to remain in an implicitly inferior social category. Accordingly, he composes a series of arguments to defend the full status of non-Jews and to oppose even the mere *insinuation* that proselyte conversion would somehow "improve" their status.

This third option, I think, fares much better in explaining the narrative in Gal 1–2. After all, if Peter, deferring to Judean interests, is leveraging his status as Jerusalem's foreign missionary in order to institute segregated meals as the general practice among all Mediterranean Christians, and if Paul regards this practice to be a perversion of the gospel along the same lines as the pro-Judaizing position earlier advocated (unsuccessfully) by a special interest group in Jerusalem, it makes perfect sense for Paul to frame himself as a parallel missionary, called personally by Jesus, who (unlike his old acquaintance Peter) continues to champion the practice of integrated meals (which, incidentally, Peter himself formerly championed) because he is immune to the social pressures at work in Jerusalem. Also, if Paul

---

49. For an insightful analysis of the issue of table fellowship, see Lee, *Politics of Difference*.

knows that non-Jews in Galatia, confronted with a segregated table, will *feel* pressured to Judaize (even without someone saying they cannot be saved otherwise), it makes perfect sense for him to accuse Peter of 'pressuring the nations to Judaize' and for him to advance a series of arguments designed to establish that Jesus-faith for non-Jews is a perfectly legitimate expression of Christian obedience and not something that should be abandoned just because segregated meals are giving the (apparently false) impression that Christian Jews, by virtue of Torah observance, are somehow more holy in God's sight than Christian non-Jews. In essence, if we treat the Antioch incident as the direct onset of the Galatian crisis—such that Peter's change of missionary policy more-or-less *is* the Galatian crisis, even if the actual implementation of segregated meals in Galatia is being handled by others—then the shape of Paul's opening narrative in Gal 1–2 very directly attacks the Galatian agitators when it attacks Peter's conduct in Antioch.

Looking beyond the opening narrative in Gal 1–2, there are further confirmations of the hypothesis that segregated meals are at the heart of the Galatian crisis. Here, I will mention only two. First, if the segregation at meals is based on the status of persons as Jews or non-Jews, rather than on more immediate and transitory factors such as washings or food choices or morality, and if the segregation is predicated on cultural notions of Israel's identity as a holy people set apart from the nations, then non-Jews in Galatia wanting not to feel impure and rejected will feel "pressured to circumcise" (Gal 6:12). The only practical alternatives are to accept the implicit message that non-Jewish Jesus-faith is a relatively less pure and less holy variety of Jesus-faith, or to reject the reliability of the Judean missionaries. Recognizing these social realities, Paul urges his non-Jewish readers to view themselves as fully equal with their Jewish counterparts in every way as equal recipients of the Spirit (3:1–5), the blessing of Abraham (3:6–14), and divine sonship and inheritance (3:15—4:11). At the same time, he reconstrues the adoption of segregated meals in terms of social status rather than purity, as a compromise whose sole purpose is to reduce the amount of negative attention that Christian Jews receive from their countrymen (6:12–16). According to Paul, the Christian movement may be Jewish through and through, but heeding the good news of Jesus nevertheless means abandoning the wrongheaded pursuit of social status or social advancement, whether within Judaism or by means of entrance into Judaism (4:12—5:12; cf. 1:13–14).[50]

50. The problem, on this reading, is not Judaism as a culture. The problem is that the

Alongside these more overtly theological passages in Galatians, a second confirmation comes in the exhortations found in 5:13—6:10.[51] These exhortations actually make very good sense as a reaction to segregated meals, provided we are willing to regard concerns about moral purity as one of the factors instigating the segregation (alongside more immediate concerns about washings or food selections, if indeed these were also factors). Let us suppose, therefore, that some Christian Jews were finding it very hard *not* to persist in viewing non-Jewish Christians as impure "sinners" (cf. 2:15), perhaps because of some incidents involving stereotypically pagan sins. With such a supposition in place, Paul's concluding exhortations can be read as an advancement of the view that non-Jews can in fact obtain moral purity without placing themselves in a position of submission to the Torah as a whole (5:14; cf. 5:3), provided they are assisted rather than denigrated by their Jewish peers.

Notice in particular how Paul does not just advocate the pursuit of purity but advocates it as a shared community activity in which *those who have concerns about a brother or sister's moral conduct are obliged to restore the other gently, avoiding the sin of pride* (6:1). With the Jew/non-Jew separation looming large, Paul insists that as with physical laborers, the burdens carried by different Christians are not all the same, and he insists that just as an employer of laborers does not forget that some carry heavier loads, neither should the laborers forget this. Out of love for one another (i.e. obedience to the law of Christ), the Galatians ought to help others with their burdens (6:2). Instead of recoiling when someone stumbles under a heavy burden (e.g. a non-Jew sins because of his or her pagan upbringing), the person who is able to teach the word (e.g. a Jew well-versed in the Torah because of his or her Jewish upbringing) should not simply carry their own load but should come alongside the struggling person and actively *partner* with them (6:3–6).[52] Not only do these exhortations relate to the Galatian crisis, they exemplify the idea that there can be two distinct Christian

---

gospel of Jesus negatively assesses social advancement, at the expense of others, both within and between social systems.

51. For an influential explanation of these exhortations and their relationship to the Galatian crisis, see Barclay, *Obeying the Truth*.

52. In other words, Paul is not suddenly concerned with financial matters when he speaks in Gal 6:6 about partnership. Rather, he is concerned that Christian Jews actively partner with Christian non-Jews so that spirit-filled Christian love can produce a holy Christian community in which those who are learning participate right alongside those who are in a position to teach.

identities—Jewish and non-Jewish—provided the two groups are willing to work together for the benefit of everyone, without any inherent superiority attributed to one group or the other. Each person carries their own load, but this must not preclude helping others.

Much more could be said about Paul's letter to the Galatians, but I must proceed or else I will not reach Rome. By what has already been said, I hope to have made it clear that the evidence of Galatians coheres quite nicely with Baur's claim that there were two major Christian missions in the first century, one overseen by Peter and the other by Paul. Indeed, the evidence of Galatians coheres quite well with the view that Paul's very strong words in his Galatian letter are directed at missionaries who, deferring to Peter's own practice and ultimately to the Judean leadership, have disrupted the communities in Galatia by implementing segregated meals. Nothing indicates that the missionaries deny the legitimacy of Paul's mission to non-Jews, or that they deny the availability of salvation to non-Jews. However, they are not actively partnering with non-Jews as non-Jews so as to encourage their positive transformation; rather, non-Jews are being segregated and hence made to feel inherently unclean, such that proselyte conversion has become a potential means of (and pre-requisite for) personal and social advancement.

Corinth

As one last stop before reaching our destination in Rome, let us look at Paul's letters to Corinth in order to consider the plausibility of Baur's view that the same group of "Judaizers" involved in the Galatian crisis was also involved in Corinth. I will begin by assessing whether the Corinthian situation resembles the Galatian situation as regards three key issues: (1) the practice of circumcision; (2) the practice of segregated eating; and (3) Judaizing as a form of social advancement.

Concerning the practice of circumcision within Corinthian Christianity, there is little to be said. What *is* often said is that there is no sign in Paul's Corinthian correspondence that the circumcision of non-Jews is a live issue, with the usual inference being that the "opponents" in Corinth are not from the same group as the "opponents" in Galatia.[53] Yet this logic does not

---

53. To some extent, this derives from matters of definition, since, as Duff correctly observes, "despite the various claims made about Judaizers in Corinth, no substantive evidence exists anywhere in the Corinthian correspondence to support such activity on the part of Paul's opponents" (Duff, *Moses in Corinth*, 56). The story changes, however,

hold. If the Galatian crisis can be plausibly explained as the result of Judean missionaries implementing a policy of segregated meals, then circumcision became a live issue in Galatia because proselyte conversion presented itself to non-Jewish Christians as an attractive means of advancement in the face of an implicitly denigrating social segregation. When exploring possible connections between the Galatian and Corinthian missionaries, therefore, we should not look chiefly for signs of mandatory circumcision. We should ask whether non-Pauline missionaries have implemented segregated meals and whether this is prompting non-Jewish Christians to contemplate proselyte conversion as a means of social advancement.

As regards the separation of Jews and non-Jews at mealtimes, the Corinthian correspondence is silent, making it difficult to say if or how this particular practice was manifesting in Corinth. Given that Paul's critical remarks in 1 Cor 11:17–34 have in view an economic disparity rather than a Jew/non-Jew disparity, we might conclude that segregation along the latter lines is not an ongoing practice in Corinth. Is it possible that the Jerusalem leadership saw the error of its ways and abandoned its policy of segregated meals prior to the composition of 1 Corinthians? Possibly, but it is also possible that segregated meals became the established practice for Judean missionaries around the Mediterranean, with Jewish and non-Jewish Christians being fully integrated in the Pauline communities but not in emerging communities under Peter's auspices. Either way, we should not expect to observe the practice of segregated meals among Paul's readers. Moreover, if we suppose a period of time has passed since the Galatian crisis, Paul may have resigned himself to the inevitability of a distinctly Jewish/Judean mission and adopted a more settled response aimed at mitigating the impact of this mission on his communities and on their understanding of the gospel. It follows that, in our efforts to determine whether or not Judean missionaries are working in Corinth under the auspices of Peter's mission "to the circumcision" (Gal 2:9), we cannot look solely for overt signs of mandatory circumcision and/or mealtime segregation.

Taking a different tack, I suggest that if Judean missionaries are active in Corinth, we should expect to see a mixed reaction from Paul himself, including both a tacit recognition of Peter's mission and an underlying warning about the need to critically assess its activities. Yet arguably, this is precisely where Paul begins 1 Corinthians. He articulates very forcefully

---

when we cease to speak of "Judaizers" in terms of circumcision and proselyte conversion and speak instead of a "mission to the Jews."

that the gospel undermines all claims to personal status and that decisions about which leaders to follow should not be influenced by anyone's perceived status. He urges his readers to embrace all would-be Christian leaders, but then observes that individual leaders will have the quality of their work assessed and that God will destroy anyone who destroys God's temple. Finally, he chastises his readers for thinking too much about whose leadership to recognize and not enough about how to follow his own humble example. Granted, amidst all of this, the focus is largely upon Apollos and his impressive wisdom and eloquence, yet there are some tell-tale references to Peter (1 Cor 1:12; 3:22), as well as a much-debated passage in which Paul seems to indicate that he has very intentionally discussed leadership with reference to himself and Apollos so as to demonstrate, by personal example, that restraint can diffuse rivalries (4:6).[54] At the very least, then, it can be said that 1 Cor 1–4 reads quite cogently as a reaction to uncertainties surrounding newly arrived Petrine missionaries. In fact, although overt references to circumcision and Torah observance and personal ties to Jesus have been "transformed" into references to wisdom and eloquence and noble birth (here again, see 4:6), the overall thrust of the discourse is virtually identical to what is found in Galatians—i.e. the cross stands as a critique over anyone who would mistakenly abandon the truth of the gospel for the sake of social advancement, and nobody should despise Paul for being unpopular.

Let us hypothesize for a moment, on the basis of these preliminary observations, that Judean missionaries have moved into Corinth and that, like the Galatian missionaries, they have the obvious upper hand as regards their ostensible legitimacy and status. Let us also suppose that, like their Galatian counterparts, the Corinthian missionaries wish to ensure that the Christian community is kept pure and that Christian Jews are regarded as faithful Jews. In Galatia, these factors prompted Paul to assert the legitimacy of "non-Jewish Christianity," to passionately warn his converts against proselyte conversion, and to encourage a partnership between Jews and non-Jews as regards the fulfilling of the law, with each person carrying his

---

54. If we take seriously Paul's eagerness to see Apollos return to Corinth (1 Cor 16:12), it is difficult to interpret the subtle warnings in 1 Cor 1–4 with reference to Apollos himself. More likely, Paul is urging his readers to be cautious and appropriately critical of other Christian leaders in Corinth, and he is using the issues surrounding Apollos as a diplomatic way to avoid overtly discussing the issues surrounding the Petrine missionaries. Ideally, Paul's readers will observe this diplomatic strategy in action and will understand the lesson that it conveys.

or her own load (and most importantly, with non-Jews being morally transformed—with the assistance of Jews—apart from their full submission to Torah). Should we really be surprised that only the last of these is clearly visible within the Corinthian correspondence? After all, Paul's non-Jewish converts in Achaia do not seem to have suffered from feelings of low status, nor do they seem to have been tempted to undergo proselyte conversion. To the contrary, Paul is working overtime to maintain even the most basic standards of Jewish morality, such as the avoidance of sexual immorality (1 Cor 5–6) and separation from pagan temples and offerings (1 Cor 8–10; 2 Cor 6:1—7:4). In fact, the pastoral force needed by the Corinthian non-Jews is seemingly the *inverse* of that needed by the Galatian non-Jews. In Galatians, Paul is urging non-Jews to resist full conversion to Judaism; in 1 and 2 Corinthians, he is attempting to pull non-Jews away from paganism, such that he himself is acting as a kind of Judaizer (loosely defined).[55] This lack of similarity between Galatia and Corinth, however, does not at all prevent us from accepting Baur's proposal that Petrine missionaries were an instigating factor in both situations—provided we grant that conditions in Corinth were remarkably different than in Galatia.

In simple terms, my reading of the Corinthian situation is as follows: Paul's so-called "opponents" are Petrine missionaries, and they are better described as "critics," with the main target of their criticisms being the impurity of the Christian community founded by Paul, in which both Jews and non-Jews are fully integrated. Because Paul himself was at the time seeking greater purity and hence forcefully "Judaizing" his own non-Jewish converts (after a fashion), he had no reason to fear a repeat of the Galatian crisis. Accordingly, his initial reaction to the arrival of the other Christian leaders was one of cautious acceptance, with 1 Corinthians quite diplomatically seeking to quash any rivalry with the command, "No more boasting about human leaders! All things are yours, whether Paul or Apollos or Cephas" (1 Cor 3:21–22). Unfortunately, Paul's critics did not adopt a similarly accepting posture, but instead launched an aggressive campaign in which they vigorously opposed the impurity of the Pauline congregation(s) and blamed the impurity on faulty leadership (i.e. on Paul, and more specifically on the Pauline mission's failure to exercise more direct oversight in Corinth). This explains why, in 2 Corinthians, Paul is rather less genial towards the Judean missionaries in Corinth. In this follow-up letter, he presents them as behaving too harshly towards his converts:

55. See the provocatively-worded arguments of Fredriksen, "Judaizing the Nations."

> If someone comes to you and preaches a Jesus other than the Jesus we preached, or if you receive a different spirit from the Spirit you received, or a different gospel from the one you accepted, you put up with it easily enough . . . In fact, you even put up with anyone who enslaves you or devours you or confronts you or slaps you in the face. To my shame I admit that we were too weak for that! (2 Cor 11:4–21)

He also quotes the other missionaries as saying, "[Paul's] letters are weighty and forceful, but in person he is unimpressive and his speaking amounts to nothing" (2 Cor 10:10), meaning that Paul is not merely absent but also incompetent.[56] It would seem that the Corinthian crisis is like the Galatian crisis in that Christian Jews are being tempted to abandon the hard work of integrated community, which explains why Paul repeatedly points out to the Corinthians that *they themselves* are responsible for the purity of their community and why he discusses mechanisms for the maintenance of communal purity (e.g. 1 Cor 5, esp. 5:11; 2 Cor 12:19—13:10, esp. 13:1). Paul is fully supportive of Christian purity and of the belief that meals should not be shared with certain people, but—as in Galatians, so also in 1 and 2 Corinthians—he wants these convictions to motivate a healthy, integrated community in which the law of Christ is fulfilled by both Jews and non-Jews.

Certainly, the situation I have just sketched differs somewhat from the one proposed by Baur. The basic contours are the same, however, in that the "two mission" arrangement of Gal 2:7–9 is taken seriously. I have even endorsed Baur's rather unpopular suggestion that the same Judean agitators lurk behind 1 Corinthians as were seen previously in Galatians.[57] The major difference is the manner in which I have interpreted the relevant tensions. Whereas Baur sees Paul's gospel as inherently opposed to Peter's "Judaism" or "Jewish Christianity," I have endeavored to take more seriously Paul's remarks in Gal 2:11–14 concerning the disagreement between himself and Peter, with the result that both Peter and Paul are regarded as "Nazarenes" and the "Ebionites" are given no major role to play.[58] That is to say, the two

---

56. As I have argued at length elsewhere (Land, *Integrity*), the most coherent way to read these (and other) texts in 2 Corinthians is to view them against the backdrop of Judean missionaries who were critical of the impurity that characterized some of Paul's non-Jewish converts in Corinth.

57. E.g. "The opponents against whom the Apostle contends are the same Judaising propagandists" (Baur, *Paul*, 256).

58. Regarding Baur's (non-)use of the Nazarene/Ebionite distinction that was being

Apostles were united in their conviction that, while non-Jews do not need to adopt full Torah-observance, neither do Jews need to cease full Torah observance. They disagreed, however, over the implications of this conviction as regards the social integration of Jews and non-Jews within Christian assemblies. For his part, Peter accommodated Judean interests by advocating at least some form of social segregation, although details concerning the motivations for and implementation of this policy remain unclear. In direct opposition to Peter and James and the preponderance of the early Christian movement, Paul insisted upon fully-integrated Christian communities, advocating the voluntary accommodation of Jewish mealtime practices on the part of non-Jews (Rom 14–15) but unequivocally *not* the visible separation of the two groups.

Before moving on from the Corinthian correspondence, I will note once again that Paul's role in the Corinthian situation does not seem to have been (in any simple sense) that of an agitator. Or at least, this is not the role evident in his Corinthian letters. With 1 Corinthians, the fury and fire of Galatians have subsided, and Paul is actively seeking to avoid a rivalry between his mission and the other missionaries working in Corinth. He does not even preclude their having an influence on his readers, provided they are mindful of the fact that Christ will judge the quality of this influence. Sadly, by the writing of 2 Corinthians, the situation has deteriorated so badly that Paul condemns the other missionaries as false apostles and servants of Satan—but even this aggressive name-calling does not entail Paul's rejection of the Petrine mission as a whole. To the contrary, the interpretation presented in 2 Corinthians is that the *other* missionaries disturbed the peace by openly and inappropriately slandering Paul and by threatening the well-being of his congregation. Paul even insinuates that they are seeking to benefit financially, presumably by attacking Paul's handling of impurities so as to win over some established Christian Jews. What this means for historical reconstructions is that we cannot cast each and every conflict between the Pauline and Petrine missions as a conflict between *opposing ideals*. In actuality, Paul's *ideal* seems to have been a cautious peace between the two missions.

---

used by some of his immediate predecessors, see the insightful discussion in Lincicum, "Baur's Place," 145–50.

The Letter to the Romans

SOME IMPLICATIONS FOR THE SITUATION IN ROME

I began this essay on the historical setting of Romans by drawing attention to Paul's sentiment that there was "no longer any place" for him to work in the regions extending from Jerusalem to Illyricum (Rom 15:23). I suggested that his zeal for frontier mission work was not unrelated to the problematic interactions he kept experiencing with other Christian missionaries in his already-evangelized territories, yet I also pointed out that Paul's priorities cannot be reduced to foreign evangelism, inasmuch as both his voyage to Jerusalem and his composing of the Roman epistle manifest a strong and abiding desire to produce unity within and among existing Christian groups. Subsequently, in the main body of this essay, I sought to reconsider and ultimately to revitalize an idea traditionally associated with Baur. I argued that Baur's *Hauptbriefe* or main letters (i.e. Galatians, 1 and 2 Corinthians, and Romans) do in fact substantiate the hypothesis that there were two major missionary movements in the earliest decades of the Christian movement, one under the leadership of Peter and the other under the leadership of Paul. I took issue, however, with Baur's conception of the two missions and with his unhelpful and inaccurate opposition between "Jewish Christianity" and "Paulinism," proposing instead that disagreements between the missions pertained chiefly to the visible segregation of Jews and non-Jews. I also argued that Paul's letters manifest both a begrudging acceptance of the alternative mission's work and a fierce and unyielding opposition to any activities that threatened the vitality of his existing, integrated communities. Thus in Galatians, Paul opposes the separation of Jews from non-Jews and the consequent migration of non-Jews towards Judaism, whereas in 1 and 2 Corinthians he rejects criticisms of his handling of typically non-Jewish sins and impurities as an attempt to win over the loyalty and financial support of his less problematic (i.e. less unruly and impure) converts.

How does this historical setting inform our reading of Romans? While this is not the place to develop a well-argued response, I will conclude with a few brief considerations. First, all of the so-called "theological instruction" in Romans is directly related to Paul's vision of integrated Christian communities. Thus the focus of Romans 1–8 is not so much to articulate a Pauline view of salvation as to show that a Christian view of salvation broadens the definition of "God's holy and righteous people" as to include both Jews and non-Jews. God's work in Christ resolves a fundamentally human problem, such that the promises given to Israel are now being fulfilled not just in a renewed Israel but in a renewed humanity. And God's renewing of humanity takes place not through Torah but through the gift of the Spirit, which enables *all* of its recipients—both Jews and non-Jews—to live a truly holy life. Notably, throughout his presentation of this expansive vision, Paul speaks over and over again in terms of two distinct groups, the circumcised and the uncircumcised, showing that the work of Christ does not efface Jewish identity but rather bestows the gift of God on both Jews and non-Jews. Long before we reach Rom 9–16, therefore, Paul is taking steps to facilitate the integration of Jews and non-Jews as distinct but equal members of God's family. He is not opposing "Jewish particularism" as an abstract ideal but as a practical social policy that rejoices in the salvation of non-Jews but treats them as "other" in a way that hinders their active participation as equal members of God's family.

Second, Paul is repeatedly on the defensive in Romans, but not with respect to his soteriology. As in Galatians and especially 1 and 2 Corinthians, he reacts to criticisms of his handling of sin, insisting that his gospel embraces non-Jews as full heirs of the Abrahamic promise without abandoning the vision of a holy and righteous people of God. His mission is very much concerned to address sin; it merely objects to the insinuation that sin is a distinctly "Gentile" problem and hence a more serious problem for the Pauline mission than for the Christian movement in general. Paul also reacts in Rom 9–11, as in Galatians and 1 and 2 Corinthians, to the claim that his missionary work is antagonizing Diaspora Judaism in a way that problematizes the Judean community's mission "to the circumcision." He underscores his deep longing for his fellow Jews, aligning himself with other servants of Israel whose efforts were at times dramatically unsuccessful (e.g. Moses, Elijah). He points out that he has not rejected the Jewish people (nor has God); rather, many Jewish individuals have rejected his message (and by implication the righteousness of God). Finally, he explicitly warns non-Jewish Christians not to antagonize Jews in the manner of which he is being accused but to desire the salvation of all Israel in the same manner that he himself does. The practical goals of the remnant theology in Rom 9–11 are thus twofold: first, to encourage Jews who are uncomfortable with conflict that they should not misconstrue the real cause of the emerging division between Paul's Christian Judaism and "unbelieving" Diaspora Judaism; and second, to discourage non-Jews who have been quick to construe this emerging division as a separation from Judaism itself. But these goals only make sense if the controversy and antagonism surrounding Paul's mission work is already manifesting itself in Rome quite apart from Paul's direct involvement, and hence the letter is likely addressed to integrated communities that are struggling to understand the nature of their relationship to wider Judaism.

Third, amidst ongoing scholarly debate concerning the ethnic makeup of the Christian communities in Rome and their relationship to Diaspora synagogues, my proposal regarding the historical setting of Romans entails a complex scenario in which different models were likely implemented by different Christian groups in Rome. In Romans, Paul would seem to be addressing integrated communities in which Jews and non-Jews share a common table, but there will have been other communities in Rome that maintained a more visible distinction between Jewish and non-Jewish members. Moreover, even within the integrated communities, the Jews themselves will have persisted in observing Torah, with the only point of debate being the acceptability of eating together at a single table with non-Jewish Christians. Against such a backdrop, Rom 14–15 reminds its readers that integrated gatherings should voluntarily observe Jewish dietary traditions for the sake of any Jewish participants who might be uncomfortable eating at a non-kosher common table, with the immediate impetus for the reminder being a growing resistance to this voluntary deference on the part of certain non-Jews. If Judean Christians around the Mediterranean were practicing segregated tables *irrespective of the willingness of non-Jews to follow Jewish dietary observances*, non-Jews within the fully-integrated communities may have begun to begrudge their standard practice of deferring to Jewish traditions, perhaps abandoning this accommodation and then antagonizing any Jews who consequently felt unable to come to the table. Inasmuch as this attitude is just as un-Christian as its corollary, however, Paul opposes it. He himself is comfortable sharing a table with non-Jews who do not observe Torah, but this degree of confidence is not universal and the common table needs to remain open to the integration of Jews who will only share a kosher common table.

Baur, it would seem, may well have been correct to see ongoing tensions between Pauline and Petrine missions behind the letter to the Romans. Yet the tensions need not entail competing forms of religion. Instead, we can make good sense of Romans with reference to internal debates concerning the ongoing importance of Jewish identity for Christian Jews and the implications of this ongoing identity for the table fellowship that was at the heart of Christian gatherings. For his part, Peter was in general agreement with the Judean leadership that a pronounced and unrestricted influx of non-Jews, with their non-observance of Torah, would not benefit his mission in the Diaspora, because the indiscriminate treatment of Jews and non-Jews as equal members would pose a threat both to the identity of the Christian movement (as a Jewish renewal movement) and to evangelistic opportunities (since many Diaspora Jews would be uncomfortable joining a movement that gave the appearance of effacing Jewish identity). Accordingly, the Petrine mission implemented a general practice of segregated tables as a visible manifestation of the ongoing relevance of Jewish identity within the Christian movement. For his part, Paul treated integrated table fellowship at mixed Christian gatherings as an extremely important and potent embodiment of the gospel of reconciliation, with all of humanity—Jew and non-Jew, master and slave, male and female—coming together as one. According to this vision of Christian unity, the cross does not efface cultural identity; rather, it effaces the inequalities that exist between these identities and hence the social statuses that inhere within them.

In sum, while Romans, in the hands of the Tübingen school, was used to denigrate Judaism as something superseded by Christianity, the letter's function in its historical setting was to defend the Pauline mission against the charge that its vision of fully integrated, mixed communities (along with the scriptural and theological arguments used to support this vision) posed a threat to Jewish identity and to the ongoing preservation of Jewish traditions. Romans provides clear evidence that, despite all the tension and conflict between Paul and the rest of early Christianity, Paul continued to pursue his vision of Christian unity, in which the nations rejoice together with the Jews (Rom 15:8–12).

BIBLIOGRAPHY

Barclay, John M. G. "Faith and Self-Detachment from Cultural Norms: A Study in Romans 14–15." *ZNW* 104 (2013) 192–208.

———. *Obeying the Truth: Paul's Ethics in Galatians*. London: T. & T. Clark, 1988.

Baur, Ferdinand Christian. "Die Christuspartei in der korinthischen Gemeinde, der Gegensatz des petrinischen und paulinischen Christenthums in der ältesten Kirche, der Apostel Petrus in Rom." *Tübinger Zeitschrift für Theologie* 4.3 (1832) 61–206.

———. *Paul the Apostle of Jesus Christ: His Life and Works, His Epistles and His Doctrine*. Vol. 1. 2nd ed. London: Williams & Norgate, 1876.

Bauspieß, Martin, et al., eds. *Ferdinand Christian Baur und die Geschichte des frühen Christentums*. Tübingen: Mohr Siebeck, 2014.

Betz, Hans Dieter. *Galatians: A Commentary on Paul's Letter to the Churches in Galatia*. Hermeneia. Philadelphia: Fortress, 1979.

Blommerde, Acton C. M. "Is There an Ellipsis Between Galatians 2,3 and 2,4?" *Bib* 56 (1975) 100–102.

Carlson, Stephen C. *The Text of Galatians and Its History*. WUNT 2:385. Tübingen: Mohr Siebeck, 2015.

Duff, Paul Brooks. *Moses in Corinth: The Apologetic Context of 2 Corinthians 3*. NovTSup 159. Leiden: Brill, 2015.

Eisenbaum, Pamela. *Paul Was Not a Christian: The Original Message of a Misunderstood Apostle*. New York: HarperOne, 2009.

Esler, Philip Francis. "Making and Breaking an Agreement Mediterranean Style: A New Reading of Galatians 2:1–14." *BibInt* 3 (1995) 285–314.

Fredriksen, Paula. "Judaizing the Nations: The Ritual Demands of Paul's Gospel." *NTS* 56 (2010) 232–52.

Goulder, Michael D. *St. Paul Versus St. Peter: A Tale of Two Missions*. Louisville: Westminster John Knox, 1994.

Harris, Horton. *The Tübingen School: A Historical and Theological Investigation of the School of F. C. Baur*. Reprint, Grand Rapids: Baker, 1990.

Hunn, D. "Pleasing God or Pleasing People? Defending the Gospel in Galatians 1–2." *Bib* 91 (2010) 24–49.

Jewett, Robert. "Agitators and the Galatian Congregation." *NTS* 17 (1971) 198–212.

Land, Christopher D. *The Integrity of 2 Corinthians and Paul's Aggravating Absence*. New Testament Monographs 36. Sheffield: Sheffield Phoenix, 2015.

Lee, Jae Won. *Paul and the Politics of Difference: A Contextual Study of the Jewish-Gentile Difference in Galatians and Romans*. Eugene: Wipf and Stock, 2015.

Lincicum, David. "F. C. Baur's Place in the Study of Jewish Christianity." In *The Rediscovery of Jewish Christianity: From Toland to Baur*, edited by F. Stanley Jones, 137–66. HHBS 5. Atlanta: SBL, 2012.

Manson, T. W. *Studies in the Gospels and Epistles*. Philadelphia: Westminster, 1962.

Miller, D. M. "Ethnicity, Religion and the Meaning of *Ioudaios* in Ancient 'Judaism.'" *CurBR* 12 (2014) 216–65.

———. "The Meaning of *Ioudaios* and Its Relationship to Other Group Labels in Ancient 'Judaism.'" *CurBR* 9 (2010) 98–126.

Murphy-O'Connor, Jerome. *Paul: A Critical Life*. Oxford: Clarendon, 1996.

Nanos, Mark D. "Intruding 'Spies' and 'Pseudo-Brethren': The Jewish Intra-Group Politics of Paul's Jerusalem Meeting (Gal 2:1–10)." In *Paul and His Opponents*, edited by Stanley E. Porter, 59–97. PAST 2. Leiden: Brill, 2005.

———. "What Was at Stake in Peter's 'Eating with Gentiles' at Antioch?" In *The Galatians Debate: Contemporary Issues in Rhetorical and Historical Interpretation*, edited by Mark D. Nanos, 282–318. Peabody, MA: Hendrickson, 2002.

Orchard, Bernard. "Ellipsis Between Galatians 2:3 and 2:4." *Bib* 54 (1973) 469–81.

———. "Once Again the Ellipsis Between Gal 2,3 and 2,4." *Bib* 57 (1976) 254–55.

Runesson, Anders. "Particularistic Judaism and Universalistic Christianity? Some Critical Remarks on Terminology and Theology." *ST* 54 (2010) 55–75.

Zetterholm, Magnus. *Approaches to Paul: A Student's Guide to Recent Scholarship*. Minneapolis: Fortress, 2009.

2

"I Have Written You Quite Boldly on Some Points"
The Register and Structure of Romans

STANLEY E. PORTER

INTRODUCTION

THIS TITULAR QUOTATION FROM Rom 15:15, in the NIV 2011 version, provides a suitable introduction to register analysis of the book of Romans. The development of the concept of register is one of the major contributions of Systemic Functional Linguistics (SFL) to twentieth-century (and later) linguistic thought. The term "register" itself has a relatively long history in linguistic (and other) research, and has come to mean a number of different things even within SFL (some of those will be touched upon if only briefly in discussion that follows). Nevertheless, when we think about how language is used, one of the ways in which we can talk about it is in terms of the language variety of the user, which often focuses upon what is called dialect or even idiolect, and language variety according to use, or register.[1] This fundamental distinction penetrates the issue that language is both an individual and a community event. It is individual in that there are individuals who use language, each in a particular way, based upon a mix of variables (such as physical location, education, etc.), but, in many ways at least as importantly (if not more so), language is used in social contexts to achieve various purposes. These can be described as various ways in which

---

1. See Halliday in Halliday and Hasan, *Language, Context, and Text*, 41. This distinction was first found in Halliday, McIntosh, and Strevens, *Linguistic Sciences*, 88–89. Cf. Catford, *Linguistic Theory of Translation*, 84–85.

meanings are exchanged between participants using language in its varied media.

Thus, language according to use is characterized on the basis of its situational context. This situational context involves those who are participating in the making of meanings, the topics that are being exchanged by them, and the various features of language and their use that make up such a meaningful exchange. These exchanges almost invariably have individual features, because each language exchange is virtually always unique. However, these exchanges can also be typified on the basis of a number of common or overlapping features and the levels of abstraction employed. This sociolinguistic characterization of language as it is used in such situational contexts is what is meant by register. Register analysis is the attempt to characterize typical uses of language on the basis of the configuration of its situational contextual features. Systemic functional linguistics has found it useful to describe the situational context in terms of three components. The first is the field of a given discourse, that is, the "what-ness" of a meaningful use of language, involving the subject matter, what the discourse is about, and the arrangement of its content. The second is the tenor of a given discourse, that is, the "who-ness" of a meaningful use of language, involving those who are involved in the exchange of meanings within the field of discourse, whether they are both contemporary participants, real or hypothetical participants, or posited participants (as in the implied speaker or hearer). The third is the mode of a given discourse, that is, the "how-ness" of a meaningful use of language, involving the means by which the various elements of language use are structured into a meaningful communicative act or set of acts, so that there is cohesion to the discourse and organization so that the discourse is about something in particular rather than about everything in general.[2]

If I may return to the chapter title of this paper, as well as my opening statement, the quotation from Rom 15:15 provides a suitable introduction to register analysis of the book of Romans. We all recognize that the book of Romans is about something—in fact, this is what the major debate of Romans has been about, its content. Is it Paul's compendium of his theology, or is it something else, such as a letter of apology for his behavior

---

2. One of the best introductions to register is Gregory and Carroll, *Language and Situation*. A recent introduction that tends to synthesize various perspectives is found in Biber and Conrad, *Register, Genre, and Style*. I draw on their work throughout this paper. For some of my own previous thoughts, see Porter, "Dialect and Register"; and now Porter, *Letter to the Romans*, 24–35.

in relationship to the Jerusalem church, or a summary of Paul's deepest thoughts, or a final word in anticipation of the close of his ministry, or something else altogether? However, even the asking of this question reveals that there is more involved in the book of Romans than simply an isolated notion of content. Paul's letter also instantiates meaningful relationships between Paul and the Roman Christians (whoever these may be), along with others common to them both, and possibly others in places such as Jerusalem. The reason that we think we know what Paul is speaking about and to whom is because he has put his meanings into a particular shape, a constellation of these meanings with not only an organizational structure but a means by which the various individual elements—at whatever level we wish to identify them, from the word on up—are placed together in relationship with each other. In other words, the statement in Rom 15:15 provides a lesson in register in miniature, because it indicates a field of discourse—some points that Paul wishes to make—a tenor of discourse—Paul writing to the Romans, that is "I, Paul" writing to "you, followers of Christ in Rome"—and a mode of discourse—writing, but more than that, writing organized in a particular way, a letter. In this paper, I will explore the register of Romans in more detail, and use register analysis as a means of addressing the question of the organization and structure of Romans as a letter. This study will thus also bring register analysis to bear on the question of literary genre, and more particularly, epistolary analysis.

THE REGISTER OF ROMANS

To ask the question of the register of Romans is to ask a question with multiple strands to it. In one sense, it requires attention to all of the issues raised in any exploration of the historical or material situation of the letter (as raised in the previous paper). In another sense, it requires even more attention to a variety of issues raised simply by the language of the letter itself as instantiations of the author's communicative intent, as the indicators of the subject matter, the characterization of the participants, and the means of formulating a meaningful communication. Whereas language use proceeds from meanings to instantiations, the analysis of a letter such as Romans must reverse engineer such a movement to determine the meanings from the instantiations.

Hughson Ong, in a recent work on multilingualism in the New Testament, characterizes my situational contextual configuration of Romans as found in some of my previous work, including a commentary, in this way:

> Porter applies register analysis to the book of Romans, profiling the context of situation of this major Pauline letter. Porter notes that Paul uses various discursive styles, such as analogies, metaphors, semantic chains, chained-like words and phrases, parallelism, alliteration, repetition, etc., as a way of organizing the topics and concepts he discusses in the letter (mode of discourse), that Paul clearly uses the diatribe or dialogical technique (question-and-answer) of conversation with either his real or his fictitious conversation partners in the letter to get his message across to his audience (tenor of discourse), and that Paul's use of the diatribe and various discursive styles was to talk about sets of progressively developing theological concepts (e.g., the human condition, justification, reconciliation, etc.) throughout the letter (field of discourse).[3]

I think that this is a fair and accurate representation of my analysis of Romans.

I wish to examine briefly each of these components of register to add some detail to what is said above. Some of my findings here will be important when I turn to the issue of the structure of Romans in the next section.

Field

The field of discourse is what a text is about, in the most general and yet also specific terms. We all know that a text is about something, even if we cannot say specifically what that "aboutness" is. The reason for that is that there is no easy or straightforward way to determine the field of discourse. There are several possible ways, however, to think about how one might do this. One is lexically and the other is grammatically.[4]

Let me examine some of the lexical matters first. One approach might be to examine the frequency of the semantic domains of the lexical items used. (I assume here that the Louw-Nida semantic domain lexicon is an adequate tool for such a study, realizing that there are problems that can and should be noted.)[5] Matthew Brook O'Donnell and I have made such a study, and discovered that LN semantic domain 33, Communication, is

---

3. Ong, "Multilingual Jesus," 105, referring to Porter, *Letter to the Romans*.

4. For many of the instances of data used below, as well as treatment of other issues in Romans, see Porter and O'Donnell, "Semantics."

5. See Louw and Nida, *Greek-English Lexicon*, used throughout and referred to as LN.

the most frequent.[6] However, it is also the most heavily populated domain in the Louw-Nida lexicon, and lexical items in LN semantic domain 33 are very frequent throughout all of the New Testament. Despite the difficulties, this is, in fact, useful information, as it perhaps indicates in a broad way that the field of discourse of the New Testament as a register is that of communication. What LN Semantic domain 33 indicates is that books of the New Testament are, in some way that needs much further definition elsewhere, concerned with communication. So much should be obvious—although I suspect the point has been lost on some New Testament scholars. However, it is not specific enough to help us with the register of Romans, as it does not differentiate the register of Romans from that of any other book of the New Testament. In other words, the frequency of a domain does not itself indicate the field of discourse, and in this case the field of discourse of Romans. This does not mean that lexical items in their respective semantic domains, and their various groupings, are not important in determining the field of discourse. However, much more is needed than simply counting such lexical items and categorizing them.

A second means of examining the lexicon for the field of discourse is to examine the most frequent words in Romans (including only content but not function words). Again, O'Donnell and I have done such a study. The following twenty most frequent words are found in Romans, with their frequencies per 1000 words: "God" (θεός; 153), "be" (εἰμί; 113), "law" (νόμος; 74), "each/every" (πᾶς; 70), "Christ" (Χριστός; 65), "sin" (ἁμαρτία; 48), "lord" (κύριος; 43), "faith" (πίστις; 40), "Jesus" (Ἰησοῦς; 36), "become" (γίνομαι; 35), "righteousness" (δικαιοσύνη; 34), "spirit" (πνεῦμα; 34), "speak" (λέγω; 34), "people" (ἔθνος; 29), "person" (ἄνθρωπος; 27), "flesh" (σάρξ; 26), "have" (ἔχω; 25), "grace" (χάρις; 24), "die" (ἀποθνῄσκω; 23), "do" (ποιέω; 23).[7] If we look at this list, I suppose that we can—but perhaps only because we already have some idea of the content of Romans—determine what the book is about. The field of discourse of Romans is concerned with God, as well as Christ, the Lord, Jesus, and the spirit, each human being, their being and becoming in relation to the law, sin, flesh, dying, and righteousness. I have not studied all of Paul's letters in this way, but I can imagine that a somewhat similar distribution may be found for some of his other letters. This may be entirely appropriate, as one might well argue that the registers of some of these letters may be similar (if for no other reason than that they

---

6. Porter and O'Donnell, "Semantics," 182.

7. Ibid., 161.

are ecclesial letters). However, this remains a fairly crude tool for determining the field of discourse of Romans, although it may set parameters for a more specific examination. There is certainly no way to differentiate major topics within Romans simply on the basis of this distribution. Field of discourse is not necessarily to be equated with the topic of a discourse, although there is often a correlation between field of discourse and topic in more technical or focused texts, arguably Romans being one of these.[8]

A third approach to the use of the lexicon is to examine the distribution of semantic domains across units within the letter, such as chapters or even epistolary structural units (assuming that these are in fact appropriate units—see below). Needless to say, this generates a significant amount of information that is difficult to differentiate and analyze appropriately. A couple of examples will suffice. LN Semantic domain 31: Hold a View, Believe, Trust, has high frequency of occurrence in Rom 3 (13 instances) and 4 (17 instances), as well as Rom 10 (10 instances). LN Semantic domain 23: Physiological Processes and States, has a high frequency of occurrence in Rom 5–8 (15, 28, 19, and 18 instances respectively), as well as Rom 14 (29 instances).[9] This would appear to indicate that the field of discourse of Romans is concerned with the relationship between belief (and unbelief) and physical states such as life and death. If we examine the twenty most frequent semantic domains in relation to traditional epistolary structure, we find that LN Semantic domain 33: Communication, is the most frequent in every section, and hence too broad a distinctive to guide our analysis. However, there are other observations worth making. LN Semantic domain 93: Names of Persons and Places, is the most frequent semantic domain in both the opening and closing of Romans (142.90 words per thousand words in the opening and 128.30 per thousand in the closing). This is what we might expect, or at least what we should expect in the opening and closing, as we will discuss further under tenor of discourse. I also note that the next most frequent domain is LN Semantic domain 12: Supernatural Beings and Persons, in the opening (90.91 per thousand words) and the closing (34.03 per thousand words). The thanksgiving portion of the letter has lexis from LN Semantic domain 12: Supernatural Beings and Persons, as its most frequent also (44.59 per thousand words), followed by Semantic domain 31: Hold a View, Believe, Trust (38.22 per thousand words). The first may well be expected, but the second probably is not, unless we see belief and trust

---

8. See Gregory and Carroll, *Language and Situation*, 29.

9. Porter and O'Donnell, "Semantics," 163.

as the object of thanksgiving. The body of Romans has highest frequency of LN Semantic domain 88: Moral and Ethical Qualities and Related Behavior (49.45 per thousand words), followed by LN Semantic domain 12: Supernatural Beings and Persons (34.46 per thousand words). I think that this pattern is completely unexpected, as one would expect LN Semantic domain 88 to be more frequent in the parenetic section of the letter. The parenesis of Romans has the highest frequency of LN Semantic domain 25: Attitudes and Emotions (43.16 per thousand words), followed by LN Semantic domain 12: Supernatural Beings and Persons (40.97 per thousand words).[10] This simple survey of the most frequent semantic domains of each portion of the letter, while remaining a relatively crude means of examination, provides some intriguing ideas. The openings and closings of the letter rightly focus upon the participants in the discourse. However, divine beings—God, Christ, etc.—are regular participants throughout the letter. I will return to this observation below.

A second approach, one that is more typical of some linguistic approaches (including SFL), is to consider the linguistic environments, or cotexts, in which the various lexical items appear, especially at the level of the clause as the primary semantic or message unit. This is probably the best means of determining the field of a discourse, as it involves a more syntactically sensitive approach to examination of what the discourse is about or what is being said about the processes or activities of the text. This approach involves what is called transitivity in SFL parlance, and is concerned with how, at the clause level (with the clause as the principal semantic/message unit), there is interaction among the people, processes, and entities, that is, who does what to whom and how.[11] Examination of the clause includes attention to agency, causality, and aspectuality, among other factors.

Agency indicates the level of participatory involvement in the event, as an instigator or recipient or the like. Agency is directly related to a number of other clausal components, including causality. There are a number of interesting patterns regarding causality. Direct causality is overwhelmingly predominant in the thanksgiving (active voice forms 95.54 per thousand words), body (121.50 per thousand words), and especially parenesis (149.96 per thousand words) of Romans. Indirect causality is found most frequently in the thanksgiving (passive voice forms 44.59 per thousand words), though still far less frequently than direct causality (not counting

10. See ibid., 181–84.
11. See Thompson, *Introducing Functional Grammar*, 88–135.

ambiguous forms, that is, middle/passives). Ergative agency is only significantly found in the opening (middle voice forms 25.97 per thousand words) and the closing (47.12 per thousand words, plus some middle/passive forms).[12] Indirect causality has the same frequency in the opening but far less in the closing. Direct causality, though still the most frequent in the opening and closing, is relatively less than in the other structural units and closer to ergative causality. The distributions of the direct causality in relation to the indirect and ergative follow the normal Pauline distribution in the body and parenesis, which one might well expect. Nevertheless, there are some interesting patterns suggested for the register of Romans. The opening and closing are less direct in causality than the other major sections of the letter. The thanksgiving, though often indicating direct causality of processes, also has significant indirect causality (the indirect causality is highest in the thanksgiving with passive forms 45.59 per thousand words).

Aspectual patterns must also be examined in relation to causality. The perfective aspect is more frequent than either the imperfective or stative in the opening (51.95 per thousand compared to 25.97 and 12.99) and the closing (73.30 in comparison to 60.21 and 5.24). However, the imperfective aspect is more frequent in the other three sections: the thanksgiving (95.54 imperfective per thousand compared to 63.69 for perfective), the body (89.51 compared to 59.74), and the parenesis (133.87 compared to 42.43). The stative aspect is found most frequently in the parenesis (15.36 per thousand), higher than in any other part but still way behind the imperfective.[13] The discourse planes of the letter are clearly shifted from the opening to the thanksgiving, body, and parenesis of the letter, before returning to the plane of the opening.

Expecting to find a simple statement about what Romans is about is complicated by the linguistic evidence. I would suggest that an adequate examination of the field of discourse of Romans must do more than simply state that it is a letter about justification or the like. Instead, Romans is a complex text about how various agents, especially divine agents, are involved in actions in relation to humanity. These complex relations are instantiated in various configurations of agency, causality, and aspectuality, among other factors.

---

12. Porter and O'Donnell, "Semantics," 178.
13. Ibid., 177.

Tenor

The tenor of the discourse concerns the social dimension of the text, that is, the social relationships instantiated by the language of Romans. We have already seen above that various participants are lexicalized within the book of Romans, including divine and human figures. The fact that these participants are involved in the discourse is important for the field of discourse, but their textual social relations, as indicated by the way that they are represented in the discourse, indicates the tenor of the discourse, or its interpersonal character. There are three major ways in which the tenor of a discourse is indicated: lexical specification of participants, indication of grammatical person, and attitudinal semantics.

Lexical specification of the interpersonal semantics of Romans is made more complex by the fact that it involves both direct and indirect participants. Direct participants are the letter author, Paul, and the letter recipients, the Roman followers of Christ. Paul is designated as the single author of the letter (note use of the third person, not first person in the opening), and the Roman recipients are specified as those who are in Rome. Paul is the single author of the letter, though a scribe is designated later (Tertius, Rom 16:22). (This raises some interesting questions regarding the mode of discourse; see below.) There are indirect participants in the letter of various types, including especially divine figures and other humans. We have already seen that divine figures include God, Christ, Jesus, and spirit. Others include those mentioned in Rom 16 that Paul wishes to greet. Romans 16 has proved surprisingly contentious in study of Romans. The primary issue is how it is that Paul appears to have known so many people in Rome, a city he had never visited.[14] However, that is not a direct problem of register so much as it is a problem of the material situation. What is significant about Rom 16 is that those whom Paul greets are invoked by name but also usually elaborated so as to identify them by means of their relationship to Paul and sometimes the Romans. In other words, Paul both defines these people but also clausally links them to his epistolary situation. He does this by means of grammatically characterizing them as the complements of the clausal constructions. Paul's typical, though not invariable (see Rom 16:1), pattern is to direct his recipients to greet those he is introducing.

Grammatical person is a means of identifying a relationship among participants, as person indicates the participatory levels of the various participants (first person is inclusive of the author, second person is

---

14. See Porter, *Letter to the Romans*, 299–300.

addressed by the author, but third person is outside of the direct personal interaction).[15] Paul identifies himself in the third person by means of the nominative case and the recipients, the Romans, by means of the dative case. The move from the nominative to the dative indicates a hierarchical relationship or superiority to inferiority (cf. some other letter prescripts, where the addressees appear in the nominative, and the addressor by a prepositional phrase). The first person does not occur in the opening of Romans (1:1–7). Paul, however, further establishes the tenor of the discourse by defining himself explicitly by full grammaticalization (Paul, servant of Christ Jesus, called apostle, designated for the gospel of God), as well as further clausal elaboration (Rom 1:2–6). The Roman recipients receive minimal elaboration in comparison (Rom 1:7). Paul uses the first person singular in the thanksgiving and only a few other times in the letter (Rom 7:7–25; ch. 9; and 15:14—16:25). For the most part, the letter of Romans is carried by the use of the third person throughout the body of the letter, and for most of the parenesis apart from Romans 12. This indicates that indirect participants have a significant role to play in the major portion of the letter, especially with the divine participants in relationship to general humanity—including but apart from the direct participants, Paul and the Romans. The first person plural is also used at a number of places, such as Rom 3:9–20, 5:1–11, 6:1–8, and 8:15–28. The first person plural includes at least Paul, probably the Romans as followers of Christ, and in some instances other followers as well.

The attitudinal semantics concern the relationship of the processes and their participants to reality. As would be expected in a letter such as Romans, the assertive attitude is used throughout the letter. However, there are several other patterns worth noting. In the opening, participial constructions (which grammaticalize factual presupposition) as part of the modification structures to elaborate the participants are used more frequently than mood (attitudinal) forms (51.95 per thousand participles to 38.96 indicative forms). In the parenesis, the directive attitude is used more than in the other major sections (23.41 per thousand), apart from the closing, where the greetings are passed on to others (44.50 per thousand). Participial constructions are also used frequently in the parenesis (54.13 per thousand), especially in the exhortative section in Rom 12:9–21. The use of the directive attitude and factual presuppositional semantics reduces

---

15. See Porter, "Register in the Greek," 223, citing Levinson, *Pragmatics*, 69.

the relative frequency of the assertive attitude in the parenesis (84.13 per thousand).[16]

One of the major questions in recent discussion of Romans is the audience of Romans. This is usually discussed in relation to the question of the constituency of the church in Rome, that is, whether it was predominantly Gentile or a mixed church.[17] This is no doubt an interesting historical question, and related to the material situation of the letter to the Romans. However, the contextual situation as indicated by Romans frames the issue differently. There are three factors to consider. The first is the way the addressees are first addressed in the letter, as noted above. They are addressed by means of the dative case as "those who are in Rome," "beloved of God," and "called saints." The epistolary introduction of Romans is an elaborated version of the standard epistolary prescript, Nominative to Dative, Greetings—but modified in various ways. The identification of the author is elaborated significantly, so as to define the Pauline author as the servant, apostle, and designatee of the good news of God. This good news is further described in a proto-trinitarian theology of God, the Son, and the Spirit (note use of vocabulary from LN Semantic domain 12). The second factor is the use of the dialogical interaction throughout the body and parenesis of the letter. The tenor of the discourse involves a hypothetical debate that draws a variety of dialogical partners into the discussion. These include the Romans (e.g. Rom 1:8–16 and elsewhere, often addressed as "brothers"; and Rom 16), judgmental humans probably including those who ought to be bound by some type of legal code or "law" (e.g. Rom 2:1–16), the Jews (Rom 2:17–29), unnamed discussion partners contemplating such issues, probably including both Jews and non-Jews (e.g. Rom 3:1–20), non-Jews who might believe in their privilege because of Jewish rejection of Jesus (Rom 9–11), those in Rome who wish to follow Paul's instructions (Rom 12–15), the strong, as opposed to the weak who follow self-imposed practices (Rom 14:1—15:13), and even God himself (Rom 16:25–27). Discussing the tenor of the discourse is quite different from trying to establish the actual recipients of the letter—and they may or may not have bearing on each other. The third factor to consider is Rom 14:1—15:13. I have mentioned the weak and strong above, but they have been the focus of much of the discussion regarding the audience of Romans. There are three primary participants within this section. These are Paul, his direct addressees, and

16. Porter and O'Donnell, "Semantics," 179.
17. See Das, *Solving the Romans Debate*, for recent discussion.

his indirect addressees or those he is talking about with his addressees. As is fitting for the parenetic section of the letter, Paul begins by directing the behavior of his addressees (note use of an imperative in the second person plural) about those who are weak in faith (note use of the accusative case for them as the complement of the clause). This clausally inclusive relationship is maintained throughout the section. Paul speaks to his addressees about the others. When he wishes to offer an example of what he is stating, he usually frames it in the third person as an example about one who eats, etc. The effect is to frame the discussion as Paul instructing others about a third party. The third party is indeed characterized by behavior that might well represent Jewish legalism of the time—rules concerning food (Rom 14:2, 3, 6, 15, 20, 21), others' behavior (Rom 14:4, 5), celebration of particular days (Rom 14:5, 6), and possibly even circumcision (Rom 15:8). The greater concern is not these practices but concern for this "other" person that the person not stumble (Rom 14:13), even though Paul (note the use of two marked stative verbs in Rom 14:14) is convinced of the rightness of his behavior. In other words, Paul instructs his direct addressees regarding their need for tolerance of his indirect addressees.

Mode

The mode of discourse is the means by which the language becomes a text. In other words, the mode of discourse is the linguistic or language-in-use means by which the field and tenor become a text. In one sense, the mode of the letter to the Romans, like all of the New Testament letters, is relatively easy to describe. It is a written text, apparently meant to be read out loud—because of economies of resources and literacy. In other words, there was not sufficient means to produce a letter for everyone and not everyone could read the letter for him- or herself in any case.

I realize, however, that having said what I have just said about a letter raises many more questions than it answers. This situation may describe the initial instance of the transmission of the letter, but it does not address the larger situational contextual features of letter writing—that is, why letters were written as opposed to other forms of communication. We have been told that letters in the ancient world were meant as substitutes for the personal presence of the author, and in fact have even been told (wrongly I think) that the letter was less important than the personal information conveyed by the letter carrier and reader.[18] This is difficult to substantiate—and

18. On Paul and the letter form, see Porter, *Apostle Paul*, 136–55.

in any case, if Romans is less important than what the reader conveyed, I find it hard to imagine what exactly it was that the reader said that was of greater importance than the content of Romans itself. This begs the question of why a letter as opposed to something else was sent, as well as the issue of subsequent use of letters within the original community, to say nothing of other Christian communities that made use of these letters (e.g. the exchange of letters between Colossae and Laodicea). We also know that letter writers of the ancient world saved copies of their letters for subsequent use. For Paul, this may well have involved subsequent use in writing of further letters or even in keeping a collection of his own letters for ecclesial reasons. And what of the use of a scribe in the authorial process? Since Tertius is grammatically invoked in the text, he is a presence to be reckoned with. In other words, without problematizing the situation further, let me simply say that I am not sure that a letter is best seen as simply a substitute for the personal presence of the author. In some regards this may be true, but I do not think that it can be the case in all instances. The situational contexts of letters were much broader than traditionally conceived. I think that the letter (best seen as a register in its own right) was selected because, within the situational context, a letter was able to structure its content in a particular way that was able to accomplish the author's purpose in ways not as easily accomplished by another written form. Some of the reasons for this include: the structure of the letter itself gave a particular type of organization and, thereby, emphasis to the content of the letter; the letter was more readily able to accomplish particular purposes and perform specific functions than other types of communication, as it was addressed to designated recipients by a particular author; the letter was better suited to particular fields of discourse than were other types of communication, such as contemporary situations and events; and the letter was suited to establishing particular tenors of discourse than were other discourse types by the way in which the author is able to characterize him/herself and the audience (recipients).

I think that all of these are found in Romans, where Paul addresses a group that he has never met. There is nothing in particular about register analysis or the letter style that is particular to writing to a group that Paul had never met. However, Paul is able to take the ancient epistolary form—itself a broad register (and literary) type—and, due to particular situational contexts, narrow the scope of the register to suit his purposes. Paul elaborates particular parts of the standard epistolary form, such as the opening, body, and closing, and even enhances and adds sections not normally found within the epistolary format, such as the thanksgiving and the parenesis, to suit his purposes. He writes letters whose context of situation is individual recipients, such as Timothy, Titus, and Philemon, and whose situation is various types of churches. Within the church letters, there are registers for those churches he has visited, such as Philippi and Corinth, and those for the churches he has not visited, such as Romans (I am not convinced that Paul had not visited Colossae).

There are other factors to consider in mode of discourse, such as cohesion, informational structure, and the like. Cohesion is based upon various formal and semantic chains formed by various linguistic elements. Others have shown that Romans, though a complex discourse, has a number of cohesive devices, especially within its various epistolary units. One of the major features not fully appreciated is the use of citations to create structural unity. Informational structure of Greek is significantly different from English, due to its nonconfigurational character as a language. Nevertheless, at each level of exponence, there are structural informational patterns that arrange the material thematically.

THE STRUCTURE OF ROMANS

This discussion of register types, and the various registers of the Pauline letters, raises the question of letter structure within the ancient world, and in particular the letter structure of Romans. In the comments made above, I designated a particular type of theological argument found within Romans, characterized by movement from the human condition to justification to reconciliation to sanctification/salvation (the field of discourse), by means of a dialogical interaction that frames the discussion between the authorial voice and his audience, often about others (the tenor of discourse), and does so in written form to be read out, and, probably, even to be read again by others whether aloud or not.

Many of these issues are typically discussed as matters of genre. Not only within the field of biblical studies, but certainly within this field, appeal is often made to genre as a resolution of matters related to the type of literature that is being discussed. There are two types of genre discussion that I have encountered in my surveying the field. To not put too fine a point on it, there is sophisticated genre study and there is naïve genre study.[19] Most genre study within biblical studies, and also within linguistic

19. For a helpful guide, see Frow, *Genre*.

study so far as I have read in much recent linguistic work, falls into the category of naïve genre study. To oversimplify, such naïve genre study treats genres as relatively fixed forms, relatively easily identifiable, defined usually on the basis of a limited number of features (if features are identified at all), and then used to label instances of literature as a means of determining their meaning. Every one of these assumptions is highly problematic—perhaps the most difficult of all being the one that says that understanding of genre provides a means of determining meaning. Only within various types of sophisticated narratological analysis and forms of literary criticism and linguistics is the problematic nature of genre realized. The result, however, is the recognition that the use of the category of genre holds little promise for discussion of the kinds of issues raised by most biblical material, and certainly not the kind of issues raised in register analysis.

In a highly insightful treatment of the issue of genre, David Perkins notes that the usual way that genres are identified is to assert their unity but then to undermine such a conception. As he states, "in dealing with genres, as with any taxonomy, the literary historian must establish a canon (what texts belong to the genre) and a concept. Both the canon and the concept are more or less uncertain." The result is that "contemporary genre theory always undermines the unity and coherence of a genre while also asserting it. Contemporary theorists emphasize that genres change over time (Fowler, Cohen), that works incorporate features of several different genres (Bakhtin, Guillen), that there are mixed genres (Colie), and that works in a genre may be linked only by family resemblance (Fowler)." The notion then achieves less than it promises, because "it seems that very different works may belong to the same genre and that a work may belong to different genres. If this is so, the actual role of genre concepts in the production and reception of works must often be less than genre theorists suppose."[20] Instead, with the Russian formalists, Perkins contends we should recognize "that there can be no definition of literature as such that is valid for all epochs." Note that he says that the "intimate letter is a literary genre in some epochs, but in others it falls into the realm of private life outside of literature." Perkins, following Tynyanov's argument, claims that "the literature of any time is a synchronic system and that over time systems succeed each other... some elements of a system may reappear in its successor;

20. Perkins, *Is Literary History Possible?*, 80, referring to many of the important recent theorists of genre. Perkins adds: "Because it depends so heavily on constructions of the literary historian, the description of a genre may be no less creative than the writing of literary history is generally."

others may not. The same form may have an altered function in the context or system of a different epoch."²¹ In language reminiscent of structuralist/linguistic thought, Perkins states that the "proper subject of literary history is not the succession of works but the succession of systems, for to describe the work without describing the system in which it functions is meaningless. When an element of a system changes, or the function of an element, the whole system changes correlatively. Succession, therefore, is discontinuous; a system takes the place of the previous one. When this happens, not only the marginal elements of the system but also the central ones may have altered; the previously central elements may move to the margin or disappear altogether."²²

Genre theory, I contend, does not have the formal apparatus sufficient to handle all of the issues that it raises. What about the ancient letter? Haven't we just been discussing the ancient letter? We have been discussing an instance of an ancient letter, one that has some resemblances to and some differences from other ancient letters, as well as other writings, even by the same author. Perhaps at the highest level of abstraction, as a feature of a cultural context, we might identify broad literary types, and we may wish to call these genres. Perhaps. However, at the less abstract level, at a level at which differences between them become meaningful, I think that we need a more robust means of categorizing and discussing differences between and among texts. Register analysis, I think, provides at least a plausible way forward in such discussion. The reasons are several. One is that register does not demand the kind of conceptual unity demanded by genre. Another is that register analysis functions at any and all levels of abstraction, as means of discussing a single text up to a large group of texts, depending upon the level of typified specificity desired. Another is that, whereas genre analysis often pays attention only to limited features of texts, often structural and sometimes content-based (e.g. "once upon a time . . ."), register analysis provides a more complex set of variables for discussion, including field, tenor, and mode, or content (aboutness), interaction (whoness), and structure (howness).²³

The Pauline letter is an instance of the register of personal letter, directed to either churches or individuals. However, the Pauline letter often

---

21. Ibid., 169, drawing upon Tynyanov, "Literary Fact."
22. Perkins, *Is Literary History Possible?* 170.
23. For some of the most developed recent work in this regard, see Martin, *English Text*, 497–508; and Martin and Rose, *Genre Relations*, 16–18.

varies in its structural components and the weightings given to these individual elements. Paul's letter to the Romans is the longest of his letters, and develops each of the five major components of a Pauline letter: the opening, thanksgiving, body, parenesis, and closing. These are of course not the only ways of characterizing the major movements within the letter. Prague school functional analysis has argued for the Functional Sentence Perspective. This approach to sentence (or clause) structure is essentially concerned with the mode of discourse, or how the field and tenor are exposited as organized text. I have argued elsewhere that an expanded form of functional perspective, what I have termed Functional Letter Perspective, may be available as a means of arguing for the organizational structure of a letter.[24] Nevertheless, even if we retain the traditional epistolary analysis, I think that we can gain insights through register analysis. Above, I noted how various components of the situational context related to these various epistolary parts. In that discussion, I assumed for the sake of classification that these were meaningful "places" (topoi, to use the rhetorical term) within the Pauline letter register. This raises a notorious problem in register analysis—the question of sub-registers. Registers within registers—whatever they are called, and this includes such things as embedded registers, micro-registers (as opposed to macro-registers), simple registers (as opposed to complex registers)—are, at least it seems to me, a major factor that must be taken into account. The tendency is to want to characterize situational contexts as complex wholes, and hence reflective of a single register (Biber and Conrad speak of this as a unidirectional movement from the situational context to register).[25] However, we must also recognize that registers can vary, in both spoken and written language. For example, within a conversation, a speaker may introduce a story or tell a joke or shift their tone or subject matter, so as to constitute a shift in register. The same may occur in writing—when within a narrative, for example, one embeds another story or shifts to reporting speech. Thus, we need to have a flexible enough analysis of register to accommodate a text as complex as a Gospel—and a Pauline letter.

Thus, within a Pauline letter such as Romans, we may well wish to speak of the register of Romans and the sub-registers that it also instantiates. These sub-registers may well relate to epistolary structure. In fact, I

---

24. Porter, "Functional Letter Perspective."

25. Biber and Conrad, *Register, Genre, and Style*, 72. They recognize sub-registers within what they call general registers (e.g. 110 and elsewhere).

think that they do, on the basis of a variety of quantifiable shifts in their contextual features. Each of the features of context will not shift with each sub-register, but each may shift as appropriate and as indicated by various moves within the text.

The opening of the letter functions to establish the relationship between author and reader, writer and recipient, and is concerned to establish the general communicative purpose of the letter, organized usually by means of traditional formal features. The thanksgiving focuses upon a particular field of discourse, thanksgiving, and with it uses a number of linguistic devices already noted, such as the imperfective aspect in distinction from the perfective aspect of the opening. The body of the letter may well shift the field of discourse again as it chooses to move from thanksgiving to other topics, such as human sinfulness and its progressive remedies. This shift in field may also result in a shift in tenor, from the epistolary audience of the opening and thanksgiving to the varied audience of the body, including both the epistolary audience and a variety of secondary participants. The parenetic section may well mark a further shift in both field and tenor of discourse, as the emphasis is placed upon the direction of behavior rather than the assertion of concepts. Finally, the closing shifts back to the epistolary audience, even if it also includes other secondary participants.

This brief summary of the book of Romans is meant to illustrate how its structure is reflective of various sub-registers, or rather, how various sub-registers help to form the structure of the book of Romans. This is not simply a reflection of more typical patterns found in the type of the letter, but reflects particular features of the Pauline letter, and in particular the letter to the Romans. These shifts are reminiscent of the same kinds of shifts that have been noted within various other registers, such as Biber and Conrad have explored in various examples (and shown to some extent in the Pauline letter corpus by Burggraff).[26]

CONCLUSION

This paper has not attempted to offer definitive analysis of any one dimension of Paul's letter to the Romans. Instead, it has attempted to lay out some of the many and diverse features that must be considered within a register analysis of this or any Pauline letter. Register analysis, not one of the standard tools of New Testament epistolary analysis, finds its roots in the recognition that situational context influences and constrains the meaning

26. See ibid., throughout; Burggraff, "Corpus Linguistic Verb Analysis."

potential and hence expression of a text. These constraints and their resulting instantiations are reflected in the various meaningful choices that an author makes in crafting a text in a particular way. Romans is such a text. There are various quantifiable and analyzable features that reflect the various features of the situational context, its field, tenor, and mode. These are instantiated in various ways within this letter that contribute to our understanding of how the situational context—as opposed to other types of constraints—influences our understanding of Paul's communicative purposes.

BIBLIOGRAPHY

Biber, Douglas, and Susan Conrad. *Register, Genre, and Style.* CTL. Cambridge: Cambridge University Press, 2009.

Burggraff, Philip D. "A Corpus Linguistic Verb Analysis of the Pauline Letters: The Contribution of Verb Patterns to Pauline Letter Structure." PhD diss., McMaster Divinity College, 2011.

Catford, James. *A Linguistic Theory of Translation.* London: Oxford University Press, 1965.

Das, A. Andrew. *Solving the Romans Debate.* Minneapolis: Fortress, 2007.

Frow, John. *Genre.* New Critical Idiom. London: Routledge, 2005.

Gregory, Michael, and Susanne Carroll. *Language and Situation: Language Varieties and their Social Contexts.* London: Routledge and Kegan Paul, 1978.

Halliday, Michael A. K., and Ruqaiya Hasan. *Language, Context, and Text: Aspects of Language in a Social-Semiotic Perspective.* Geelong, Victoria: Deakin University Press, 1985.

Halliday, Michael A. K., Angus McIntosh, and Peter Strevens. *The Linguistic Sciences and Language Teaching.* London: Longmans, 1964.

Levinson, Stephen C. *Pragmatics.* CTL. Cambridge: Cambridge University Press, 1983.

Louw, Johannes P., and Eugene A. Nida. *Greek-English Lexicon of the New Testament Based on Semantic Domains.* 2 vols. New York: United Bible Societies, 1988.

Martin, J. R. *English Text: System and Structure.* Amsterdam: Benjamins, 1992.

Martin, J. R., and David Rose. *Genre Relations: Mapping Culture.* London: Equinox, 2008.

Ong, Hughson T. *The Multilingual Jesus and the Sociolinguistic World of the New Testament.* LBS 12. Leiden: Brill, 2015.

Perkins, David. *Is Literary History Possible?* Baltimore: Johns Hopkins University Press, 1992.

Porter, Stanley E. "Dialect and Register in the Greek of the New Testament: Theory." In *Rethinking Contexts, Rereading Texts: Contributions from the Social Sciences to Biblical Interpretation*, edited by M. Daniel Carroll R., 190–208. Sheffield: Sheffield Academic, 2000.

———. "Register in the Greek of the New Testament: Application with Reference to Mark's Gospel." In *Rethinking Contexts, Rereading Texts: Contributions from the Social Sciences to Biblical Interpretation*, edited by M. Daniel Carroll R., 209–29. Sheffield: Sheffield Academic, 2000.

———. "A Functional Letter Perspective: Towards a Grammar of Epistolary Form." In *Paul and the Ancient Letter Form*, edited by Stanley E. Porter and Sean A. Adams, 9–32. PAST 6. Leiden: Brill, 2010.

———. *The Apostle Paul: His Life, Thought, and Letters.* Grand Rapids: Eerdmans, 2016.

———. *The Letter to the Romans: A Linguistic and Literary Commentary.* New Testament Monographs 37. Sheffield: Sheffield Phoenix, 2015.

Porter, Stanley E., and Matthew Brook O'Donnell. "Semantics and Patterns of Argumentation in the Book of Romans: Definitions, Proposals, Data and Experiments." In *Diglossia and Other Topics in New Testament Linguistics*, edited by Stanley E. Porter, 154–204. Sheffield: Sheffield Academic, 2000.

Tynyanov, Yury. "The Literary Fact." In *Texte der russischen Formalisten*, vol. 1, *Texte zur allgemeinen Literaturtheorie und zur Theorie der Prosa*, edited by Jurij Striedter, 417–23. Munich: Wilhelm Fink, 1969.

Thompson, Geoff. *Introducing Functional Grammar.* 2nd ed. London: Hodder Education, 2004.

3

Deliverance and Demographics
The Pastoral Riches of "Romans Righteousness" (Romans 1–4)

ROBERT W. YARBROUGH

INTRODUCTION

MY ASSIGNMENT IN THIS essay is to examine Rom 1–4 under the heading of "salvation." But is that what these chapters are about? The book *The Romans Debate* reminds us that the subject of the whole book of Romans, never mind these chapters, was declared uncertain in scholarly discussion near the end of the twentieth century.[1] Further, the by now somewhat old discussion called "the New Perspective" had the effect for many of declaring previous readings of Paul and in particular readings associated with Reformation understandings of salvation largely mistaken. The saving message of Romans concentrated in Rom 1–4 is at the core of what has been called in question and for many cast in doubt.

And what about Rom 1–4? They contain 117 verses. The first fifteen are introductory and could front a treatise on various topics.[2] That leaves 102 verses. Of these, Rom 1:18—3:20 contains 64 verses. That is 63 per cent of 102. It may be doubted whether anyone reading Rom 1:18—3:20 in isolation would exclaim, "This is about salvation." It is rather about the wrath of God, if we take the opening words of v. 18 as the theme. Or the verses

---

1. Donfried, ed., *The Romans Debate*.

2. This is not to deny that Rom 1:1–15 serves well as an introduction to a treatise that turns out to be largely about salvation. See Holland, *The Divine Marriage*, 27 n. 1.

are about human sin or fallenness, if we think of the reason for the wrath. In either case, mathematically Rom 1–4 is about hamartiology, or maybe eschatology if we take seriously the meaning of ὀργὴ θεοῦ ("wrath of God"; cf. Rom 1:18), not soteriology.

And yet, "God . . . gives life to the dead and calls into being things that were not" (Rom 4:17).[3] Just *one* verse out of 102 that conveys salvation would be enough to tint the whole verbal landscape in that shade, given that the author speaks of a message that "is the power of God that brings salvation to everyone who believes" (1:16). This is because by that message "the righteousness of God is revealed" (1:17). Also, that God has power to do what he promises (4:21), which includes granting salvation even to the ungodly by his righteousness (4:5; 5:6).

Alert to the fact, then, that we must not let the heading "salvation" blind us to the gritty details of what we are actually looking at, we proceed as follows. First, we will survey some recent trends in the discussion on salvation in Rom 1–4, arriving at a summary of Pauline theology as articulated in Romans. Second, we will comment on implications of the deliverance afforded by God's righteousness for certain pastoral applications, thinking demographically in two senses: the demographics of the world church, and the demographics of congregations we may lead or belong to. By demographics I mean simply what is true, statistically, about large groups of people regarding their beliefs and behaviors.

ROMANS 1–4 AND SALVATION IN RECENT STUDIES

Among pastors and scholars, who *doesn't* have a pretty clear idea of what constitutes salvation in Rom 1–4? But neither scholarship nor ministry stands still, because both society and we as individuals grow and change, whether for good or ill. That means new studies are constantly appearing that can shape and perhaps shake our understanding even of such a seemingly settled topic.

One source of fresh air in what could seem a stale discussion comes from the series The Church's Bible edited by Robert Louis Wilken. In this series, in 2012 there appeared a volume called *Romans: Interpreted by Early Christian Commentators* by J. Patout Burns Jr.[4] This is comparable to the older volume by Gerald Bray in the Ancient Christian Commentary on

---

3. Unless otherwise noted, Scripture quotations are from the NIV 2011. Parenthetical Scripture references lacking a book name are from Romans.

4. Burns, *Romans*.

Scripture series.⁵ Both volumes try to distill from patristic commentators the gist of views on Romans that prevailed in the church's earliest centuries. The difference is that whereas Bray's citations of the church fathers tend to be terse and are derived from a lengthy roster of figures, many of whose extant writings cite Romans only sporadically, those in the Burns volume are fewer in number but more extensive in scope. This is because Burns focuses on those who wrote "extended commentaries on the Pauline letters."⁶ This means Origen, John Chrysostom, Theodoret of Cyrrhus, and Cyril of Alexandria on the Greek side, and in Latin the unknown person called Ambrosiaster, Pelagius, and Augustine. The happy result is not just insight on phrases or verses but a sense of the larger currents of conviction in a given church father and in Romans as patristic commentators viewed it.

Burns contributes to our understanding of Rom 1–4 by confirming that in the fathers' readings, Romans "was focused on the unity of the divine plan of salvation."⁷ He notes that the fathers speak of "the universal need for salvation, the relation between divine promise and human faith," and "the roles of Christ and the law . . ."⁸ All of these matters, one notes, are discussed in Rom 1–4. Whereas contemporary discussion has questioned in what sense or even whether Romans is about personal salvation, Burns confirms that this was a given among patristic interpreters.

Burns also alerts us that Origen and most others in that period upheld "human autonomy and free choice—though carefully limited—because they considered this essential for safeguarding the human moral responsibility essential to their understanding of God's justice in condemning sinners and rewarding the faithful."⁹ Less prominent but in historical perspective equally important were Augustine and some others who "emphasized the sinfulness of humanity and the absolute gratuity of all God's operations which led chosen individuals to that salvation provided in Christ."¹⁰

Burns' selections from the fathers assure us that we are not necessarily far off track, Reformation retrogrades, or dupes of some glitzy revivalism if we see in Rom 1–4 the foundations for a plan of salvation through which a

---

5. Bray, *Romans*. On the history of exegesis of Romans up through about 1970, see Cranfield, *Romans*, 1:30–44.

6. Burns, *Romans*, xxvii.

7. Ibid., xxiv.

8. Ibid., xxiv.

9. Ibid., xxv.

10. Ibid.

confessing sinner may find justification and peace with God though faith in Christ. That is probably not *all* we should find in Rom 1–4 or in a full-scale Romans soteriology. But as a starting point it seems to be a significant aspect of what the earliest extant commentators saw there.

A second newer source for insight into Rom 1–4 is the "union with Christ" discussion that has emerged in recent years. Note just these nine studies:

1. *Covenant and Salvation: Union with Christ* by Michael S. Horton (2007)

2. *Union and Communion with Christ* by Maurice Roberts and Joel Beeke (2008)

3. *Union with Christ: A Biblical View of the New Life in Jesus Christ* by Lewis B. Smedes (2009)

4. *Union with Christ: Reframing Theology and Ministry for the Church* by J. Todd Billings (2011)

5. *Union with Christ: In Scripture, History, and Theology* by Robert Letham (2011)

6. *Paul and Union with Christ: An Exegetical and Theological Study* by Constantine R. Campbell (2012)

7. *One with Christ: An Evangelical Theology of Salvation* by Marcus Peter Johnson (2013)

8. *Found in Him: The Joy of the Incarnation and Our Union with Christ* by Elyse M. Fitzpatrick (2013)

9. *Union with Christ in the New Testament* by Grant Macaskill (2013)

These works do not of course point to a single uniform truth or result. But they do signal for some the end of fixation with "justification" or "the righteousness of God" or related subtopics as these dominated discussion of Romans in recent decades. Constantine Campbell ventures that "justification occurs as an outworking of union with Christ, and the two concepts ought not be set against each other, but rather, must be understood in their relatedness."[11] He further explains that "the justification of believers stems from their participation in the death and resurrection of Christ;

---

11. Campbell, *Union with Christ*, 405. For a helpful review with critique of this book by Michael Bird see http://www.patheos.com/blogs/euangelion/2013/03/official-launch-of-con-campbells-book-on-paul-and-union-with-christ/.

his vindicating resurrection becomes the vindication and righteousness of those united to him."[12] And he concludes: "Finally, the theological conception of imputation is understood as the unmerited reception of Christ's righteousness, which is received through union with him."[13]

In a burgeoning investigation of "union with Christ" currently underway, then, we are seeing the Old Perspective/New Perspective impasse transcended by rediscovery and exploration of an overlooked theological emphasis. As Chris Tilling observes, the New Perspective "diagnosis of the problem confronting readers of Paul is one-dimensional and its prescribed reinterpretation of Paul" does not always deal adequately with "the real interpretative difficulties involved."[14] Maybe Luther and Calvin did not get everything right, but neither did E. P. Sanders, N. T. Wright, James Dunn, and other leading lights of the New Perspective, in the view of an increasing number of often younger scholars. Salvation in Romans involves more than a scholarly consensus regarding the New Perspective, beyond which the guild has now begun to shift with emphases like union with Christ.

A few more words about this important turn in Pauline studies are in order. Whereas there has been a strong tendency (going back at least to Adolf Deissmann) to assign a single overarching meaning to union with Christ, connecting it with phrases like ἐν Χριστῷ ("in Christ"), and to import that meaning into every context where the phrase or close analogies appear, Campbell finds "union with Christ" to be polysemic—diverse in meaning. While "union" is often what Paul seeks to communicate, other times what is conveyed is participation (i.e., "partaking in the events of Christ's narrative"),[15] other times identification (i.e., believers' location in the realm of Christ and their allegiance to his lordship),[16] and still other times incorporation (i.e., "the reality and entailments of corporate membership in Christ's body").[17] Moreover, this four-fold meta-theme summarized by the term "union with Christ" occurs in passages that connote a range of emphases, from locality to instrumentality to trinitarianism to eschatology to, finally, spiritual reality.[18]

12. Campbell, *Union with Christ*, 405.
13. Ibid., 405.
14. Tilling, ed., *Beyond Old and New*, 1.
15. Campbell, *Union with Christ*, 420.
16. Ibid., 420.
17. Ibid., 420.
18. Ibid., 29, also 406–14.

Campbell points out that this Pauline meta-theme is not Paul's own invention but is anticipated in and informed by antecedent concepts "in Jewish theology and the Old Testament, but most profoundly in the words of Jesus, beginning with his words to Paul on the Damascus road."[19] Yet Paul's "conception remains boldly original in its language, scope and pervasiveness."[20]

Campbell denies that union with Christ is the "center" of Pauline theology. In fact he thinks that the quest for such a center has not arrived at consensus, because there is no center. Rather than viewing Paul's theology as a wheel, in which case there must be a hub or center, Campbell suggests it is web-like. Union with Christ is a key, or to change the metaphor "the essential ingredient that binds all other elements together; it is the webbing that connects the ideas of Paul's web-shaped theological framework."[21] He points out that "virtually every topic that Paul addresses is in some measure connected to union with Christ."[22] Campbell also notes that union with Christ was prominent in Luther and Calvin but came to be neglected in traditions associated with their names in subsequent generations and centuries. In that respect, Campbell does not claim to have arrived at new insight so much as to have "discovered a route back to an understanding of Paul . . . that has remained elusive for a time."[23]

If Campbell and other "unionists" are correct to any considerable degree, it is arguable that we have moved beyond the New Perspective debate wiser but also ready to recognize fuller dimensions of Paul's doctrine of salvation than may have been typical not many years ago.

A third source of insight into Rom 1–4 and its doctrine of salvation comes from recent commentaries.[24] Here I mention but two. The first is by Tom Holland, a 2011 publication called *Romans: The Divine Marriage*.[25] Interacting extensively with Dunn and Wright, and thus cognizant of New Perspective insights, Holland offers a reading of Romans that highlights God's pursuit of a people in the Old Testament called Israel, "God's bride

---

19. Ibid., 29; see also 414–20.
20. Ibid., 29.
21. Ibid., 442.
22. Ibid., 441.
23. Ibid., 441.
24. For a searching analysis of dozens of Romans commentaries more generally, see Porter, "Commentaries on the Book of Romans," 365–404.
25. Holland, *The Divine Marriage*.

because she was called to a unique, personal relationship" with him.[26] In the New Testament, Holland thinks, "the theme of the divine marriage (which is the culmination of the new exodus)" continues to dominate, but with a major modulation.[27] That is the new covenant, through which "believing Jews and Gentiles have now become the true bride of God," both drawing "from the same divinely-appointed stock as they share the promises given by God to Abraham."[28]

Holland's work sharpens understanding of Romans in six ways, among others.[29] (1) He stresses the need to check what he calls "Hellenistic baggage" that scholars tend to carry along with the West's populist individualism, in order to reaffirm the Old Testament heritage that Paul seeks to explicate in Romans as a primary means of presenting Christ. (2) Holland stresses the corporate dimension of Romans, as addressed to churches not primarily to autonomous individuals. If we do not hear in Romans the call to be joined to the people of God, not just isolated souls saved from our sins, we aren't hearing Romans. He emphasizes, "This commentary seeks to correct the faulty reading that results from placing the individual at the center of the message of Romans."[30] (3) Romans 1 highlights the Old Testament seedbed for the emergence and growth of Christ's kingdom, a kingdom desperately needed due to humanity's rebellion against its Creator (1:19–32). (4) Romans 2 speaks of justification as inclusion in the eschatological community, toward which people must strive, as John the Baptist called for the act of repentance. Chapter 2 as a dialogue with a "representative of the Children of Abraham" is not about personal justification in the fullest Pauline sense. (5) Chapter 3 develops exile themes showing how Christ by his death becomes "the atoning Passover sacrifice," that is, "the eschatological Passover" in which "there is no special status for Jews and Gentiles." (6) Chapter 4, Holland thinks, shows clearly that "there has been failure in understanding" Paul's theology of justification. It is about God's "covenant-making" which was sealed for Abraham on Mount Moriah, not by the act itself but through "the faith that made his obedience possible." New Testament believers are called to an analogous proactive attachment to God's saving work in raising Jesus and constituting them "a spiritual

26. Ibid., ix.
27. Ibid., ix.
28. Ibid., ix.
29. See ibid., 483–84.
30. Ibid., xii.

family as a result."[31] If we read Romans as about believing in Jesus but not about becoming children of Abraham, we are missing the message.

More could be said about Holland's rich treatment, informed by recent scholarship and replete with substantial excurses on topics like Paul's use of the word δίκαιος ("righteous"), justification in Paul's theology, and baptism into Christ. But this commentary is a commendable example of how historic Christian understanding of Paul's gospel continues to be articulated and sharpened in the academic marketplace.

A second recent commentary contributing to understanding of salvation in Rom 1–4 is by Colin Kruse in the Pillar New Testament Commentary series.[32] Kruse is less enamored of the Old Testament as the hermeneutical key to Romans than is Holland. Where he excels is, for example, in his interaction with the commentaries by Brendan Byrne, C. E. B. Cranfield, James Dunn, Joseph Fitzmyer, Robert Jewett, Douglas Moo, and N. T. Wright. Kruse affirms and integrates recent scholarship more painstakingly and effectively than most. This is seen in his careful and substantial introductory section, "The Influence of 'the New Perspective,'"[33] as well as in his lengthy discussion of theological themes.[34] It is here, by way of summary, that Kruse opens a window into the larger understanding of salvation to which Rom 1–4 contributes. After discussing proposed "centers" of Pauline theology in the light of which Romans should be interpreted—those centers include justification by faith, salvation history, the work of Christ as the center of redemptive history, Christ or christocentric soteriology, reconciliation, the triumph of God, and combinations of all of the above—Kruse offers this:

> In respect to what may be deduced from Romans itself . . . note should be taken of the overwhelmingly theocentric nature of the letter . . . The gospel Paul expounds is the gospel of God in which the righteousness of God, the grace of God, and the love of God are revealed. God's sovereign will is determinative in the matter of salvation as he exercises the divine prerogative to have mercy upon whom he will have mercy. God himself is the primary agent of salvation, and he effects it through the redemptive activity of his Son whom he put forward as the atoning sacrifice for sins. Accordingly, the focus of Paul's exposition of God's saving activity

---

31. For all quotations in this paragraph, see ibid., 483–84.
32. Kruse, *Romans*.
33. Ibid., 14–22.
34. Ibid., 22–33.

is upon the work of the Son. Perhaps it may be said, then, that, as far as Romans is concerned, the center, heart, and organizing principle of Pauline theology is the action of God through the person and work of Jesus Christ to deal with the effects of human sin, individually, communally, and cosmically. In brief, as far as Romans is concerned, the *centrum Paulinum* is the gospel of God comprehensively conceived.[35]

Those words may be taken as summative and suggestive for our topic of salvation in Rom 1–4. Following Kruse, we may say that salvation is theocentric; it is christocentric; it is comprehensive. Romans' theocentricity is a challenge to interpretations that seek to center anything other or less than God himself. Romans' christocentricity calls in question readings that might cast the spotlight on something other than the finished work of the one highlighted so graphically along with the Father in Rom 1:1–6 and 16:25–27. Romans' comprehensiveness is a challenge to reductionist interpretations that view Romans as merely a source for verses about personal salvation, or as testimony chiefly to complications in first-century social relations, or as a repository of puzzles to fuel endless scholastic debates. Romans really is about the gospel, for "in the gospel the righteousness of God is revealed" in saving ways (1:17). The implications of Romans for human deliverance, to "free us from all ills, in this world and the next,"[36] deserve careful and constant reflection. That is our focus in the next section.

THE PASTORAL RICHES OF "ROMANS RIGHTEOUSNESS"

Academic study of Romans naturally emphasizes the intricacies, conundrums, and disputations associated with the letter. This is on display in the recent volume edited by Chris Tilling, *Beyond Old and New Perspectives on Paul: Reflections on the Work of Douglas Campbell*. If both perspectives, old and new, got things wrong, what contrasting option might remain? Douglass Campbell claims to have discovered one, notably in *The Deliverance of God: An Apocalyptic Rereading of Justification in Paul*. Tilling's work documents responses offered by many scholars at many levels to what Campbell has proposed. Here I wish only to observe how daunting and sterile Romans could seem for the everyday work of pastoral ministry, most notably ministry of the word, if Romans and its saving message truly were so elusive, so debatable, and consequently so unstable in nature and impervious

35. Ibid., 33.
36. The words are from the Martin Rinkart's hymn "Now Thank We All Our God."

to application as it might seem based on contemporary Romans scholarship. As Graham Tomlin observes in interaction with Campbell, "We must admit a little nervousness about any approach that makes the Scriptures incomprehensible to the 'ordinary reader'—in other words, one relatively unversed in the nuances of contemporary NT scholarship."[37]

In a volume bearing the name of the pastor H. H. Bingham, and endowed by his daughter Mrs. Doris Kennedy "as an act of admiration and appreciation for a wonderful father and minister,"[38] it is fitting that we include here a few pastoral implications of Romans, or of "Romans Righteousness" as I am terming the dynamic that encounters readers or hearers of this epistle as a whole. We do not need here to enter into the technical debate of what "righteousness of God" means in Scripture or in Romans; we can simply observe the clear statement of 1:16–17 that the gospel message, which I will define here as the fulfillment of God's promises in the death and resurrection of his Son Jesus the Christ, *is* God's power to deliver, because by or in it *God's righteousness* is revealed.

What might that mean at the North American local church level? What should make a pastor's heart beat a little faster when he or she thinks of Romans or reads through the first four chapters? I am thinking not just of "salvation" there in terms of the doctrine or even in the populist sense that "I am saved; I have salvation" because of Christian belief. I am thinking of σωτηρία[39] ("salvation") in the sense of rescue from mortal peril, deliverance from grave threat, possibly by someone's personal intervention, who would in that case become a σωτήρ[40] ("savior").

At the world church level, Romans' saving message offers those who receive it hope in the face of unimaginable trial. I say "unimaginable" advisedly. There are things like combat, or less exotically bearing a child, that you must experience really to understand. I have read much about combat and been in the proximity of a child entering the world, but every combat veteran and mother knows that I am an outsider to things they share with fellow soldiers or other moms, however much I read about and mentally grasp what they have endured.

37. Tomlin, "Luther and the Deliverance of God," 25.
38. "Bingham Colloquium," [n.d.].
39. The word occurs in Romans at 1:17; 10:1, 10; 11:11; 13:11. The cognate verb σῴζω ("I save, rescue") occurs at 5:9, 10; 8:24; 9:27; 10:9, 13; 11:14, 26. A near synonym is ῥύομαι found in Romans at 7:24; 11:26; 15:31.
40. In Paul, the word occurs at Eph 5:23; Phil 3:20; 1 Tim 2:3; 4:10; 2 Tim 1:10; Titus 1:3, 4; 2:10, 13; 3:4, 6.

The world church today has many divides, but one is between the millions who live with real heavenly hope because there are few earthly assurances, on the one hand, and those whose co-dependency on earthly assurances renders talk of heavenly hope pure theory, on the other. Affluent Christians in the west and elsewhere flirt with a co-dependency akin to what Scripture calls idolatry, with the aid of a technique historians of religion call syncretism. We may be about as willing to give God's righteousness free rein as Jeremiah's co-religionists were in his day.

But in other locations there are those like Nigerian believers who are making their peace with God under the pall of Boko Haram, or Arab background believers in Sudan, or believers in South Sudan where there is war and as I write a cholera outbreak, whose daily survival is problematic. The God whose revealed righteousness enabled Paul to make the lockdown case of Rom 1–4 leading to the glorious confession of peace with God despite sufferings in the opening verses of Rom 5 is still at work in those places and others like them. Beleaguered believers know his consolation.

While servants of the word in places of ease and security bang their heads against walls of indifference to the savory meat served up in Rom 1–4, the Romans message *is* God's power for deliverance for those who are attuned to eternal life because it is all they have to drown out the chomping of the maws of death.

Some time ago I received an e-mailed prayer request from a friend of nearly twenty years, a pastoral leader in a Muslim country in Africa, who sat with fellow converts from Islam recently as they held a sort of church business meeting over this question: "Are there steps that may be taken to overcome fear?" I quote my friend:

> Our church asked this question last Sunday after a [local] court sentenced a woman to hang for apostasy—the abandonment of her religious faith—after she married a Christian man. The judge also sentenced the woman to one hundred lashes after convicting her of "adultery" because her marriage to a Christian man is not considered to be valid under Islamic law. Please remember to pray for this brave . . . lady who changed her name to Miriam ("Mary").

These believers live, you see, in the city where this international media drama has unfolded. In a follow-up letter this pastor reminded me of how stressed his wife and all wives in that region's numerous underground cell groups are. For they are all guilty of the same crime. Where does that leave them? What hope do they have?

It leaves them, they concluded, with deliverance. Here's how the business meeting ended:

> Finally at our church we concluded that we should stand on God's Word, His promises. God is as good as His Word. He will do whatever He has promised. This is our security and anchor; we can know that whatever does come into our life does not have to shake us because of what Jesus has done.

I cannot think of a better application of the message of salvation in Rom 1–4. And as far as the power of that message, this pastor continues as follows:

> The Islamic government . . . is taking all these actions to stop the Gospel from spreading, but what actually is happening is exactly the opposite. The Gospel is spreading fast! For example, within the last couple of months, God blessed me and my team . . . as we have planted another church, and now we have thirty-one souls! In addition, we have an opportunity to help raise yet another church in another nearby town where there are already eleven believers. These 11 asked me to help provide them with a teacher and a preacher. The bottom line: the harvest is plentiful and the Father is drawing people to Christ.

For the sizable demographic of today's persecuted church, Romans righteousness in the sense of a sustaining consciousness of relatedness to God through faith in Jesus is graphic, tangible, and life-sustaining. This might not be surprising given Paul's location as he wrote: within scant months before writing Romans he would have recounted his own sufferings in 2 Cor 11 and 12. And he would have been anticipating adversity in returning to Judea and Jerusalem just after Romans was complete. It is perhaps this consciousness of suffering for the faith, yet Christ upholding him, that helps explain why it bubbles to the surface here and there in the epistle.[41]

This is not to say that overt persecution is required for the revelation of Romans righteousness with pastorally rich potential. I offer three benefits from Romans for those living for now in less dire straits, the demographic more familiar to most of us.

First, Rom 1–4 offers deliverance in the form of *intellectual stimulation* to those with the will and tools to explore its varied terrain. A young pastor recently blogged this to his congregation:

---

41. E.g., Rom 5:3; 8:17–18, 35.

> When we [reduce] Christianity to [a few] statements, then I only need to read the Bible until I understand them. I only need to read it enough so I can say that I believe those ... statements. After that, I'm covered. There's no need for me to open the Bible again; no need to look into hard passages; no need to let the Bible grow me or challenge me. There's no need to memorize anything except arguments that prove the Bible's inerrancy against liberals and atheists. So someone coined the phrase, "We believe the Bible, but we don't read the Bible," to express our current situation.[42]

Romans 1–4 has the potential to transform brain-dead fideists into Bereans who search the Scriptures with new zeal. The "Romans Road" can be more than a tidy set of stepping stones to a sense of spiritual security.[43] In this sense, Rom 1–4 is a prolegomenon to the command of 12:2 to be transformed by the renewing of the mind.

Second, Rom 1–4 offers deliverance in the form of *hamartiological diagnosis*. We have already commented that over 60 per cent of these chapters is about what brings down divine wrath. Happily, Rom 3:21 contains perhaps the most important adversative δέ ("but") in all of Scripture: "*But* now apart from the law the righteousness of God has been made known ..." But much cutting-edge Romans scholarship is pursued by scholars who regard with skepticism the notion of universal divine wrath for sin. This is dangerous for their own souls and for students or readers tempted to affirm their God whom sinners need not fear. For those schooled in spiritual growth through repentance by conviction of sin, Rom 1–4's harrowing depictions of human depravity are a tonic against self-righteousness, a goad to self-examination, a field guide for identifying maladies proliferating even in the hearts of God's people, and a springboard for doxology when chapter 3 assures readers of a person and place where wrath has been propitiated, making accessible "the righteousness of God through faith in Jesus Christ for all who believe" (3:22).

---

42. Tuck, "Our View of Scripture" (blog).

43. See, for example, Fairchild, "What is Romans Road?" [n.d.]. Over the years, arrays of verses from Romans have been deployed by evangelistic workers effectively to lead people to confession of faith in Christ. Typical steps and supporting verses are: 1. Who needs salvation (3:10–12, 23); 2. Why we need salvation (6:23); 3. How God provides salvation (5:8); 4. How we receive salvation (10:9–10, 13); 5. The results of salvation (5:1; 8:1).

Finally, Rom 1–4 offers deliverance in the form of *nurture for diverse spiritualties*.[44] Alice Mathews speaks of different learning styles that people have; I would observe that Rom 1–4 with its literary versatility draws readers or listeners into its force-field with graphic description, diatribe, Old Testament citation, inexorable logic, metaphor, and narrative reference to Abraham and Sarah. Add to this the graces of apostolic God-consciousness and Spirit-taught profundity. Mathews also speaks of the necessity for faith to have an object. She finds this in Rom 1:17 and its citation of Hab 2:4, which she notes is rendered by some scholars as "the just shall live by faith in God's faithfulness." "Faith grows," Mathews avers, "as our knowledge of the faithfulness of our God grows."[45]

Yet Mathews flags two unsatisfactory ways of presenting faith, either of which could appeal to Romans. One is to stress only "the faith," "a body of doctrine to be believed."[46] Another is "to preach 'simple trust' without a strong biblical vision of God as the mighty and the trustworthy."[47] Mathews asserts:

> Preaching is a call to faith. But faith in what? The Bible is clear that it is faith in a faithful God. That calls for both a knowledge of the Holy One and a confidence in him. This is the essence of Christian spirituality. Preaching to women [and I would add: to men] of all epistemologies calls for preaching a faithful vision of God that listeners are able to trust. Once then will they be able to love him with all their minds.[48]

On that strong theological note with resonances throughout Romans, we conclude this brief investigation of salvation in Rom 1–4. The explication of the righteousness of God in Christ found there is a focus of voluminous recent studies. And those chapters continue to serve their historic and eternal role in anchoring God's administration of redemption in our world across the full range of cultural and individual diversities.

BIBLIOGRAPHY

Billings, J. Todd. *Union with Christ: Reframing Theology and Ministry for the Church.* Grand Rapids: Baker Academic, 2011.

44. The expression is from Mathews, *Preaching That Speaks to Women*, 109.
45. Ibid., 111.
46. Ibid., 110.
47. Ibid., 110.
48. Ibid., 111.

Bray, Gerald. *Romans*. ACCS 6. Rev. ed. Downers Grove, IL: IVP, 2005.
Burns, J. Patout, Jr. *Romans: Interpreted by Early Christian Commentators*. Grand Rapids: Eerdmans, 2012.
Campbell, Constantine R. *Paul and Union with Christ: An Exegetical and Theological Study*. Grand Rapids: Zondervan, 2012.
Campbell, Douglas. *The Deliverance of God: An Apocalyptic Rereading of Justification in Paul*. Grand Rapids: Eerdmans, 2009.
Cranfield, C. E. B. *The Epistle to the Romans*. ICC. 2 vols. Edinburgh: T. & T. Clark, 1975–1979.
Donfried, Karl, ed. *The Romans Debate*. Rev. ed. Peabody, MA: Hendrickson, 1991.
Fairchild, Mary. "What is Romans Road?" [n.d.], http://christianity.about.com/od/conversion/qt/romansroad.htm [n.d.].
Fitzpatrick, Elyse M. *Found in Him: The Joy of the Incarnation and Our Union with Christ*. Wheaton, IL: Crossway, 2013.
Holland, Tom. *Romans: The Divine Marriage*. Eugene, OR: Pickwick, 2011.
Horton, Michael S. *Covenant and Salvation: Union with Christ*. Louisville: Westminster John Knox, 2007.
Johnson, Marcus Peter. *One with Christ: An Evangelical Theology of Salvation*. Wheaton, IL: Crossway, 2013.
Kruse, Colin G. *Paul's Letter to the Romans*. PNTC. Grand Rapids: Eerdmans, 2012.
Letham, Robert. *Union with Christ: In Scripture, History, and Theology*. Phillipsburg, NJ: P&R, 2011.
Macaskill, Grant. *Union with Christ in the New Testament*. Oxford: Oxford University Press, 2013.
Mathews, Alice. *Preaching That Speaks to Women*. Grand Rapids: Baker Academic, 2003.
McMaster Divinity College. "Bingham Colloquium" [n.d.], https://mcmasterdivinity.ca/bingham [n.d.].
Porter, Stanley E. "Commentaries on the Book of Romans." In *On the Writing of New Testament Commentaries: Festschrift for Grant R. Osborne on the Occasion of His 70th Birthday*, edited by Stanley E. Porter and Eckhard J. Schnabel, 365–404. Leiden: Brill, 2013.
Roberts, Maurice. *Union and Communion with Christ*. Grand Rapids: Reformation Heritage Books, 2008.
Smedes, Lewis B. *Union with Christ: A Biblical View of the New Life in Jesus Christ*. 2nd ed. Grand Rapids: Eerdmans, 2009.
Tilling, Chris, ed. *Beyond Old and New Perspectives on Paul: Reflections on the Work of Douglas Campbell*. Eugene, OR: Cascade, 2014.
Tomlin, Graham. "Luther and the Deliverance of God." In *Beyond Old and New Perspectives on Paul: Reflections on the Work of Douglas Campbell*, edited by Chris Tilling, 23–33. Eugene, OR: Cascade, 2014.
Tuck, Tag. "Our View of Scripture," *Grace Community Church Blog*, May 21, 2014, http://www.cvillegrace.org/Our-View-Of-Scripture.

4

Changing Allegiance

Set Free and Spirit-led (Romans 5–8)

Cynthia Long Westfall

INTRODUCTION

WHEN WE PREACH OR teach through Romans, we can take different approaches in how we handle the text. Often we will hear a series of sermons on Romans that preach through the great theological themes that have made such a tremendous contribution to our theology, so that a sermon drawn from Rom 5–8 might focus on a robust theology of sanctification, making significant connections with other great passages on sanctification or talk about the theological question of original sin.[1] Other times we may enjoy a focus on those special passages that may have played such a

---

1. The message, topics, and epistolary characteristics of Romans often have been lost through a tendency to treat it as if it were a systematic theology. In part, this is because Romans has played such a central historic role in Protestant theology, and its contents are the primary basis for central doctrines in churches and groups. For example, Douglas Moo states, "Because the main body of Romans is a 'theological tractate,' outlines of the structure of the letter tend to resemble the headings in systematic theologies" but acknowledges that there is a problem when "scholars subsume everything in the letter under a single theological doctrine (e.g., justification by faith) or attach the labels of later dogmatic structures to the letter" (Moo, *Epistle to the Romans*, 32). Furthermore, as Robert Jewett notes, "the tendency has been to burden each word and phrase with theological content held with absolute certainty by particular churches and groups" (Jewett, *Romans*, 2). This study reflects a shift away from understanding Romans as a "theological tractate" (see, for example, Becker's argument in *Paul the Apostle*, 64–69), and understands its words and phrases through how Paul uses them in the text of Romans and through the context of the language and culture.

vital role in our spiritual walk, such as Rom 8:35: "Who can separate from the love of Christ?" or the encouragement in Rom 5:3–5 that teaches suffering is vital to character formation, so that we may develop our sermon around great pastoral topics in Romans. However, a third way to preach from the text is to fully preach the message of the entire section of Rom 5–8 as it is developed with each passage and attempt to reflect what Paul was trying to accomplish when he wrote to the first readers.[2] We will see that Paul is not simply describing the process or theology of sanctification, but that he is urging the members of the church at Rome to transfer or change their allegiance to God in every part of their lives in a way that is consistent with what God has done for them.[3]

Without question, the section in Rom 5–8 describes sanctification and righteousness in the Christian life.[4] However, instead of arguing the traditional view that it primarily consists of theology which teaches doctrines about the Christian life, this study argues that Paul is attempting to persuade the believers in the Roman church to make a change, not only in thought, but in their commitments and behavior in response to God's gracious work and free gift in Jesus Christ.[5] Paul exhorts the believers to

---

2. It is generally held that either Rom 5–8 forms a section (e.g. Jewett, *Romans*, viii, 344–554; Moo, *Epistle to the Romans*, 33–34, 290–95), or that Rom 6–8 forms a section, usually with Rom 5 functioning as "bridge" between chapters 1–4 and 6–8 (e.g. Dunn, *Romans 1–8*, 242–44; Wilckens, *Romer*, 286–87). Elliott argues that "Romans 5 is the pivot on which the letter's argument turns" (Elliott, *Rhetoric of Romans*, 346). While chapter 5 has many ties with chapters 1–4, there is a distinct formal shift at 5:1 after which Paul introduces major topics that will be developed so that it is more than a bridge or transition.

3. This study suggests a unique theme for this section that may appear to be distinct from other studies. However, it combines, incorporates, and/or reflects elements from the suggested themes in other studies such as "Life Promised for Those Who Are Righteous by Faith" (Cranfield, *Romans*, 28); "The Outworking of This Gospel in Relation to the Individual and to the Election of Grace" (Dunn, *Romans 1–8*, viii–ix); "Justified Christians are Reconciled to the God of Love; They Will Be Saved through Hope of a Share in the Risen Life of Christ" (Fitzmyer, *Romans*, ix–x); "Life in Christ as a New System of Honor" (Jewett, *Romans*, viii); "Righteousness and Sanctification: The New Life in Christ" (Osborne, *Romans*, 25); "Hope as a Result of Righteousness by Faith" (Schreiner, *Romans*, 26; cf. Moo, *Epistle to the Romans*, 33–34). The difference is that the focus of this study is not on the results directly achieved by the believers' comprehension of doctrine, but rather on Paul's persuasion to respond with specific actions.

4. See Osborne, *Romans*, 124–26 as a clear and simple representation of the traditional view that sanctification is the theme of chapters 5–8.

5. This study is influenced by a text-critical decision based on a strongly supported variant in 5:1, and the methodology of discourse analysis in which the text is constrained

change their allegiance from sin and death to righteousness with the appropriate life and service that it entails.

The section begins with an exhortation to believers to have peace with God through a faithful response to his work of reconciliation. This peace with God is fully realized through three essential changes on the part of the believer. First, they must make an essential change in their values by taking pride in three things: the hope of the glory of God, suffering, and God himself. Second, they must make a change in loyalty and service/slavery from sin and death to a new life with righteousness as their Lord and master. Third, rather than being controlled by their selfishness, they must live a life that is led and controlled by the Spirit of God that is living in them. Paul concludes the section by looping back to the three things in which he wanted the believers to take pride, showing how their hope in the glory of God and their relationship with God through the Spirit fully reframes their response to suffering so that "in all these things" they are more than conquerors over any circumstances.

This paper is organized in sections that correspond to the four chapters. Each section begins with essential background information by answering questions that equip a preacher or teacher in their interpretation and explanation of the passage. Next, the message of the passage is summarized. Finally, further insights for preaching and teaching are offered.

LET'S HAVE PEACE WITH GOD (ROM 5:1–21)

The first passage begins with either a statement that we have peace with God or, what is more likely, a command: "Let's have peace with God."[6] Up

---

by and interpreted in its context.

6. This is an application of the insights of textual criticism and demonstrates implications for preaching. Porter has argued for the hortatory subjunctive variant (first person plural command) and is followed by Jewett (Porter, "The Argument of Romans 5"; Jewett, *Romans*, 344). According to Metzger, the hortatory subjunctive has "far better external support than the indicative" (Metzger, *Textual Commentary*, 452), and the hortatory subjunctive was favored by Tischendorf among others. Why did the variant occur? In Greek, the omicron and the omega were pronounced in virtually the same fashion, so it could be scribal error. Why has scholarship privileged the indicative reading? Possibly because of the influence of the KJV, but also because of "internal evidence" which assumes that this is a doctrinal section and concludes that a hortatory subjunctive is out of place and "in this passage it appears that Paul is not exhorting but stating facts" (Metzger, *Textual Commentary*, 452; cf. the circular argument of Verbrugge, "ΕΧΩΜΕΝ in Romans 5:1," 569). However, if Romans 5 is taken together with Romans 6, there is a pattern of exhortation as well as the use of the indicative.

until this point, Jews have been contrasted and compared with Gentiles. Now the two groups are treated together as God's people, and the experience of peace between God and his people is maintained by a reciprocity that Paul is going to describe for the Roman believers. As the Psalmist says,

> I will listen to what God the LORD says. For he will make peace with his people, his faithful followers. Yet they must not return to their foolish ways. Certainly his loyal followers will soon experience his deliverance; then his splendor will again appear in our land. Loyal love and faithfulness meet; deliverance and peace greet each other with a kiss. Faithfulness grows from the ground, and deliverance looks down from the sky (Ps 85:8–11 NET).

God fully provides reconciliation and makes peace with his people, but his people need to change their former ways and demonstrate loyalty or faithfulness to appropriate and experience that peace. This is completely consistent with the context.

Similarly, the primary verbs in Rom 5:2 and 3 could be translated as exhortations instead of statements (because the form of the present indicative and subjunctive are the same). Therefore, instead of "we boast in the hope of the glory of God" and "we boast in our sufferings," this verse ought to be translated "let us boast in the hope of the glory of God," or better, "let us take pride in the hope of the glory of God," and "let us take pride in our sufferings."[7] The exhortation in 5:1 would make it likely that these also would be exhortations, and the contents of both are hardly statements of fact or assumed universal practices of believers. Believers had to be exhorted to rejoice in trials in James, 1 Peter, and elsewhere in the Pauline Epistles. Therefore, the message of this passage would be mapped on the exhortations. On the basis of their justification through faith by grace, Paul exhorts the Roman readers to have peace with God. I will show that the entire section in Rom 5–8 explains how this peace with God is realized, but Rom 5:1–11 contains three basic attitudes or practices that accompany peace with God: Paul exhorts that believers take pride in the hope of the glory of God, take pride in our sufferings, and take pride in God through our Lord Jesus Christ. Romans 5:12–21 will expand on why we should take pride in God.

---

7. See explanation below for use of "take pride."

The Letter to the Romans

Background Information

Why would we have a different section at Rom 5:1? How does this passage relate to Rom 1–4? Though some scholars group Rom 5 with the previous section, at this point, there is a decisive turn in the text.[8] Up until now, the focus has been on people (Jew and Gentile alike) who were locked up in sin and how God makes them righteous through faith. Now the focus in chapters 5–8 is on what should happen on the basis of justification through faith.

How does this passage address or reflect the context of the church in Rome? Peace and reconciliation with God have immediate implications for factions, divisions, and competition between Jews and Gentiles for power or some kind of ethnic priority or headship.[9] The common problem of sin and equal access to God renders competition between groups fundamentally invalid. The sort of boasting in status and achievement that created competition between groups is replaced by taking pride in the hope of the glory of God, sufferings, and God himself—and the issue at hand should not be the problem of the differences between believers, but the resolution of the differences between us that place us outside of God's peace, a challenge which all of God's people have in common. Conversely, peace with

---

8. According to Moo, *Epistle to the Romans*, 292, four arguments show that Paul transitions: (1) The opening phrase summarizes the argument of Rom 1:18—4:25; (2) the shift in style from a polemical tone to a more confessional style; (3) the shift in key words to "life" and "to live" (righteousness continues but interacts with ethics and eternal life rather than status attained through faith, and "faith" and "believe" are discontinued); (4) 5:1–11 provides a more convincing teaching of what is happening with chapters 6–8. In addition, as mentioned in n. 2, major themes are introduced in chapter 5 that are developed in the following text.

9. There was a tension between Jews and Gentiles in the church in Rome, which accounts for Paul's argument in Rom 1–4. According to Ambrosiaster (c. 366) the earliest Christians in Rome were law-abiding Jews who were worshipping Jesus in the synagogues (CSEL 81.1.5–6). See Fitzmyer, *Romans*, 25–33 for a discussion of the evidence for Jews and Christian Jews in Rome. Christianity could have been brought to Rome by Roman proselytes present in Jerusalem at Pentecost, or by trade, servants, or slaves. However, in AD 49, Claudius expelled the Jews from Rome (Suetonius, *Claud.* 25.4). Therefore, there was a vacuum of Jewish Christian leadership for five years until the Jews were allowed to return (AD 49–54). The churches must have continued as household congregations with Gentile leadership—four of the Christian groups in Rom 16 fit this description (and the Gentile references in Rom 1:5, 15) but one group is led by Priscilla and Aquila (Rom 16:4–5). When Paul writes, the Jewish refugees have returned: 12 or 13 of the people mentioned in Rom 16 are Jews. The situation together with Paul's argument indicates that there has been a development of a power struggle and sectarian splintering along the ethnic lines of Jew and Gentile.

God is realized in a corporate peace among his people. Taking pride in God's glory draws attention away from the future status of one's own group and the status or achievements of the group. God is not the possession of any one group. Up until this point, Paul has been differentiating between Gentiles and Jews, but now on the basis of the fact that all believers are justified by faith, Paul shifts to the inclusive first person plural.

How does the passage interact with Greco-Roman beliefs or values? Clear connections with the imperial cult are central to the passage in a way that was relevant to readers located in Rome. Paul builds his argument on Greco-Roman concepts of allegiance and reciprocity between patron and client that were foundational for understanding the function between the Roman emperor and his people as established by Augustus.[10] On the other hand, some aspects of the imperial cult are reversed. According to Roman court etiquette, access to a Roman emperor required high status, a special position, or the possession of money and/or power.[11] Access to God through faith by grace reverses this cultural expectation. Taking pride in suffering reverses Greco-Roman and Jewish attitudes toward value, honor and shame, success, and adversity.[12] Similarly, the culture placed a high value on endurance, but it is redefined—it is no longer a property of the elite which was an exclusively masculine virtue that comes through human effort but rather it is achievement through suffering.[13]

---

10. See Jewett's discussion of honor and the civic cult (Jewett, *Romans*, 46–51). For the connection of honor and the civic cult with reciprocity and allegiance, see deSilva, *Honor, Patronage*, 97, 179–80.

11. Προσαγωγή occurs in the Pauline corpus only here and Eph 2:18; 3:12 (cf. Heb 10:18–25). Jewett states that it typically appears in a context of entrée to kings, dignitaries, and shrines (Jewett, *Romans*, 349). However, in the LXX it is used for approaching the altar with an offering.

12. Roman celebrations of victories and triumphs over enemies/parades offer an extreme illustration of a shame/honour environment.

13. Endurance was manly resistance to contrary pressure. Jewett likes "fortitude" because he believes that it brings out the masculinity of the quality (Jewett, *Romans*, 354). In the Greco-Roman world, it was assumed that women lacked essential traits that contributed to honor, so that her "status" was shame. However, Paul clearly considers masculine responsibilities and virtue as the standard and outcome of faith. When Christian women were forced to exhibit these qualities because of their faith, they had no question about what their faithful response could be, but exhibited a lot of tension between their Christian call and their cultural role. In stories of martyrdom, women are depicted as putting on Christ in a way that is comparable to assuming a masculine persona or becoming a man.

Message of Romans 5:1–21

The message of the passage (Rom 5:1–21) is that we need to have peace with God, and in order to experience peace, we need to take pride in the right things.[14] Jews and Gentiles had been at enmity with God (e.g. 1:18; 2:5), and consistently had targeted, among other things, arrogance and misplaced pride or boasting (1:30; 2:17, 23; 4:2). Paul now gives the reasons that we can have peace with God and an explanation of what we should be proud of and why (5:1–11). What lies beneath these reasons and explanation is the rule of God's grace that has replaced the rule of sin (5:12–21).

God's people, Jew and Gentile, slave and free, male and female, can have peace because we are standing in the sphere of grace.[15] Why is that and so what? Paul's explanation of why we stand in grace is compact and summarizes, applies, and extends the preceding section.[16] We are in a position to have peace with God because we are made righteous through faith in Jesus Christ and we have access to God through Jesus Christ. We are now God's people. There is a question as to whether "faith" applies to our faith in Jesus or the faithfulness of Jesus.[17] The near context would constrain it to refer to our faith (in parallel to Abraham's faith, Rom 4). However, Jesus is the means of our access, and both our faith in him and his faithfulness are essential to that access. The fact is that grace both refers to the reliability of

---

14. Peace here means the absence of hostility (once we were his enemies but now we are his friends), but also probably carries the Hebrew sense of *shalom*—a general sense of harmonious well-being and ultimately salvation (Moo, *Epistle to the Romans*, 299). Jewett says that it introduces the theme of reconciliation (Jewett, *Romans*, 349). Some will stress the status of peace over subjective feelings, but the subsequent discussion does involve pride, hope, and security which have emotional components. As Moo says, "It is an inner sense of security and serenity that wells up in our hearts when we appreciate the blessings we enjoy in Christ" (Moo, *Epistle to the Romans*, 174).

15. Grace, sometimes defined as "God's unmerited favor," is conveyed to the undeserving and comes by means of faith rather than performance. Standing in grace is a metaphor for entering a sphere and remaining—it could have an Old Testament connection with a priest standing before God (Lev 9:5; 2 Chr 29:11), and high ethical qualification (Ps 24:3–4—"who will stand?"). Grace is now a constant state in which we live. Equal access renders competition between groups inappropriate.

16. This carries forward the preceding argument. Jewett states the author is "summing up the burden of the preceding proof . . . Paul insists that such righteousness never comes through works but only by faith in the gospel" in this clause (Jewett, *Romans*, 348).

17. For "faithfulness of Christ," see Hays, *Faith of Jesus Christ*, 141–60. For "Faith in Christ" see Lee, "Against Hays." For discussions of both sides of the debate, see Bird and Sprinkle, eds., *Faith of Jesus Christ*.

the benefactor who bestows a gift, the gift itself, and the recipient's response to the gift.[18]

In Romans, a certain attitude accompanies the goal of having peace with God: we must take pride in the right things.[19] If we understand Rom 5:1 to be a command to have peace with God, the three clauses on boasting should also be treated as first person plural commands, and this makes sense, because what Paul commands (or models) is corrective in intention because it is counter-cultural and counter-intuitive. I suggest that there is a better gloss for the three commands than the word "boast" which is common in most translations: the word "boast" is pejorative, and tends to create dissonance in the passage, and there is no way that Paul intends to promote arrogance. "Taking pride," as opposed to being proud, can be either good or bad, depending on value or object of the pride. Paul tells the Roman believers to take pride in three things: the hope of the glory of God, their sufferings, and God through Jesus Christ. These three things replace the values and advantages claimed by both Romans and Jews: it confronted the arrogance, pride, and selfish ambition of the Greco-Roman ideology, and it confronted the Jews' pride in the Law and their assumed leadership as teachers and moral police.

So, Paul commands us to take pride in the hope of the glory of God (Rom 5:2b).[20] Paul defined the hope of the glory of God in Rom 2:6–8 in a way that contrasts the trajectory of peace with God with the trajectory of those who are the target of the wrath of God: "He will reward each one according to his works: eternal life to those who by perseverance in good works seek glory and honor and immortality, but wrath and anger to those who live in selfish ambition and do not obey the truth but follow unrighteousness." The hope in the glory of God is in direct opposition to human pride, arrogance, and factions that manifest in human competition, which Paul has effectively clarified. However, it is not clear at this point how

18. deSilva, *Honor, Patronage*, 118.

19. This is the same word that is translated as "boast" in Rom 2:17, but is invariably pejorative in English. However, taking pride in appropriate things is not pejorative. Many translations use the word "rejoice," but that misses the semantic ties with the previous statements about boasting and arrogance. According to Jewett, it is clear that Paul "is recommending a revolutionary new form of boasting to replace the claims of honorable status and performance that mark traditional religion in the Greco-Roman world" (Jewett, *Romans*, 351).

20. "Boasting was oriented to one's own glory or the glory of one's family or group; it was an essential aspect of the social competition by which the 'dyadic personality' defined itself" (ibid., 351). Glory was effective assurance of immortality.

anyone can hope for the glory of God on the basis of perseverance in good works. Paul introduces the concept here.

The next command in Rom 5:3 is to take pride in our suffering.[21] This command is directly tied to our ability to hope that we are and will be at peace with God. Our suffering is the primary means that equips us to play our part in the act of reconciliation: suffering produces endurance,[22] and endurance produces character.[23] This would be the kind of character that patiently does good, thereby contextually fulfilling 2:7—that is why it produces hope, that would be hope in sharing the glory, honor, and immortality of God.[24]

The certainty of our hope is supported by a number of statements about the work of God. The theology could distract us from the essential message of our responsibility to do our part to have peace with God. The point of Rom 5:5–10 is that God has already lavishly and unconditionally completed every necessary aspect on his part to reconcile and have peace with us, so that if we play our part in the act of reconciliation, there is no way that our hope for glory will be disappointed—it is completely secure. Such a hope will never put us to shame[25] because it is grounded in the love

---

21. This is an important reversal of cultural values: to take pride in something that is often a source of shame, our sufferings. Taking pride in suffering or tribulation reverses Greco-Roman and Jewish attitudes toward honor and shame, success and adversity, superior virtue, and status. It is followed by a beautiful progression of how God uses our sufferings to build qualities of great value in our lives. Afflictions are suffered in the context of Christian commitment, which Jewett insists must refer to specific experiences of the Roman congregation. Ibid., 353.

22. Endurance is an important virtue in the culture. Plato, Socrates, Philo, Stoics, and Hellenistic Judaism all placed great value on it. Paul eliminates human effort by making it a product of suffering. The Greco-Roman culture assumed it was not available for females.

23. "Character" doesn't occur in Greek literature before Paul, but some cognates do appear. According to Jewett, the key to meaning is the testing of qualifications by performance in battle or public life. "Its meaning . . . is close to 'approbation,' that is, a faith that has been tested and found to be authentic" (Jewett, *Romans*, 355).

24. According to Jewett, this does not mean approbation creates more confident hope, though that is exactly the argument that supports the phrase—now that we are reconciled and made righteous through Christ and the process of suffering, we have more of a basis for hope than we had when we were ungodly, helpless, sinners, and enemies of God. Still, Jewett's comments of what it does mean are worth considering: Hope "arises instead from the approbation that comes from God's providential working and thus eliminates another form of human boasting [in professional superiority]" (ibid.).

25. Καταισχύνω (to shame) in v. 5 belongs to the honor/shame register, so the avoidance of shame is accomplished in a revolutionary manner. It reflects a major theme in

of God that is poured out in our hearts through the Holy Spirit,[26] and it is grounded in God demonstration of his love for us in Christ's death. There are two arguments from lesser to greater that validate our hope:[27] if he died for us while we were helpless sinners, he will certainly save us from God's wrath since we are made righteous through his blood. If we were reconciled by Christ's death when we were his enemies, we will certainly be saved by his life.[28]

Therefore, it follows that we must not only to take pride in the hope of the glory of God (5:11) and in our sufferings, but also we must take pride in God through our Lord Jesus Christ through whom we received the reconciliation.[29] In order to have peace with God, pride, praise, and honor are directed Godward, the human standards of shame and honor are inverted, and we fulfill our part in reconciliation through our endurance and character formation that produces acts of righteousness.

---

the Old Testament: "don't let me be put to shame because I have hoped in you" (Ps 24:20; see 1 Cor 1:27–30). Paul explains why hope will not disappoint us in vv. 5–10. We can be certain that we will receive what we hope for in Christ given Paul's reasoning. According to Jewett, "[d]ivine love addresses shame at its deepest level and reveals the motivation behind 'peace' and 'reconciliation'" (ibid., 356).

26. The pouring out of love is paralleled with the pouring out of the blood of sacrifice and of the Pentecost pouring out of the Holy Spirit (Joel 2:28/Acts 2:17–18)—Paul is often struck by the lavish generosity of God in terms of his love, grace, and Holy Spirit. This is the first place after the salutation (1:4) that the Holy Spirit is mentioned, being made conspicuous by his absence. The Holy Spirit will play a major role in Rom 8.

27. This is in contrast to the Greco-Roman culture and particularly to the Roman civic cult, where the hero dies for the honored fatherland. Jesus died for undeserving sinners. Jewett, *Romans*, 561.

28. Reconciliation combines traditional themes of appeasement of God's wrath with transformation: our enmity is abolished and we will be saved through his life (see 2 Cor 5:20).

29. This phrase is not a command such as in Rom 5:2b and 3, because it is a participial phrase, subordinate to v. 10. However, it is climactic in the description of hope, God's love, and reconciliation. It also has strongly marked parallels with v. 3 in the lexical repetition of a conjugation of καυχάομαι with οὐ μόνον δέ, ἀλλὰ καί. Consequently, the phrase is treated as parallel to the two commands on the basis of formal features other than the repetition of the hortatory subjunctive. The question that needs to be answered is why Paul chose to use a participle. To claim that this is an imperatival participle is unsatisfactory because it fails to recognize that the author's choice is significant and meaningful. I would suggest that God's actions on our behalf in past, present, and future leave us no honorable option but to take pride in him.

In Rom 5:12–21, Paul further explains the reason that we now stand in grace.[30] Grace now rules where sin formerly ruled because of Jesus Christ's one action. The goal of the passage is to magnify our pride in God through Jesus Christ. Paul illustrates the rule of grace through a series of comparisons between Christ and Adam, which describe how grace now rules where sin formerly ruled. In the first comparison (5:12–14), Adam is established as a type or pattern of Christ.[31] Sin and death entered the world through the one individual, Adam, it passed to all people, and consequently death ruled or reigned. In the comparisons in 5:15–19, Paul clarifies that though Adam is a type of Christ, the "gift" of grace/favor (χάρισμα) is not like the transgression.[32] The similarity between Adam and Christ is built on how "the many" were affected by one person through one act in both cases.[33] The difference that Paul stresses through repetition is the "surpassing quality of Christ's influence"[34] that he expresses with a lesser to greater comparison (vv. 15, 17).[35] However, most of the contrasts consist of antonyms or opposite counterparts, all of which illustrate that Adam functions as an "antitype." Adam's one act is represented by a range of words that refer to disobedience, Christ's one act is obedience.[36] Paul presents a number of contrasting results: judgment and condemnation came through Adam, justification came through Christ; death came through Adam, life came

---

30. The exhortations in the previous passage (5:1–11) are supported by this passage (5:12–21). The theology in this passage is often referred to as the believer's forensic righteousness.

31. For a discussion on Old Testament typology in the New Testament, see Goppelt, *Typos*, 17–18. While there is no Old Testament quotation in Rom 5:12–21, this passage contains numerous allusions to Gen 1 and 3.

32. In contrast, Porter claims that vv. 15 and 16 are actually introduced with diatribal questions missed by translators: "Isn't the gift just like the trespass?" Porter, "The Argument of Romans 5," 673–74. This could be more consistent with the context where v. 14 just stated that Adam was a type or a pattern of the one who was coming and yet there is a contrast between the gift and trespass.

33. The parallelism between "the many" who died and "the many" who will be made righteous has led some to claim this verse supports universalism where all experience salvation. However, there are clear statements to the contrary (Rom 1:18—3:20; Rom 2:12; 2 Thess 1:8–9), and this is a relatively weak connection.

34. Fitzmyer, *Romans*, 419.

35. The Rabbinic form of argument from the lesser to the greater (*a minori ad maius*) permeates this passage with the question "how much more?" and other parallel comparisons.

36. Jesus lived an entire life of obedience. However, the "one righteous act" Paul had in mind was probably his death on a cross.

through Christ; many were made sinners through Adam, many were made righteous through Christ; death or sin in death reigned because of Adam, grace reigns and the recipients of the gift reign in life.

Next, in Rom 5:20–21, two temporal spheres are distinguished from each other and yet connected. In 5:14, Paul explains that until Moses, there was no law and so no commands were broken so sin "was not charged to anyone's account"—no law, no foul. Therefore, when the law came it "increased trespasses." That refers to the case of Israel. By definition, sin increased with the giving of the law, but through God's provision grace increased all the more for God's people. So sin reigned in death, but it corresponds to grace, which now reigns through righteousness to bring eternal life through Jesus Christ our Lord. On the one hand, 5:12–21 sets the table for chapters 6 and 7 by identifying two competing rulers or masters: sin and grace. However, on the other hand, the passage explains why we can now have peace with God, and the theology is meant to define and promote that relationship with God: we are to take pride in God through Jesus Christ. Thus the entire chapter introduces three goals that the author has for the believers in response to what he has written in the first four chapters: to take pride in the hope of the glory of God, to take pride in sufferings, and to take pride in God himself through Jesus Christ

Insights for Preaching and Teaching

In preaching or teaching this passage, it would be prophetic and powerful in a North American context to approach the material with a comparison between the values in which Canadians or Americans take pride and these values in Rom 5:1–11 that promote peace with God: taking pride in the hope of the glory of God, taking pride in our suffering, and taking pride in God through our Lord Jesus Christ. Each one of these biblical values has fallen on hard times among various Christian groups: our anticipation of eternal life is sometimes characterized as ludicrous or unrealistic; the vital role of suffering in the Christian life is openly denied in favor of a health, wealth, and prosperity gospel; and the exclusive claims of Jesus Christ are relativized. That is, they make much more sense as exhortation than they do as statements of fact. Perhaps the challenge is not as much in teaching that contradicts these central values, but their neglect as priorities in life and worship. While 5:12–21 can definitely be included in the contrast in values in focusing on the incomparable value of Christ's act and gift of grace, it could also be a separate teaching or sermon that contains some pertinent illustrations of the pragmatic consequences of the reign of sin and death that brings home the contrast between the human condition under Adam's headship and the headship of Christ and the rule of grace—this contrast is essential in setting up Rom 6–8. It is important to keep 5:12–21 connected as a support for the surrounding contexts.

THE NEXT LEVEL: CHANGING LOYALTIES, PATRONS/ RULERS, AND CITIZENSHIP (ROM 6:1–23)

While Rom 8 is a climax and conclusion for this section, Rom 6 provides an interpretive key or a sort of map that is necessary in order to understand and contextualize the rest of the section, which is why the title of this paper corresponds so closely to the content of this chapter. Unfortunately, the semantic contributions of the chapter are usually obscured or lost because biblical scholars and theologians have tended to be distracted by theological concerns/controversies and particularly by the strong references to baptism at the beginning of the chapter. However, the message of the chapter consists of understanding our new life in Christ as forming a personal and exclusive reciprocal relationship with God as our Lord and master. Paul is referring to the Greco-Roman patron-client relationship with God which is in direct competition with the reign of sin (introduced in 5:12–20). The language and concepts that are associated with patron-client relationships include the paradigmatic patronage relationship (6:1–14), the master-slave relationship (6:15–23), the husband-wife relationship (7:1–6), and the parent-child relationship (8:1–17). This provides an interpretive key for Rom 5 in that the exhortations to "take pride" exhort believers to give God the honour that is due a patron for the benefits received in chapters 1–4. Chapter 6 is particularly important for the interpretation of chapter 7, because it defines and constrains the terms and phrases that will be used. Believers have transferred their allegiance to God so that they are set free from sin (6:18a), they are slaves to righteousness (6:18b), and sin must no longer be their master because they are under grace (6:14).

Background Information

Why is Rom 6 controversial? It is controversial because it touches on issues and vocabulary that are central to different theological systems and traditional practices, such as the role of grace versus human effort in sanctification, and controversies about the meaning and form of baptism.

How are metaphors and symbols from the culture used by Paul? The use of a metaphor or a symbol is powerful. As Paul himself says, "I am speaking in human terms because of your natural limitations." Paul's use of imprecise but appropriate and relevant first-century analogies/symbols/metaphors gave his language and argument power, but it requires recontextualization by the contemporary expositor in order to have a comparable meaning and impact. However, until recently, much of biblical studies and theology has placed a priority on the proposition and abstract logic over the power of narrative and symbols, but the biblical cultures communicated deep truths with narratives (Torah, stories that embed Israel's culture and identity, Gospels, parables) as well as symbols (circumcision). In Rom 6:1–23, Paul utilizes the metaphors of baptism, death, and the patron-client relationship expressed in allegiance to a ruler and the transfer of ownership and obedience in slavery.

Paul therefore uses powerful cultural metaphors to illustrate our new life in Christ. The metaphor of the patron-client relationship is primary to the passage. David deSilva asserts, "The patron-client relationship is the basic building block of Greco-Roman Society."[37] The patronage involved a personal connection between the patrons and clients of favors and loyalty, as well as privilege and dependency. The principle of reciprocity that existed between patrons and clients permeated all levels of society and relationships, from Caesar on down to slaves. The person's worth within the social system was that person's honor, which is the "affirmation of one's worth by one's peers and society, awarded on the basis of the individual's ability to embody the virtues and attributes that his or her society values."[38] Since the Roman Empire had the patron-client relationship as its basic building-block, which included honoring the established authorities, it is supported by the threat of irrevocable dishonor for ingratitude, disloyalty, or non-conformity. In the militaristic center of the Roman Empire, the believer would probably have associated "sin" at least in part with Caesar and Rome, and the provocative exhortation to not offer the parts of your body as weapons to sin but rather to God is the center of an extended metaphor that draws on the warp and woof of Rome's history and militaristic culture—and it competes with that culture.

The second powerful metaphor is slavery. There is often an aversion to the reference to the metaphor of slavery. Many do not relate to Paul's

37. deSilva, "Patronage," 766.
38. deSilva, "Honor and Shame," 518.

references to slavery because they have not personally experienced any aspect of it or others have been devastated by slavery in their family history, and any positive reference to it is offensive. On the one hand, the offense against the existence of slavery has to be set aside in order to read it in the context of the first century, but on the other hand, being a slave was pejorative in the Roman Empire—it did not have a positive meaning by any means. Slaves in the Roman Empire could be found at all economic levels, but they had no honor. Slavery has been described as a "dynamic process of alienation and dishonor termed *social death* . . . Social death means denying a person all dignity (as understood in that particular culture) and ties of birth in both ascending or descending generations . . . Although they are not biologically dead, slaves, in effect, are socially dead to the free population."[39] Therefore, in Rom 6, Christians assume the identity of the lowest on the totem pole in the patronage system—but, according to Paul, slavery is part of the human condition: you are either a slave of sin or a slave of God.

Message of Romans 6:1–23

The message of Rom 6:1–23 is that our new life with Christ requires an intentional change in our master or ruler (in the Greco-Roman culture, both are included in the function of a patron).[40] This allows us to appropriate the peace that God provides, and is in direct contrast with the rule of sin that wages war on the believer (Rom 7:23). Paul's first point in 6:1–11 is that our death to sin should result in the experience of new life in which we are set free from sin, not just its consequences, but the very actions of sin. Paul asks a rhetorical question: since the increase of sin caused the increase of grace, does it follow that we should go on sinning to make grace increase?[41] His emphatic answer is no, we have died to sin and this is clearly

---

39. Harrill, "Slavery," 1125.

40. Paul's metaphor is in contrast with Moo's metaphor of transfer to a new realm (Moo, *Epistle to the Romans*, 352). Moo's description alters a description of a relationship to a depersonalized metaphor that is directly related to an understanding of the kingdom of God, but loses the rich correlations with the first-century patron-client relationship that was a building block of the Greco-Roman culture and characterizes the passage (as in Tannehill, *Dying*, 17; Jewett, *Romans*, 396).

41. Paul is using the diatribe style as he did in Rom 1–4, but the imaginary dialog partner is now a Christian. The next diatribal question in 6:15 forms vv. 1–14 into a unit; the first person span forms a sub-unit in vv. 1–10, and the second person span forms a sub-unit in vv. 11–14 (though you will notice that many break at v. 12). Paul's

depicted in our baptism,[42] which unites us with Christ in his death and his resurrection.[43] We were slaves to sin, but we have been crucified, put to death, and buried.[44] Consequently, we are no longer slaves to sin, but rather we have been set free because we are dead.[45] We have also been united with Jesus in his resurrection, so that we may be able to live a new life—that is,

---

rhetorical question is inferred from what Paul said in 5:20–21: "Where sin increased, grace increased all the more." The reasoning would be that if grace is so wonderful, sinning would maximize grace (Schreiner, *Romans*, 302). Paul's opponents had protested that his gospel led to libertinism. However, I am not convinced by Moo that the driving force here is to argue against libertinism and the charges against him, but he rather equips his readers with a powerful metaphor to live a new life of righteousness, and set the record straight about his theology at the same time

42. The baptism metaphor works because, as Jewett observes, "Both baptism and burial entail being covered over" (Jewett, *Romans*, 398). Baptism would have been understood by the readers as water baptism by immersion and all Christians would have been baptized. It represents union with him and incorporation into him (cf. Gal 3:27). That which incorporates believers into Christ involves all the senses in complex symbolism.

43. Romans 6:5 says that we are united in the "likeness" of Jesus' death, which makes a comparison—our participation in his death is obviously not like his in every respect. Some have said that this is a reference to baptism, and perhaps this should not be entirely dismissed. Our baptism is an enactment of the death that we are participating in. Romans 6:10 states "The death he died, he died to sin, once for all." How did Christ "die to sin"? Schreiner appears to hit the mark when he says that it has to do with the dominion of death over him that corresponds to his triumph over it where he shattered its authority and ended its mastery (Schreiner, *Romans*, 320). Remember the Genesis association between death and sin that Paul explored in Rom 5.

44. Sin is represented as a power by Paul. What does it mean to be "dead to sin" (νέκρους τῇ ἁμαρτίᾳ)? Cranfield's four views are: (1) forensic or judicial: we die to sin in God's sight; (2) sacramental: we died to sin and were raised with him in baptism; (3) moral: we mortify sin in our bodies; and (4) we die to sin when we actually die physically (Cranfield, *Romans*, 299–300). However, Moo is more on target when he emphasizes the decisive shift in state which is dramatic as a change from life to death (Moo, *Epistle to the Romans*, 354). Schreiner also says that the emphasis in on sin's power, and dying to sin stresses the believer's power over it (Schreiner, *Romans*, 305). Our union with Christ and Christ's death to sin break its power in our life.

45. Bodies are depicted as susceptible to domination by sin—this metaphor continues with the idea of presenting body "parts" as instruments of righteousness or unrighteousness. The body imagery is a metaphor for our moral and ethical behavior, and is not to be confused with a Platonic view of the physical nature. While Moo states that 6:1–14 has the dominant motif of freedom from sin's tyranny (Moo, *Epistle to the Romans*, 350), the freedom is not absolute—it is only freedom from sin. Like the adultery metaphor in 7:1–6, freedom involves dying to the first spouse of sin and being free to be bound to God.

"walk" (περιπατήσωμεν) in a new life, which refers to a tangible change in our conduct.[46]

On that basis, in Rom 6:11–14 Paul tells us to consider ourselves dead to sin but alive to God—that is the new life that Christ's resurrection made possible.[47] Note that Paul's language is by no means forensic. We realize our new life by deliberately transferring our allegiance, loyalty, and obedience to God as our new master or patron/ruler. We must refuse to let sin rule us;[48] it must no longer be our master so that we would obey its cravings.[49] In a patron-client relationship, in exchange for services or goods, the client would often "present arms" to the patron—that is, they would participate in military service on behalf of their patron.[50] Paul uses this imagery when he commands that we must not offer any part of ourselves to be used by sin as a weapon of unrighteousness. Instead we must offer ourselves to God so that every part of us serves as a weapon of righteousness.[51] Allegiance and loyalty is therefore directly connected with having peace with God in terms of an alliance in war—we are either weapons of sin at war with God or weapons of God at war with sin.

---

46. The believer's new life is grounded in Christ's resurrection, but our resurrection with Christ is suspended, which Dunn calls an "eschatological reservation" (Dunn, *Romans 1–8*, 316).

47. There is a shift to the second person imperative and the commands in Rom 5:1–3 are linked. As Moo says, "[w]hat God has done for us is the basis and stimulus for what we need to do for God" (Moo, *Epistle to the Romans*, 199). Dying to sin and being alive to Christ further describes the new life which is a metaphor that correlates to changing allegiance. Death frees us from our entangling alliances and our obligations. We need to think of ourselves differently; we need to see ourselves as people are dead to sin and its demands as the basis of action.

48. This is where sin is particularly personified as a powerful patron who must not be allowed to "rule" (βασιλευέτω) in Rom 6:12.

49. "Lust" (ἐπιθυμία) tends to be sexual, and while sexual behavior is a major issue for Paul in moral and ethical conduct, the desires or cravings of personified sin in Rom 6:12 encompass and extend beyond sexual lust.

50. The word ὅπλα refers to "weapons" rather than instruments (a metaphoric gloss of the word). "Weapons" fits more closely with the metaphor of the client's obligations to bear arms for the patron. This is part of a powerful illustration from the patron-client relationship, in which the patron supplies the clients' needs and the client reciprocates with loyalty, honor, and service. For example, a client may be expected to fight for the patron in a war or even a street fight against a competitor.

51. Understand weapons here as "all our capacities and abilities" (Moo, *Epistle to the Romans*, 211) in service to God for spiritual warfare.

Paul utilizes the metaphor of slavery in Rom 6:15–23: slavery was a familiar system to the Greco-Roman culture and also part of the patron-client relationship. Paul uses the transfer of ownership in slavery to illustrate the change of allegiance from sin to God.[52] He explains that a person is the slave of the one whom he or she obeys.[53] Slavery to sin ends in death (or as Paul says in 6:23, death is the wages that sin pays) and slavery to righteousness leads to sanctification/holiness and ends in eternal life—and yet that eternal life is the free gift of God.[54] Believers have been set free from sin, but the freedom is relative because the ownership has been transferred to righteousness. Paul thanks God that the Roman believers have come to obey from the heart the pattern of teaching "to which authority you have been transferred" (Rom 6:17 TNIV).[55] The imagery expresses the transfer of a slave's ownership.[56] He says that they in fact have been set free from sin and have become slaves to righteousness.[57] On that basis, Paul exhorts them to now offer themselves as slaves to righteousness to the same extent that they used to offer themselves to impurity and to ever-increasing wickedness.[58]

Through the use of metaphors, in Rom 6:1–23, Paul continues to describe the reciprocal nature of the peace with God that he wants the Roman believers to experience. This peace includes aspects of justification,

---

52. The freedom from sin does not result in either autonomy (the freedom from all outside powers and influences) or the freedom to sin, but a change of allegiance (Jewett, *Romans*, 397). What is interesting about this in the context of Paul's greater argument is that we were unable to be obedient in the context of the law. The problem is our relationship with Adam. We are able to be obedient because of our relationship in Christ. Obedience is not following the rules, but a result of relationship.

53. "Don't you know" in v. 16 would appear to signal that the readers do know, or they are in a position where they should know, that they become the slaves of what they obey. In one sentence, Paul has captured one of the central features of fallen humanity: the tendency of addiction—it appears that virtually anything can be habit-forming which can result in essential idolatry.

54. Interpretive position: "holiness" is a state or the process of sanctification. Again, the interpretation of this passage as forensic indicating status neglects the force of the argument and the application to "now." The result of our allegiance is "God-likeness."

55. Moo refers to vv. 17–18 as a "once/but now" contrast, which is semantic rather than formal here (Moo, *Epistle to the Romans*, 397).

56. Dunn, *Romans 1–8*, 344. Cf. 1:24, 26, 28; 1 Cor 5:5; 13:3; 15:24; 2 Cor 4:11.

57. Some read righteousness as forensic or eschatological, but the context would indicate ethical and moral conduct that pleases God.

58. Here in Rom 6:20–22, as Moo observes (Moo, *Epistle to the Romans*, 407), there is another "once/but now" contrast; but this one is formal with the markers ὅτε (v. 20) and νυνί (v. 22).

sanctification, and eternal life which are all God's gracious gifts due to the once and for all act of Jesus Christ and there is nothing that humanity can do to earn them. However, the possession of peace and the constellation of benefits that comprise that peace are not accomplished by a once and for all act of conversion on the part of the believer. As Dunn argues,

> Conversion-initiation, the point at which this present train of thought began, is not an isolated and once-and-for-all event in its character of grace meeting obedience. Rather for Paul that first act characterizes the whole of the believer's life as believer. The newness of life there entered upon must be received as a gift of grace ever and again throughout life in this mortal body and beyond in the fullness of resurrection life.[59]

At the very least, the believer needs to be a conscious participant in the transfer of ownership from sin to righteousness, and then conduct themselves consistently with their new identity. Peace and sanctification are realized in a reciprocal relationship consistent with the patron-client relationship.

Insights for Preaching and Teaching

I would particularly caution anyone who wants to adequately reflect the message of God's word to avoid making this passage all about the meaning of baptism. The best thing that we can do in our ministry and teaching is to communicate the importance of the message that each believer must intentionally transfer loyalty and allegiance from whatever is in their lives that competes with God for the position of Lord and master. A real problem for preaching this passage exists because the metaphors that were relevant for the first-century Christians cannot have the same impact on the contemporary reader in North America. The impact of the metaphor of baptism is obscured by controversies, individualism, self-actualization, entitlement, and a belief in freedom for the pursuit of happiness that compete with any visceral connection with the metaphors that are inherent to this illustration drawn from a patron-client system. The preacher/teacher who wishes to communicate the message of Rom 6 will carefully meditate on the ways in which sin enslaves people in our culture and on the people or things that compete for our allegiance. This requires that we facilitate the imagination of students and congregants in recreating the Greco-Roman socio-cultural

---

59. Dunn, *Romans 1–8*, 357.

THE PROBLEM OF THE LAW WITHOUT THE SPIRIT (ROM 7:1–25)

Since Paul's bombshell in Rom 5:20 where he asserted the law was brought in so that trespasses might increase, Paul has all but ignored the law. However, with Rom 7:1, he brings it back front and center. It is possible that Paul is addressing the Jews only, as he says, "I am speaking to those who know the law," but the alleged background of the Roman church holds that the early Gentile believers kept the Jewish law as well.[60] It is important to understand Rom 7 in context with the previous two chapters, and to understand how its terminology of sin, righteousness, ruling, death, slavery, and war/peace are defined or constrained—they should be read in the context of the two camps outlined in Rom 6. However, Paul adds the Spirit to the discussion for the first time.

Background information

There is extensive background material that provides the context for Rom 7, but for the purposes of this paper we will limit it to Jewish law and practice, marriage in the Jewish law, and the meaning of σάρξ (Rom 7:18) and σάρκινος (Rom 7:14), which are glossed in traditional translations as "flesh" and "fleshly."

Concerning Jewish law and practice, the phrase the "letter of the law" shows the Palestinian interest in exact wording and lettering (vs. interpreting laws according to principles). It will be the contention of this paper that "I" in Rom 7 represents Paul's previous experience under the law in a sense that is paradigmatic for anyone who attempts to become a righteous person by means of obedience to the Law (7:5–8). The command "You must not Covet" is a quotation from the Ten Commandments (7:7//Exod 20:17//Deut 5:21). It is the last commandment in the series, and it is the only one that deals with the state of the heart. Jewish oral tradition believed that the study of the law helped you overcome sin and that the law brings life. Paul says rather that the law became the vehicle of his death. In fact, Paul makes an allusion to Eve's deception correlating sin and the law with the serpent

---

60. C.f. n. 9 above.

and the "opportunity" presented by prohibition to eat the fruit (7:11). In contrast, Jews believed that repentance and learning the law were the only present cures for the evil impulse. Paul argues that one must receive righteousness (including the power to live rightly) as a gift of God's grace, not as an achievement of human effort. Paul's seemingly contradictory statement that the law is "spiritual" means that the law is inspired by the Spirit. However, the redemptive activity of the Spirit is otherwise completely absent from the passage so that the means of freedom from sin that are outlined in Rom 8 are not applied in chapter 7. The individual in 7:7–25 does not have the Spirit of Christ, and therefore does not belong to him (8:9).

A brief note on the background of marriage is in order. Marriage in the Jewish law and custom is in view rather than Greco-Roman law. Marriage provides something like a case study for Paul but is also another aspect of the patron-client relationship, which is part of the culture of Second Temple Judaism. The status of a wife is in view. According to Jewish law, death of the husband or divorce by the husband severed the marital bond.[61] The relationship of the husband to the wife is not in view because a man might have more than one wife but a woman could not legally have more than one husband. As in the other references to the patron-client relationship, the believer corresponds to the client/inferior.

The meaning of "flesh" (σάρξ) and the way that it should be glossed in translation and explained is an important issue. According to Louw and Nida, "flesh" has eight meanings: flesh, body, people, human, nation, human nature, physical nature, and life.[62] According to BDAG, in the Pauline epistles, "all parts of the body constitute a totality known as . . . *flesh*, which is dominated by sin to such a degree that wherever flesh is, all forms of sin are present, and no good thing can live in the σάρξ."[63] However, do not forget the previous Pauline metaphor where you could present the members of your body either to sin or to righteousness—here the self is ruled by the needs and urges of the body as opposed to the Spirit, which indicates that it is self-centered rather than God-centered. It is the source of the range of our desires, which on their own have little discretion and are easily and invariably enticed by sin. What appears to be in view here is human nature, which is created to serve God with the instinct of self-preservation but as a result of the Fall is subject to a range of weaknesses as well as mortality. When the

---

61. See Instone-Brewer, *Divorce and Remarriage*, for an excellent study on this topic.
62. Louw and Nida, *Greek-English Lexicon*, 2:220.
63. *BDAG*, 915.

human nature is served, we can only be selfish and self-centered—it was not made to be our God and is automatically corrupt without him.⁶⁴

Message of Romans 7:1–25

Paul describes the believers' relationship to the law from a Jewish point of view. With the metaphor of marriage in Rom 7:1–6, he argues that the believer's death with Christ sets us free from the law. He then in Rom 7:7–25 dramatically illustrates exactly how the law causes sin to increase by describing a person's relationship to the law apart from Christ and the work of the Spirit. It is a vicious circle of sin and failure which is characterized as slavery to sin. It concludes with a rhetorical question of who will free such a person from his body of death. He proceeds to describe how the Spirit sets us free in Christ in the next chapter.

Paul explained in Rom 6:7 that our death with Christ set us free from sin, and similarly in 7:1–6 he explains that our death with Christ sets us free from the authority of the law, parallel to marriage in Jewish law and practice.⁶⁵ The law has jurisdiction over a person only during one's lifetime, and similarly, marital law is binding only until death.⁶⁶ That is, if a husband dies, the wife is released from the marriage. If she is with another man while her husband is alive she will be called an adulteress, but if her husband dies, she will not be called an adulteress if she is with another man because she is released from the law that bound her to him.⁶⁷ Similarly, we died to the law with the death of Christ's body because of our identification with him in

---

64. For an argument in favor of "sinful human nature," see Erickson, "Flesh," 304–5.

65. Though some take this as allegorical or analogical, Jewett, influenced by Kümmel, argues that this is a syllogism (Jewett, *Romans*, 428). A syllogism is identified by Aristotle. It is "a kind of logical argument in which one proposition (the conclusion) is inferred from two others (the premises) of a certain form. The syllogism is at the core of deductive reasoning, where facts are determined by combining existing statements, in contrast to inductive reasoning where facts are determined by repeated observations" (Wikipedia): All humans are mortal, Socrates is a human, Socrates is mortal. 7:1–3 lays down the premises, and 7:4 is the inference.

66. The major premise is highlighted with the diatribal question, the nominative plural of direct address, and the assertion that the readers are adept at the law—this is definitely a zone of turbulence that sets this apart in some way from the previous argument that it is connected with.

67. The Greek is γένηται ἀνδρὶ ἑτέρῳ (is with another man), which is generally taken to be a euphemism in Greek for a probable reference to having sex. However, it is more understated than most translations of being "joined" to another man—so our own euphemism of being "with" someone fits well.

baptism (Rom 6:4). Now we are free to be with another, "the one who was raised from the dead," the resurrected Christ, so that we might bear fruit for God.[68] Note the transparent sexual metaphor where our union with Christ produces offspring (fruit).[69] "Fruit of your womb" is a common Old Testament metaphor that links back to God's command in Gen 1:28 to be fruitful and multiply, and parallels are drawn between the fruit of the body, the fruit of the cattle, and the fruit of the ground (Deut 30:9; cf. Deut 28:4, 11, 18).[70] In this passage, Paul is much more interested in the pragmatic sanctification of all believers, than in reinforcing a masculine gender role.

In Rom 7:5–6, Paul tells us in a nutshell what he is going to talk about in the rest of our section. In 7:5, Paul expands what he meant when he said that the law caused trespasses to increase (5:20): when we were controlled by our own self-interest, the law aroused sinful passions in every part of us, so we produced fruit for death.[71] This succinctly summarizes what he is going to describe in detail in 7:7–25 and clearly places that material as an experience in the past before our identity with Christ's death—it describes a relationship with the law apart from Christ consistent with death, sin, and slavery. In 7:6, Paul creates a bridge for what he will describe in detail in chapter 8: now in the present, we have been freed from the law by dying to what held on to us, so that we can replace the old way of the written code with serving as slaves in the new way of the Spirit.[72] Significantly, this is the first mention of the Spirit in the book of Romans.

---

68. This conclusion is also heavily emphasized by discourse markers and extra words: "Consequently, my brothers and sisters, you also."

69. As Jewett suggests, "a figurative form of productivity in a general sense including childbearing is in view" (Jewett, *Romans*, 435). Bearing fruit is in a metaphorical relationship here with the natural consequences of sex: bearing children. Here, we had sin's babies, now we have God's babies, so to speak.

70. Contra Dunn who argues, "It is neither necessary nor appropriate to give it a special sense of childbearing as a way of pressing for more points of contact with vv 2–3" (Dunn, *Romans 1–8*, 363). Given the powerful Old Testament connections with fruit and childbearing and the sinful passions bearing fruit for death in v. 5, and the explicit correlation with marriage, sex, and adultery in vv. 1–3, the sense of childbearing in v. 4 is constrained.

71. The sexual innuendo is even more obvious, talking about arousing passions and bearing metaphorical children.

72. Often "slave" is translated as "servant" because it is believed that a positive reference to slavery would be offensive to many in our culture, and probably outside of the experience of many. However, in many ways the metaphor was equally difficult in the first century, as the believer is compared to female slaves who were used for breeding (bear fruit) and arguably held the lowest status of any people group in the first century.

Romans 7:7–25 is one of the most controversial passages in the book. I argue that it is characterized by the "rhetorical 'I'"—that is, the first person singular does not refer to Paul's unique experience as an individual but rather is paradigmatic. There are five views on the identity of "I": (1) autobiographical—Paul is giving his own experience of the law and sin;[73] (2) Adam and his experience in the garden;[74] (3) Israel before and after receiving the Law;[75] (4) the typical Jewish person;[76] and (5) the general unregenerate human predicament.[77] As I have argued elsewhere, Adam and Israel do not adequately account for the argument.[78] Given the general nature of the information, in contrast with true Pauline autobiographical information such as 1 Tim 1:13, the "I" is rhetorical and typical of any individual that encounters the law or any law or rule (view 4): with relevance to Paul, the Jewish Christians in Rome, and the Gentile Christians in Rome who were taught to keep the law, and purportedly had had a relationship with Judaism. But as he explained in Rom 3:16, apart from Christ every human could say with Paul, "I am a wretched human being" (7:24).

Crucifixion was even more offensive as an icon for Christianity.

73. Those who are associated with identifying "I" with Paul's personal history and experience include Gundry, "The Moral Frustration of Paul," 228–45; Schreiner, *Romans*, 363–65; Segal, *Paul the Convert*, 226–27; and Theissen, *Psychological Aspects of Pauline Theology*.

74. This position is proposed by Käsemann (*Romans*, 196): "There is nothing in the passage which does not fit Adam, and everything fits Adam alone."

75. Though Moo states that ἐγώ refers to Paul himself, he writes: "I suggest that Paul in vv. 7–11 is describing his own involvement, as a member of the people Israel, with the giving of the law to his people at Sinai" (Moo, *Epistle to the Romans*, 431). See also Sloan, "Paul and the Law," 55–56.

76. Longenecker offers a variation suggesting that the "I" represents the unbelieving Jewish community. He states: "The Mosaic law was contained within the single commandment given to Adam. Paul sees in this identification of the Mosaic law and the Adamic commandment a corresponding identification of the ethnocentric Jew and Adam who sins unto death" (Longenecker, *Eschatology and the Covenant*, 238).

77. This position that the "I" is the general unregenerate human predicament was first articulated in Kümmel, *Römer*, 7. Cranfield holds a similar view: "We may recognize Paul's use of the first person singular here as an example of the general use of the first person singular, but at the same time we shall probably be right to assume that his choice of this form of speech is, in the present case, due not merely to a desire for rhetorical vividness but also to his deep sense of personal involvement, his consciousness that in drawing out the general truth he is disclosing truth about himself" (Cranfield, *Romans*, 343–44). Fitzmyer suggests "It is more likely a device that Paul uses to describe humanity under the domination of the Mosaic law" (Fitzmyer, *Romans*, 463).

78. Westfall, "Discourse Analysis on Romans."

The Letter to the Romans

The line of thought flows out of Rom 5:20 and 7:5–6, which both address the relationship of the law to a person in an unregenerate state in contrast to the believers now who are united with Christ in his death and new life in the Spirit. Paul explains the place and function of the law in 7:7–12. The law is certainly not sinful.[79] However, virtually any law or rule provides the knowledge of sin, because of the "Dennis the Menace Principle": being told you cannot have something or do something immediately produces an uncontrollable desire to possess it or do it.[80] Therefore, a commandment brings sin to life[81] and sin seizes the opportunity, deceives us, and effectively kills the human being.[82] Nevertheless, the law and the commandment are holy, righteous, and good.[83]

Paul shows in Rom 7:13–25 that without the Spirit, any human attempt to live under the law produces conflict and guilt.[84] Sin produces death but at the same time the real nature of sin is revealed: it is shown to

---

79. The passage begins with two diatribal questions and an emphatic negative, which emphasize the point. Paul is not saying the Law is an evil thing. By maintaining the goodness of the Law he keeps continuity with the Old Testament.

80. "Dennis the Menace" refers to an American comic strip that was created in 1951, and subsequently several TV shows and series, films, and plays were based on its characters. As the comic strip has been distributed to 48 countries in 19 languages, it should be reasonably accessible to most readers.

81. Paul suggests that sin is virtually dormant without the Law to turn it into transgression.

82. Osborne (*Romans*, 175) states that this is a military metaphor for establishing a base of operations in an enemy territory. Sin is an active force taking the initiative and going to war. "Deceived me" is an allusion to Eve in Gen 3:13, where Eve was deceived by the serpent which corresponds to sin here.

83. The purpose of the Law is to restrain sin and produce life. It was meant to make people right with God.

84. A major question is who exactly the referent is in Rom 7:14–25, that is, precisely what stage of spiritual life the person is in. The options are: (1) Paul before his conversion; (2) Paul in his present experience as a Christian/the general experience of a Christian; (3) the typical Jewish person; (4) the Christian who is living a defeated life; (5) the general unregenerate human predicament. The passage is in the present tense, which leads some to assume that Paul is describing his present experience. However, in Greek, aspect theory (Porter, *Verbal Aspect*) suggests that the tenses don't indicate time, but rather point of view. The present tense is "foregrounded," or stands out in comparison to the use of the aorist, consistent with the rhetorical emphasis (Porter, *Verbal Aspect*, 196; Fanning, *Verbal Aspect*, 237–38, though Fanning states that this was one of the uses of the present). The condition Paul describes is the direct opposite of what he said the normal Christian condition should be in Rom 6. In Rom 8 Paul explains how the Spirit and being in Jesus Christ sets us free from this condition.

be "utterly sinful."[85] The law remains good and spiritual.[86] However, it highlights the problem of humanity: unregenerate humans are unspiritual and sold as slaves to sin, and their own failure to follow their own resolutions is a complete mystery or dilemma to them.[87] The function of "I" (ἐγώ) in this passage is consistent with the rhetorical usage. The same information could have been written in the third or second person. However, the use of the first person creates more interpersonal involvement than the third person and is less confrontational than the second person. The author chooses the present tense to emphasize a set of actions that involve a vicious circle of sin and failure and the state of being a slave of sin.

In Rom 7:17–23, Paul uses word play to describe the relationship between God's law, sin, and the human being so that he refers to God's law and the law of sin in conflict with the law of the mind—the law of sin refers to its nature and how it works (as a rule) and the law of the mind could represent human rules, philosophies, ideals, or resolutions. Paul identifies sin, which lives in an unregenerate person, as the problem and holds sin to be responsible for ethical failure. Any attempt to do good is frustrated—the person fails to do what they want to do and ends up doing evil that they do not want to do.[88] So Paul depicts an unregenerate person as capable of good intentions and godly values that agree with the law, but the law of sin wages war, defeats, and emerges victorious over human effort/will and logic ("the law of the mind"), and takes the human prisoner as a slave. Paul summarizes this condition in the same terms that he used in his description of humanity under the power of sin: "I am a wretched human being!"[89] He

---

85. Osborne (*Romans*, 180) says, "Through the Law the depth of [sin's] perversity is realized."

86. Jewett suggest that this means "Paul intends to imply that the Torah was created, activated and authorized by the Spirit" (Jewett, *Romans*, 461).

87. There is a distinct problem with identifying this as a believer's experience whether it is Paul or a "carnal Christian." The description of any believer's experience as "unspiritual" is problematic given the context. In Rom 8, Paul will describe the normative Christian life as essentially spiritual, led by the spirit of God. In 1 Cor 2:15, he uses the same word "spiritual" for the believer with the Spirit, though he does say he needs to address the Corinthians as "unspiritual" in 1 Cor 3:1–3. Romans 6:18, 22 explicitly says that we are set free from sin. 6:14 says that sin shall no longer be the believer's master. One may surmise that a person who is described as sold as a slave to sin is not a believer. Later in 8:1, 15 the same concept of freedom from slavery by the Spirit is reiterated.

88. The verb "to want" is repeated seven times in this passage. The repetition underscores the futility of the person under sin's power.

89. Ἄνθρωπος (human/person), though often translated as "man" particularly if they

asks the rhetorical question: Who will rescue him from the vicious circle of sin and death?, but he has already given part of the answer in Rom 5–6. Paul's following thanksgiving to God through Jesus Christ our Lord answers the question from the context because it links back to taking pride in God through our Lord Jesus Christ because of Christ's one righteous act that results in life and justification and places the believer under grace.[90] Before he goes on to describe the way of the Spirit, he recapitulates the dilemma of someone who is committed to following the Torah with self-will: one thinks that he or she is a slave to God's law, but selfish human nature is enslaved to sin.[91]

Insights for Preaching and Teaching

It is common for Christians to equate this passage with struggles in their Christian walk or to talk about the existence of "carnal Christians," but that would be completely missing Paul's point. Paul does not want Christians to identify with this struggle as normative. He wants them to recognize the difference between the futility of a life that attempts to do "good" or the "right thing" for any motivation other than serving God and living the new life that comes out of a full identity and relationship with Jesus Christ.

Instead, it would be more helpful to compare this struggle with following Law to our culture's use of self-help literature or courses to give economic, intellectual, or emotional self-improvement, or the struggle to achieve a certain standard for our quality of life or our dependence on technological advancement. Our attempts to improve ourselves or our condition as individuals ultimately fail when they do not serve God and they are not Spirit-led. This can be an opportunity to contrast our culture's siren lure to self-actualization, materialism, narcissism, and entitlement with call to a complete devotion to the Lordship of Christ, the service of God's righteousness, and the centrality of our relationship and identity within the family of God. Preaching through Rom 7 would be well-served by constant

---

understand it to refer to Paul's experience.

90. Those who think that this passage depicts a Christian experience will cite this thanks as proof—only a Christian could give thanks to Christ for deliverance. However, as in the diatribal dialogue, Paul can provide answers to rhetorical situations.

91. Again, being "a slave to God's law," if the Mosaic law is in view, would not be consistent with Paul's vocabulary of the normal Christian life—certainly it is not his goal for the Gentile members of the congregation.

anchoring and reference to the contrast with the preceding and following context, to keep the option of a vital life in Christ in the foreground.

THE CHRISTIAN LIFE IN THE SPIRIT (ROM 8:1–38)

Paul brings together the preceding themes of Rom 5–7 and beyond and explains more fully how we are set free from sin and our own selfish tendencies and how and why we are able to have peace with God and what that peace entails. The essential work of the Spirit is connected to the new life, and a complex of new metaphors fills out the description of sanctification as a relationship, all of which require participation on the part of the believer and have tangible, subjective, and experiential effects. Finally, Paul looks at a panoramic scope of suffering that believers face and reframes it all in the light of the themes that he has covered.

Background Information

As with the other chapters, theological topics can obscure the message of the passage. Romans 8 is best known in for its claim in v. 28 that all things work together for good, and the references to God's foreknowledge and predestination in v. 29 in terms of the role they have played in the debates between Calvinists and Arminians.[92] These topics may be of primary inter-

---

92. "Foreknew" can mean in most cases to know beforehand or can mean to select in advance (virtually a synonym to predestine). This is a key term in the debate between Calvinists and Arminians. Calvinists take foreknowledge to be synonymous with predestination for six reasons: (1) foreknowledge is relational and means to enter a relationship; (2) it relates to his preordained plan in Rom 8:28; (3) it is a foreknowledge that determines rather than just knows what will happen; (4) the emphasis is on predestined, and the first verb just prepares for it; (5) it means that God knew his people, not just about what he decided to do; (6) it involves intimate knowledge of believers and is synonymous with God's choice before the creation of the world. Osborne considers these reasons but observes (1) the Calvinist view is not the most natural understanding of the word; (2) none of the other of the five stages are synonymous; (3) God's knowledge doesn't mean he determines their decisions beforehand (cf. 1 Pet 1:2); (4) the passages about knowing before the creation of the world more likely connote God's foreknowledge of who would make a faith decision. "Therefore, it is better to link this with the emphasis on faith decision in 3:21—4:25 (17x) and interpret it as God's knowledge regarding those who would respond in faith to his call . . . So it means that on the basis of divine foreknowledge of each one's faith decision [or the group of those who would believe], God chooses those who turn to Christ to be his children" (Osborne, *Romans*, 222). Keener also says that the predication of predestination on foreknowledge does not cancel free will. Most of Judaism accepted both God's sovereignty and human responsibility. The idea that one has to choose between them is a post-New Testament idea based on Greek logic. Keener,

est to a well-informed congregation and they can dominate discussions in study groups. On the other hand, the Reformed issues are of less interest in contemporary theological discussions, and they present a significant distraction from Paul's message.

The primary focus in the background information should be the numerous links with the preceding context, how they interpret the passage, and also how Rom 8 interprets the preceding context. An overview of the main points of Rom 5–7 would help students and congregations to see the chapter as an integral part of a larger discussion rather than a self-contained passage. It is particularly important to review the meaning of "flesh" (σάρξ) as self-centeredness or selfishness.

Information about the baptism, indwelling, and filling of the Holy Spirit should be offered before covering this chapter or immediately after teaching or preaching on it. Whether the information is offered to the group or to the individual should be determined on a case-by-case basis. The group could be encouraged to read Acts, John 14:15–31 and 15:26—16:15.

In preparation for Rom 8:18–22, which discusses the suffering of creation, a discussion of the Old Testament background in Gen 3:17–19, which describes the curse of the ground as a result of the fall, would be helpful with students or congregants that have little background in the Bible.

Paul's list of things that are unable to separate us from the love of Christ in Rom 8:38–39 includes powerful and mystical forces that were common topics in Second Temple Jewish literature. "Principalities and powers" with "angels" and the cosmic context refer to the spiritual forces ruling the nations and bringing opposition against God's people. "Height" and "depth" may personify heaven and Hades, but other scholars think they are astrological terms: "The spiritual forces who ruled the nations were often believed to do so through the stars, and most first-century Greeks feared the inevitable power of Fate working through the stars."[93] Lists of hardships were common in Greco-Roman literature—they were used to show that the wise man had passed all tests and lived what he believed.[94] Students might brainstorm to gather a comparable list of forces that pose a primary threat or challenge.

Background Commentary, 431.

93. Keener, *Background Commentary*, 432.

94. Ibid.

Message of the Passage

Paul begins with the statement that there is no condemnation to those who are in Jesus Christ, which restates the point in Rom 5:11–21, which in vv. 16 and 18 says humanity is under condemnation because of Adam's act. However, Paul continues the wordplay on "law" and instead of repeating our unity in Christ's death and resurrection, he states that there is no condemnation because the law of the Spirit who gives life sets believers free from the law of sin and death.[95] The appeal to our unity in Christ's death and resurrection was forensic, but the work of the Spirit that sets us free from the wretched condition of slavery to sin and death is definitely experiential and subjective.[96]

In Rom 8:3–4, Paul summarizes the basics of the believer's forensic righteousness. The law was powerless to set humanity free from sin and death because of human selfishness. God did it by sending his own Son, who was in the likeness of sinful humanity in order to be a sin offering. This way, God both condemned sin in selfish human nature and met the righteous requirement of the law through Jesus Christ. However, this applies to those who live according to the Spirit not those who are controlled by selfishness.

Paul contrasts life according to the Spirit with life controlled by oneself (Rom 8:5–8).[97] The Spirit and selfish humanity have completely different goals and outcomes. The mind controlled by selfishness is set on selfish desires.[98] The outcome is death. It is hostile toward God—it cannot submit to him and it cannot please him. The mind controlled by the Spirit is set on

---

95. Whether the law brings life or death depends on whether it is written on one's heart by the Spirit (Ezek 36:27) or practiced as an external standard of righteousness, which is unattainable by human effort (ibid., 428). This is based on understanding it as the Mosaic Law. There is a big debate on whether the law is metaphorical as a "rule" or "authority" or a reference to the Mosaic Law.

96. As far as the forensic nature of sanctification, Osborne says it is not either/or: "The true purpose of the law is fulfilled when justification launches sanctification, that is, when Christ's sacrificial death enables these requirements to be *fully met in us*" (Osborne, *Romans*, 197).

97. While some take this as a contrast between two approaches to the Christian life, the whole argument would indicate that this is a contrast between the converted and the unconverted. See Moo, *Epistle to the Romans*, 486–87.

98. Dunn's description of "undue dependence on satisfying merely human appetites and ambitions" belongs here in the description of living according to the human nature (Dunn, *Romans 1–8*, 448).

what the Spirit desires.[99] Its outcome is life and peace—and since this is in contrast to hostility toward God this would be peace with God. So setting the mind on the Spirit is one of the essential means of having peace with God.

Alongside being united with Christ in baptism, belonging to Christ also must involve being in the Spirit or having the Spirit of Christ in you (8:9–11).[100] The Spirit is now identified as the source of life and is the eschatological guarantee of our physical resurrection—according to 8:23, the spirit is the first fruits of what is coming.[101] It is living by the Spirit that results in a new relationship with God (8:12–17). In view of that, we must participate in the reversal of control: we have an obligation to put to death the practices of the body instead of being under its influence—or as Paul says in 1 Cor 9:27, he punishes his body and makes it his slave in order to exercise self-control.[102]

Being led by the Spirit has a number of tangible effects on our lives. The Spirit does not make us slaves in the same way that sin does, but rather takes away our fear associated with enslavement.[103] Instead, the Spirit brings about our adoption so that we are enabled to call God "Father." The Spirit also assures us that we are God's children, God's heirs, and co-heirs

---

99. Underlying Paul's reasoning is the conviction that the human nature is created to be under God's control. The Spirit re-establishes the proper relationship between the human nature and God. It doesn't involve an empty mind, but reason directed by the Spirit/God's inspiration.

100. The Greek here is "in the Spirit." While the idea of being "controlled by God" is certainly in Rom 6, it seems to overstate the metaphor of the Spirit living in us that corresponds to us being in the Spirit. The problem of using "controlled by the Spirit" here is tantamount to saying that if you aren't "controlled" by the Spirit you don't belong to God, which depicts an all or nothing situation in which you are always questioning your salvation, or the idea of being controlled becomes meaningless.

101. "First fruits" was the first installment of the Palestinian harvest (Lev 23:10). It is a metaphor here for the Spirit in believers being the beginning of the future world.

102. "Body" here is not "flesh" (σάρξ) but σῶμα, which is our physical body that is prone to undermine our self-control (Rom 6:6). The practices or deeds in view here would include everything that has been described in Rom 1, 3, 5, 7. Jewett points out that the passage is not individualistic, but corporate, and makes a connection with 12:2, where this is an ongoing activity not to be conformed to this world in its bodily service. "A cosmic struggle to the death is here envisioned within the community and between the community and the world. Under the power and guidance of the Spirit . . . the community through its discernment and ethical actions is to kill the actions of the old age as they crop up as alternatives over and over again" (Jewett, *Romans*, 495).

103. The contrast of fearful slavery with adoption, inheritance, and intimacy with God involves a contrast between shame and honor.

with Christ. This informs us of what specifically is involved in taking pride in the hope of the glory of God (Rom 8:16//5:2). However, Paul says that we will share in Christ's glory only if we share in his sufferings.[104] So we see Paul making direct links between the presence of the Spirit in us and having peace with God that is realized by taking pride in God through our Lord Jesus Christ, taking pride in the hope of the glory of God and taking pride in our sufferings.

Finally, in Rom 8:18–39, Paul looks again at the suffering of the believer and reframes it with those three primary themes that he has highlighted at the beginning of his discussion of sanctification in Rom 5:1–11. The suffering of the children of God is hopeful when we take pride in the hope of the future glory of the children of God (8:18–30). Meanwhile, the Spirit is there to help us in our weakness (caused primarily by suffering) by assisting in our communication with God—as we groan in our suffering the Spirit groans for us (8:26–7).[105] The pride in suffering which produce character in Rom 5:3–5 is recapitulated in 8:28–30—that is why we know God is using all things, including present sufferings, to conform believers to the image of his son. Finally, our pride in God through our Lord Jesus Christ through whom we received reconciliation relativizes every threat that we face—if God is for us, who can be against us? Nothing will be able to separate us from the love of God that is in Jesus Christ our Lord.

Insights for Preaching and Teaching

The leader, teacher, or pastor needs to be sure that the teaching on the indwelling and leading of the Holy Spirit reassures the students and congregants rather than creates invalid anxiety and doubt. At the same time, individuals and groups should be challenged to recognize, acknowledge, and experience the spiritual realities that are contained in the message

---

104. The share in Christ's glory in 8:16 is directly linked to being heirs. The seemingly added stipulation of sharing in his suffering could link to the struggle against sin and killing the deeds of the flesh, but it also definitely looks ahead and anticipates the following discussion in vv. 18–30.

105. Note here the human nature is still weak when in the Spirit, but the Spirit helps our weakness when we are led by the Spirit. This provides continuity with the weakness of the human nature that is prone to sin and error when independent from God. This is the only place Paul clearly mentions the Spirit's intercession. He overcomes human limitations and struggles in communication to the Father. Some believe this is tongues, but the word "unspeakable" would argue that the help is inarticulate, especially on our part. As Burge says, this "focuses on the believer's human inability to express what they should pray but cannot because of their finiteness and weakness" (Burge, "Intercession," 438).

of Rom 8 and the entire section on sanctification. In order to adequately challenge others, it is imperative that leaders internalize and practice Paul's teaching on the Spirit and having peace with God as well as cultivate a biblical response to suffering and threats that communicates authentically.

In a North American context, it might be helpful to expose the group to issues of poverty, plague, and crisis in the majority world, as well as to lead them to ponder the range of suffering and crises that they and others have experienced. Reflect on the comparison of the real and present sufferings with the coming glory. Similarly consider how real and present suffering is sharing in Christ's sufferings and becoming conformed to his image.

CONCLUSION

Does it make a difference if we start this section on sanctification with exhortations rather than indicative statements in Rom 5? Understanding Rom 5:1 as an exhortation is not only better from the perspective of textual criticism, but it is much more consistent with the entire argument of the section. While the typical translations might have a comparable rhetorical impact, we must resist any assumption or impression that according to Paul, the believer has no real responsibility in maintaining a relationship with God except learning the facts and making a correct confession about them, or that the great theological truths of Rom 1–4 automatically produce the benefits that Paul describes in chapters 5–8. The primary teaching of Rom 5–8 is that sanctification is realized in a vibrant relationship with God in which we are active participants, not passive recipients. We must go beyond theological understanding and creedal confession in order to realize peace with God. In Rom 5–8, Paul structures the description of the believer's relationship with God and appropriate response around three exhortations which are expanded to incorporate a rich tapestry of knowing, being, and doing: take pride in the hope of the glory of God, take pride in our sufferings, and take pride in God himself through Jesus Christ. Metaphors and the cultural values of reciprocity and honor/shame associated with the first-century patron-client relationship permeate the passage. The skillful contemporary expositor will look for relevant cultural parallels that accomplish a comparable impact on any audience. Finally, I suggest that the entire section forms a well-defined and tightly knit argument that would best be read and preached as a unit in which the parts mutually interpret each other.

BIBLIOGRAPHY

Becker, Jürgen. *Paul: Apostle to the Gentiles*. Translated by O. C. Dean, Jr. Louisville: Westminster John Knox, 1993.

Bird, Michael, and Preston M. Sprinkle, eds. *The Faith of Jesus Christ: Exegetical, Biblical, and Theological Studies*. Grand Rapids: Baker, 2010.

Burge, G. M. "Intercession." In *Dictionary of Paul and His Letters*, edited by Gerald F. Hawthorne et al., 436–8. Downers Grove, IL: IVP, 1993.

Cranfield, C. E. B. *The Epistle to the Romans*, vol. 1. ICC. Edinburgh: T. & T. Clark, 1975.

deSilva, D. A. *Honor, Patronage, Kinship & Purity: Unlocking New Testament Culture*. Downers Grove, IL: IVP, 2006.

———. "Patronage." In *Dictionary of New Testament Background: A Compendium of Contemporary Biblical Scholarship*, edited by Craig A. Evans and Stanley E. Porter, 766–71. Downers Grove, IL: IVP, 2000.

———. "Honor and Shame." In *Dictionary of New Testament Background*, edited by Craig A. Evans and Stanley E. Porter, 518–22. Downers Grove: IVP, 2000.

Dunn, James D. G. *Romans 1–8*. WBC 38. Dallas: Word, 1988.

Elliott, Neil. *Rhetoric of Romans: Argumentative Constraint and Strategy and Paul's Dialogue with Judaism*. JSNTSup 45. Sheffield: Sheffield Academic, 1990.

Erickson, R. J. "Flesh." In *Dictionary of Paul and His Letters*, edited by Gerald F. Hawthorne et al., 303–6. Downers Grove, IL: IVP, 1993.

Fanning, Buist M. *Verbal Aspect in New Testament Greek*. Oxford Theological Monographs. Oxford: Oxford University Press, 1990.

Fitzmyer, Joseph A. *Romans*. AB 33. New York: Doubleday, 1993.

Goppelt, Leonhard. *Typos: The Typological Interpretation of the Old Testament in the New*. Grand Rapids: Eerdmans, 1982.

Gundry, Robert H. "The Moral Frustration of Paul before His Conversion: Sexual Lust in Romans 7:7–25." In *Pauline Studies: Essays Presented to Professor Bruce on His 70th Birthday*, edited by Donald A. Hagner and Murray J. Harris, 228–45. Grand Rapids: Eerdmans, 1980.

Harrill, J. Albert. "Slavery." In *Dictionary of New Testament Background: A Compendium of Contemporary Biblical Scholarship*, edited by Craig A. Evans and Stanley E. Porter, 1124–27. Downers Grove, IL: IVP, 2000.

Hays, Richard B. *The Faith of Jesus Christ: The Narrative Substructure of Galatians 3:1—4:11*. 2nd ed. Biblical Resource Series. Grand Rapids: Eerdmans, 2002.

Instone-Brewer, David. *Divorce and Remarriage in the Bible: The Social and Literary Context*. Grand Rapids: Eerdmans, 2002.

Jewett, Robert. *Romans: A Commentary*. Hermeneia. Minneapolis: Fortress, 2007.

Käsemann, Ernst. *Commentary on Romans*. Translated by Geoffrey W. Bromiley. Grand Rapids: Eerdmans, 1996.

Keener, Craig S. *The IVP Bible Background Commentary: New Testament*. Downers Grove, IL: IVP Academic, 1994.

Kümmel, Werner Georg. *Römer 7 und die Bekehrung des Paulus*. Leipzig: Hinrichs, 1929.

Lee, Jae Hyun. "Against Richard Hays's 'Faith of Jesus Christ.'" *JGRChJ* 5 (2008) 51–80.

Longenecker, Bruce W. *Eschatology and the Covenant: A Comparison of 4 Ezra and Romans 1–11*. Sheffield: Sheffield Academic, 1991.

Metzger, Bruce M. *A Textual Commentary on the Greek New Testament*. 2nd ed. Stuttgart: Deutsche Bibelgesellschaft, 2006.

Moo, Douglas. *The Epistle to the Romans*. NICNT. Grand Rapids: Eerdmans, 1996.
———. *Romans*. NIVAC. Grand Rapids: Zondervan, 2000.
Osborne, Grant R. *Romans*. IVPCS. Downers Grove, IL: IVP, 2004.
Porter, Stanley E. "The Argument of Romans 5: Can a Rhetorical Question Make a Difference?" *JBL* 110 (1991) 655–77.
———. *Verbal Aspect in the Greek of the New Testament with Reference to Tense and Mood*. SBG 1. New York: Peter Lang, 1989.
Schreiner, Thomas R. *Romans*. BECNT. Grand Rapids: Baker, 1998.
Segal, Alan. *Paul the Convert: The Apostolate and Apostasy of Saul the Pharisee*. New Haven: Yale University Press, 1990.
Sloan, Robert. "Paul and the Law: Why the Law Cannot Save." *NovT* 33 (1991) 55–56.
Tannehill, Robert C. *Dying and Rising with Christ: A Study in Pauline Theology*. Repr., Eugene, OR: Wipf and Stock, 2006.
Theissen, Gerd. *Psychological Aspects of Pauline Theology*. Translated by John P. Galvin. Philadelphia: Fortress, 1987.
Verbrugge, Verlyn D. "The Grammatical Evidence for EXΩMEN in Romans 5:1." *JETS* 54 (2011) 559–72.
Westfall, Cynthia Long. "A Discourse Analysis of Romans 7.7–25: The Pauline Autobiography?" In *The Linguist as Pedagogue: Trends in the Teaching and Linguistic Analysis of the Greek New Testament*, edited by Stanley E. Porter and Matthew Brook O'Donnell, 146–58. Sheffield: Sheffield Phoenix, 2009.
Wilckens, Ulrich. *Der Brief an die Römer*. Neukirchen-Vluyn: Neukirchener, 1978.

5

What Is the Future of Israel in Romans 9–11?

AUGUST H. KONKEL

ACCORDING TO THE APOSTLE Paul, the future of Israel can only be understood as the revelation of a divine mystery (Rom 11:25).[1] This mystery concerns the divine purposes in the hardening of Israel. Understanding this mystery excludes all human wisdom; according to human intelligence, the unbelief of Israel would be either a pure enigma or a temptation to arbitrary rational conclusions. The obduracy of Israel can only be understood in terms of its eschatological significance, within the context of a μυστήριον ("mystery"). Paul does not appeal to a revelation imparted to him. The revelation he interprets is based on the election of Israel, which seems to be contradicted by the present circumstance. Most of those belonging to Israel are enemies of the gospel. The inaccessibility of this mystery to human investigation elicits the exclamation of the closing wisdom hymn: "O, the depth of the riches, wisdom, and knowledge of God" (v. 33).[2] The revelation of this mystery is understood through the interpretation of Scripture. The logical conclusion of the argument (vv. 28–32) is complemented by a liturgical counterpart ascribing praise to the omnipotent God.

The procedure of the apostle Paul in articulating the revelation of the mystery learned from the Scripture should properly be called argument. *Argumentatio* in antiquity is the rhetorical terminology used for a particular kind of discourse that has been developed in accordance with an

---

1. Bornkamm, "μυστήριον," 822.
2. Johnson, *Function of Apocalyptic*, 173.

orthodox procedure.³ Paul does not engage in this kind of rhetoric in his letter to the Romans. Closer to Paul's method is the Latin *argumentum*, the provision of evidence or proof. Argument is that which supports an assertion; the procedure of argumentation is a linguistic genre, the articulation and exposition of argument.⁴ Greek has fewer examples of this than classical Latin, but Siegert has a lengthy section in which he provides examples from the Septuagint.

In Christian thought, argument is expressed by Peter as being prepared to provide a defense (ἀπολογίαν) of the hope of the faith to anyone that should ask (1 Pet 3:15). If one searches for the equivalent Greek word expressed in the Latin part of speech termed *argumentation*, one discovers the word πίστις.⁵ The plural πίστεις means argument in the anticipated sense of factual reason, evidence of truth, or proof of fact.⁶ Paul can call the message which demands faith the "word of faith" (ῥῆμα τῆς πίστεως; Rom 10:8); he can describe the hearing of faith (ἀκοὴ πίστεως) as "the preaching which demands faith" or opens up the possibility of faith (Gal 3:2, 5).⁷ Since faith is the divinely demanded relation of humans to God and is the divinely provided way of salvation, the apostle can speak of the "law of faith" (νόμος πίστεως; Rom 3:27). Law is meant in the sense of the divine ordinance which describes faith as the right human response, excluding any claims toward God. Paul can simply speak of "preaching the faith" (εὐαγγελίζεσθαι τὴν πίστιν; Gal 1:23); the Christian message properly understood leads to faith.

In writing to the Romans, the apostle expresses his readiness to preach the gospel in Rome, and in so doing states the theological theme which will be worked out in the main body of the epistle (Rom 1:16–17). The gospel is God's saving power to everyone who believes, to the Jew first and also to the Greek.

---

3. "*Argumentatio* hieß in der rhetorischen Terminologie der Antike ein bestimmter Teil einer Rede, wenn sie schulmäßig aufgebaut war" (Siegert, *Argumentation bei Paulus*, 16). Siegert has adopted this definition from Lausberg and Öhlschläger.

4. "'Argument' sind hier also das, was einen Anspruch stützt, 'Argumentation' hingegen ist de sprachliche Gestaltung, Äußerung, Darlegung der Argumente" (Siegert, *Argumentation bei Paulus*, 17).

5. Ibid.

6. "Der Plural davon, πίστεις, meinte 'Argumente' in dem vorhin erwähnten Sinn von 'Sachgründe', 'Beweisgegenstände', 'Beweistachsachen'" (ibid.).

7. Bultmann, "πιστεύω, πίστις," 213.

"To the Jew first" is very important to the apostle. He repeats it in expressing the consequences of forsaking steadfast perseverance: "There will be tribulation and distress on every individual person who works what is evil, to the Jew first and also to the Greek" (Rom 2:9). The converse is also true; there is "glory and honor and peace for everyone who works what is good, for the Jew first and also for the Greek" (Rom 2:10). The priority of the Jew in the interpretation of the apostle Paul has to do with the elective purposes of God. To Israel is the adoption and the glory, the covenants and the legislation, the worship and the promises; the fathers are of Israel, and so far as human reality is concerned, so also is Christ (Rom 9:5). These are the irrevocable gifts and calling of God (Rom 11:29). This priority of the Jew is foundational to understanding the mystery that is disclosed in the revelation of God.

There is both a consistency and a complexity in the apostle Paul coming to understand the mystery of the gospel. Paul must insist to the Galatians that the gospel which he preached was a revelation of Jesus Christ (Gal 1:12), given to him apart from any other human influence. This revelation transformed his understanding of the Scriptures, as he had pursued them in Judaism (vv. 13, 14). God revealed his Son to the apostle so he might make known the good news among nations; this was quite contrary to what he had believed as a Jew. But at the revelation of the Son of God, the apostle did not confer with those that had come to know the Christ before him; instead he went away into Arabia and then returned to Damascus. It was not until three years later that he went up to Jerusalem to become acquainted with Peter. The only other apostle he knew was James the brother of the Lord. From Jerusalem the apostle spent time in the regions of Syria and Cilicia, not being familiar with the churches in Judea. They were only aware that the one who had formerly ravaged the church was now proclaiming the faith. Fifteen years later the apostle went up to Jerusalem, taking with him Barnabas and Titus, to explain privately, to those of repute, the gospel he preached to the nations.

The mystery revealed to the apostle after three years of pondering the Scriptures was that the gospel was for the nations. This was a point he needed to defend to the churches in Judea. The mystery revealed in Christ was the divinely ordained execution of the hitherto concealed plan of salvation (Eph 3:9).[8] The revelation was a mystery because it was concealed within the Scriptures, eternally hidden in God, the creator of all things, until it was

---

8. Bornkamm, "μυστήριον," 821.

made known in Christ. Grace was given to the one who was the least of all saints, to make known the unsearchable riches of Christ.

The mystery of the gospel in bringing the good news to the nations created a tension with the promises of God to Israel. The book of Romans addresses two problems in the apostle's articulation of the mystery of the gospel: Jewish unbelief and Gentile belief.[9] The coming of the Gentiles to faith could not deny the promises of God to Israel. The gospel was still to the Jew first and also to the Greek. God's irrevocable election of Israel is directly juxtaposed to his impartial judgment and redemption of all. At stake in Rom 9–11 is God's faithfulness to Israel and God's trustworthiness as the God who elects and redeems impartially.

The apostle Paul, in concluding his argument, expresses it this way in Rom 11:28–32:[10]

> As regards *the progress of* the gospel, they are enemies for your sake, but as regards the election they are beloved for the sake of the fathers; for the gifts and calling of God are irrevocable. For as you once were disobedient to God but now have received mercy by their disobedience, so these now have been disobedient in order that they too may now receive mercy by the mercy shown to you. For God has imprisoned all in disobedience, in order that he may have mercy upon all.

The translation by Cranfield carefully provides a balanced correspondence between the protasis and apodosis in the argument that mercy received by the Gentiles is the means by which the Jews will also receive mercy (vv. 30–31).[11] You (Gentiles) were formerly disobedient to God; these (Jews) now are disobedient to God. Now you (Gentiles) have received mercy by their disobedience; now these (Jews) will receive mercy by the mercy shown to you. The mystery of the gospel is that the Jews will receive mercy because the Gentiles have received mercy. So all Israel will be saved.

THE IDENTITY OF ISRAEL AND JEW IN ROMANS

Israel is a highly multivalent term. It has the potential of almost innumerable referents because of its vast associations in ethnic, political, or religious

---

9. Johnson, *Function of Apocalyptic*, 146.
10. Cranfield, *Romans*, 2:572.
11. Ibid., 2:582.

identity. In Rom 9–11 Israel is employed by Paul in at least three ways.[12] Israel is all ethnic Israel (9:1–5, 31; 10:1–3; 11:11–36). Israel is the remnant, composed of faithful Jews, of whom the apostle is an example (11:1–6). Israel is also the children of promise (9:8, 24; cf. 4:16–17), Abraham's spiritual descendants, including those of Jewish and Gentile heritage. Israel for Paul is a single reality created by God's mercy of election, and cannot be limited by ethnicity. Each of these three perspectives of Israel in Rom 9–11 is never exclusive; each is regarded as inclusive of the other.

Each of these referents for Israel needs to be carefully distinguished in understanding Paul's argument in Rom 9–11. At the same time, it is important to note how these referents for Israel are one single reality in Paul's case for the salvation of Israel, which is the goal of the whole section.

In Paul's understanding of God's program of salvation, there is an Israel that is not identified with the church, an Israel that is part of God's elective purposes to bring about salvation, an election that is as yet unfulfilled. Its fulfilment depends on the full accomplishment of the Gentile mission, which will bring about the completion of the elective purposes of Israel. It is a mistake to think that the triumph of the Gentile mission and the growth and success of the church accomplishes God's elective purposes. This is to misunderstand God's purpose and method in election. Election included Israel and the nations; therefore, the success of the latter must not displace the role and function of the former.

There remains an Israel elected by God that must fulfill its purpose for all salvation to be complete. The church unfortunately in its early stages did not understand this. The church perceived itself to be the fulfilment of salvation, displacing any role there may have been for Israel. In the Church of the Annunciation in Nazareth, in the lower level containing the grotto of the annunciation, believed by many to be the original childhood home of Mary, is inscribed a menorah which has been defaced; it now manifests clearly only five lamps instead of seven. The statement for all pilgrims to see is that there is no longer a role for Israel. The original shrine goes back to the middle of the fourth century; it is impossible to say that the menorah was defaced when it was part of the original shrine. However, the conception that the fullness of the gospel was realized in the growth of the church, that the church itself fulfilled all the promises to Israel, is one that goes back to very early times. This is a complete failure to understand the mystery of

---

12. Johnson, *Function of Apocalyptic*, 141.

the gospel according to Paul. The gifts and calling of Israel are irrevocable and all Israel will be saved.

In Paul's argumentation, there is an ethnic component to Israel, represented in no less a person than Paul himself: "I am an Israelite, of the seed of Abraham, of the tribe of Benjamin" (Rom 11:1). But the ethnic Israelite is further qualified in two ways. Quoting Isa 10:22, Paul says Israel is the trusting remnant, as the Lord carries out a complete and decisive sentence upon the earth (Rom 9:27–28). This is complemented by a further quotation from Isa 1:9, in which Israel is not destroyed like Sodom and Gomorrah because the Lord had left them a seed, as it is expressed in the Greek. This remnant is now ignorant of the righteousness of God, seeking to stand in its own righteousness; they are not subject to God (Rom 10:3). But Christ is the goal of the law for righteousness to all who believe (v. 4). Christ stands as a synecdoche for the entire gospel.[13] The gospel announces the impartial righteousness of God. Israel has heard and Israel does know. God will use a nation that is not a nation to make them jealous, and a foolish nation to make them angry (Rom 10:19, quoting Deut 32:21). God continues to stretch out his hands to a disobedient and contrary people (Rom 10:21, quoting Isa 65:2).

The other term important for understanding the mystery of the gospel is Jew. (Paul is unique in his use of this term.) In the Synoptists Ἰουδαῖος is used rarely and is never used as a proper name for the people to whom Jesus comes. In this sense it is found only in the expression "king of the Jews." The expression however is only used by aliens, never by Jesus or the Evangelists themselves.[14] In contrast, John uses the term Ἰουδαῖος seventy times, where Jesus is called a Jew, and Jew is used frequently to denote the inhabitants of Palestine.[15] This is especially true in explaining Jewish customs or expressions. Jews oppose Jesus when he seems to reject the temple. Jew is also a name for those who reject the claims of Jesus and remain Jews because they do so. The use in Acts is similar to John. But in Acts the term Jew pertains also to the diaspora.[16] Jews bear this name as members of a particular religious community. When members of this community are called Jews, it is usually to explain particular circumstances or to denote they are members by birth.

13. Johnson, *Function of Apocalyptic*, 155.
14. Gutbrod, "Ἰσραήλ, Ἰσραηλίτης," 3:375.
15. Ibid., 3:377.
16. Ibid., 3:379.

Paul is unique in his use of the term Jew. He tends to use the singular Ἰουδαῖος even when he is not thinking of the individual Jew. He often uses Ἰουδαῖος without the article, which is infrequent in other writings. For Paul, Ἰουδαῖος has a type of spiritual or religious importance.[17] He does not have in mind specific adherents of this nation and religion. He is thinking of a type abstracted from individual representatives. Paul can speak of the true Jew as distinct from the person that is only formally a Jew. The true Jew is the one that keeps the law (Rom 2:17). For Paul the term Jew describes someone with a relationship and attachment to the law. When Christians play the part of a Jew in observing their practices of law, they remain Jews (Gal 2:13). This typical use of Ἰουδαῖος is used as an antithesis to the term Greek. The distinction is not one of race or nationality, it is grounded in revelation.[18] Paul uses Ἰουδαῖος in an essential supra-personal aspect, whether negatively in the rejection of Christ or positively in the commitment to the law. But the ethnic designation of Jew is not lost; the concept of Jew includes membership in a particular ethnic people.

In Rom 9–11 Jew and Israelite refer to a particular ethnic identity, but always in their relationship to the law. These may misunderstand the law and its teaching of salvation, or they may affirm its benefits. Israelites are Paul's kinsmen; they are the ones who have received the adoption, the glory and the covenants, the lawgiving, the worship and the promises; the fathers are of them as is Christ in human relationship. At the same time the point to be emphasized is that God's mercy is equal to Jew and Gentile; both have been called (Rom 9:24), and there is no distinction because God is Lord of all, giving riches to all those that call upon him, whether Jew or Greek (Rom 10:12). While the Jew has the privilege of the gifts and calling of God, there is no advantage in receiving the mercy of salvation.

THE ELECTION OF ISRAEL

The argument of the apostle for the redemption of Israel is developed in three stages. First is the response to the question as to whether the word of God might have failed (Rom 9:6–29). The answer to this question is that God's mercy has always been accomplished through his elective purpose, in which God creates those individuals that are the means of carrying out his salvation. There are those that were dishonorable, that were not included in the elective mercy. They are fully culpable in being excluded; God in mercy

17. Ibid., 3:380.
18. Ibid., 3:381.

has carried out his salvation through the elect. This includes the salvation of the Gentiles (Rom 9:24–26, quoting Hos 2:25, 1). It also includes the faithful remnant of Israel (Rom 9:27–29, quoting Isa 10:22; 28:22; 1:9). They are not all Israel who are of Israel, for some have stumbled on the rock causing offense.

The second argument addresses the question of the current situation concerning Israel (Rom 9:30—10:21). How is it that the Gentiles should have found righteousness, while Israel in pursuit of the righteousness of God did not attain that righteousness (Rom 9:30–31)? The answer comes in two parts; the first concerns the nature of the gospel (9:32—10:13) and the second God's relation to Israel through the gospel (10:14–21). Israel has stumbled at the stone of scandal in pursuing a righteousness of works. The reason that Israel stumbles is in the nature of the gospel. Christ is the goal of the teaching, the *tôrāh* (Rom 10:4); righteousness comes to all those that have faith in him. God is impartial in the mercy of righteousness. Israel was ignorant of this impartiality of righteousness, and so has stumbled on the rock causing offense in Zion.

Paul goes on to demonstrate covenant renewal in Rom 10:6–11.[19] Paul reads Deut 30 as a prediction of covenant renewal following judgment and exile. He explains this renewal in terms of what is happening through the gospel of Jesus Christ and through faith in that gospel shown by Jews and Gentiles alike. The covenant "exile" predicted by Deuteronomy had gone on right up to the time of the Messiah. That time of exile has been brought to an end, precipitating the long promised renewal in Deut 30. The mark of membership in this renewed covenant is the faith that confesses Jesus Christ as Lord. Christian faith is like the Abrahamic faith, open to Jew and Gentile alike. The "law" was not up in heaven or across the sea so that it would be out of reach and impossible to keep. Paul applies what is said of the law to the Messiah; he has come down from heaven, so when the word about him is in your mind, it is the sign that the new covenant work has taken place in the believer.

Paul believed that God had fulfilled the covenant promises to Abraham, and the promise of covenant renewal in Deuteronomy, in and through Jesus Christ. The exile, as in Deut 29, was being undone. In Rom 10:6–11, Paul has the larger context of Deuteronomy in mind.[20] In alluding to Deut 30, Paul has in mind the whole narrative of the latter chapters of

---

19. Wright, "Romans 9–11," 45.
20. Ibid., 47. Wright here refers to Richard Hays, *The Faith of Jesus Christ*.

Deuteronomy. He sees them as a prophetic description of the entire story from Moses to his own day and beyond. Paul believed that the exile of Deut 29 continued to his own day, like the author of the Qumran document 4QMMT,[21] and that he was experiencing at long last the unique restoration of Deut 30.

The relation between Rom 10:5 and 10:6–8 must be understood in terms of paradoxical fulfilment.[22] Romans 10:1–13 is asking and answering the question of how Jews can be saved (vv. 1, 9, 13). The answer is through the doing of the law, which is what Moses went on to say in Deut 30. For those for whom the covenant is renewed, the *tôrāh* is not high in the heaven, but is near that they may do it. Deuteronomy offers a fresh vision of doing the law, a new covenantal vision. What the law could not do is performed by Christ and by the Spirit. The mind of the Spirit can and does fulfil the law (Rom 8:5–8). Confessing Christ as Lord is for Paul the sign that Deut 30 is happening at last. Faith in Jesus Christ is the paradoxical and surprising doing of the *tôrāh* indicated in Deut 30. Righteousness is reckoned when one believes, because that belief is the sign of covenant membership.

The stumbling of Israel is not outside of the sovereign working of God (Rom 10:14–21). God continues to extend his hands to a disobedient and contrary people (Rom 10:21, quoting Isa 65:2). God's method is to provoke them to jealousy through a nation that does not understand (Rom 10:19, quoting Deut 32:21). The gospel has been offensive to Israel while the Gentiles believed so as to make Israel jealous that God may reach out to the people he foreknew.

The third argument comes in answer to the question as to whether God could have rejected his people (Rom 11:1). The first part of the answer is found in Rom 11:1b–6 with a series of quotations about Elijah in 1 Kgs 19:10–18. In Elijah's day God had left a remnant; Elijah was not the only one who had not bowed the knee to Baal. Paul, as Elijah, is representative of that Israel that has remained faithful to God. The hardening of Israel is

---

21. Elisha Qimron and John Strugnell, *Miqṣat Ma'aśe Ha-Torah*, 59: "we have [written] to you so that you may study (carefully) the book of Moses and the books of Prophets . . . And it is written that [you will stray] from the path (of the Torah) and that calamity will meet [you]. And it is written 'and it shall come to pass, when all these things [be]fall you,' at the end of days, the blessings and the curses, ['then you will take] it to hea[r]t and you will return unto Him with all your heart and with all your soul,' at the end [of time, so that you may live . . .]" (4QMMT C 10–16).

22. Wright, "Romans 9–11," 47.

also the work of God (Rom 11:8-9, quoting Isa 29:10; 6:9-10; Ps 69:23-24 [68 in the Greek Psalter]). But this is not a permanent condition (Rom 11:11). The mercy shown to the Gentiles will bring about the restoration of Israel (Rom 11:11b-16). If their first fruits are holy, so also is the whole, if the root, so also the branches. All this is illustrated by the grafting in of a wild olive to a cultivated olive tree (Rom 11:17-24). The Gentiles have been grafted in to this cultivated olive tree; how much more possible is it for Israel to be grafted in to its own olive tree.

THE SALVATION OF ISRAEL

There is hardness and blindness that has affected a part of Israel until the fullness of Gentiles comes in. Then all Israel shall be saved. The hardness and the salvation of Israel is explained by a quotation from Isa 59:20 (cf. Rom 11:26). The prophet lamented the sad state of Israel in which the action of God was pre-empted because Israel did not know how to do what is good. Their hands were stained with blood and their fingers with iniquity (Isa 59:3). Deliverance is far from their grasp because of their transgressions (vv. 9-12). The chapter is constructed as a sermon.[23] In the manner of a preacher, the writer is attempting to convince these Israelites that the lack of God's intervention is due to their own behavior. The community acknowledges its responsibility (Isa 59:9-15a), which will at last elicit a response from God (vv. 15b-20). Yahweh will come to Zion as a redeemer for those in Israel who turn from transgression. The promised redemption is limited to those who turn from transgression. Zion will be delivered for the penitent ones as the divine warrior exercises his vengeance and judgment in delivering his people. He will come like a pent up torrent, driven on by Yahweh's breath; he will come to Zion as redeemer (Isa 59:19b-20a).[24]

The action of God in the redemption of Zion is interpreted as messianic. In Isa 59:21 God endows his prophet with his word; the gift of the spirit and the gift of communicating the will of God are bestowed by covenant on an individual prophet. In its context, Isa 59:21 serves as a kind of colophon to Isa 56-59, legitimating the prophetic witness and claiming descent from the servant of chapter 53.[25] Paul seems to have made this messianic association in his interpretation of the coming of the deliverer to Zion. The servant of Isaiah is Jesus in his mission; the coming of the redeemer from Zion is

23. Blenkinsopp, *Isaiah 56-66*, 191-92.
24. Ibid., 194.
25. Ibid., 202.

understood to be the *parousia* of Christ.²⁶ The quotation confirms the salvation of Israel as an eschatological event. The turning of the ungodly from Jacob (Rom 11:26), the Greek rendering of the words of Isa 59:20, indicates the nature of the deliverance that will be accomplished. It will consist in turning back ungodliness from the nation of Israel. The messianic work is further affirmed in a quotation from Isa 27:9, which affirms the restoration of Israel as the removal of their sins (Rom 11:27). The composite quotation dashes Israel's self-centered hopes of putting a claim upon God and putting him under obligation.²⁷ The nation's final salvation will be a matter of the forgiveness of its sins by the sheer mercy of God.

In the mind of Paul, the salvation of all Israel is the redemption of the nation collectively, though not including every individual member. Redemption comes to the repentant ones of Jacob. This restoration of the nation as a whole to God comes at the end; it is an eschatological event in the strict sense. Zoccali, in a thorough review of the interpretations of the salvation of all Israel, refers to this interpretation as "eschatological miracle."²⁸ He opines that Paul's meaning is that 'all Israel' refers to the complete number of elect from the historical/empirical nation.²⁹ Without providing an exegesis of Isa 59, he contends that Paul is following Jewish oral tradition in which Isa 59:20 and Isa 27:9 have already been conflated and adapted as an explanation of Yahweh intervening on behalf of his oppressed people Israel.³⁰ It is strange to conclude that Paul's exegesis on such a critical point would be that of a Jewish oral interpretation. Isaiah is central in New Testament interpretation of Christ, and hardly dependent on Jewish oral tradition. The argument that οὕτως in Rom 11:26 should be understood in its modal sense, rather than having a temporal nuance, does not contradict an eschatological interpretation if Isaiah is interpreted as messianic, as indicated in the Pauline exegesis of this passage.

The salvation of Israel according to Paul dashes any hopes of his contemporaries, as well as those of our own contemporary time, for the reestablishment of an independent national state with political power.³¹ The

---

26. Cranfield, *Romans*, 2:578.
27. Ibid., 2:578–79.
28. Zoccali, "And So All Israel will be Saved," 290.
29. Ibid., 303.
30. Ibid., 311–12.

31. Dekar asks the question in his article ("State of Israel," 31–46). Most of the article reviews the flaws of a dispensational approach to prophecy in which the state of Israel has

salvation of Israel is a receiving of the mercy of God in forgiveness of sins, parallel to that of the Gentiles. It is an eschatological event, associated with the coming of Christ, in which Israel will receive mercy by the mercy that has been shown to the Gentiles. This is the great mystery. If their transgression, by the grace of God, came to be the salvation of the Gentiles, their defeat riches for the Gentiles, then how much more shall be their fullness (Rom 11:11–12). If their rejection means the reconciliation of the world, what can their acceptance mean but life from the dead? (Rom 11:15). The salvation of Israel will be their being grafted in again to their own cultivated olive tree. Salvation is complete when Jews and Gentiles are united in Christ. The mystery of redemption will be realized in the coming of Christ.

The final consequence of God's impartiality and faithfulness is in bringing mercy to Jew and Gentile equally. Paul gives thanks not just for God's sovereignty, his mercy, and his faithfulness, but his wisdom (Rom 11:33–36). In this wisdom the mystery is brought to fullness, the time of the redemption of Israel when the fullness of the Gentiles has taken place.

BIBLIOGRAPHY

Blenkinsopp, Joseph. *Isaiah 56–66: A New Translation with Introduction and Commentary.* AB 19.2. New York: Doubleday, 2003.

Bornkamm, G. "μυστήριον, μυέω." In *TDNT* 4:802–28.

Bultmann, Rudolf. "πιστεύω, πίστις, πιστός, πιστόω, ἄπιστος, ἀπιστία, ὀλιγόπιστος, ὀλιγοπιστία." In *TDNT* 6:174–228.

Cranfield, C. E. B. *A Critical and Exegetical Commentary on the Epistle to the Romans.* 2 vols. ICC. Edinburgh: T. & T. Clark, 1975–1979.

Dekar, Paul R. "Does the State of Israel have Theological Significance?" *Conrad Grebel Review* 2 (1984) 31–46.

Gutbrod, Walter. "'Ἰσραήλ, Ἰσραηλίτης, Ἰουδαῖος, Ἰουδαία, Ἰουδαϊκός, ἰουδαΐζω, Ἰουδαϊσμός, Ἑβραῖος, Ἑβραϊκός, ἑβραΐς, ἑβραϊστί." In *TDNT* 3:356–91.

Johnson, E. Elizabeth. *The Function of Apocalyptic and Wisdom Traditions in Romans 9–11.* SBLDS. Atlanta: Scholars Press, 1989.

Qimron, Elisha, and John Strugnell. *Qumran Cave 4 V: Miqṣat Ma`aśe Ha-Torah.* DJD X. Oxford: Clarendon, 1994.

Siegert, Folker. *Argumentation bei Paulus gezeigt an Röm 9–11, 16.* Tübingen: Mohr Siebeck, 1985.

Wright, N. T. "Romans 9–11 and the 'New Perspective.'" In *Between the Gospel and Election: Exploration in the Interpretation of Romans 9–11,* edited by Florian Wilk and J. Ross Wagner, 37–45. Tübingen: Mohr Siebeck, 2010.

---

a particular eschatological significance. His conclusion is that the state of Israel does not have theological significance, but the establishment of the state of Israel revives a whole area of theological inquiry regarding the complex relationships between peoplehood, land, statehood, and the kingdom of God.

Zoccali, Christopher. "'And So All Israel will be Saved': Competing Interpretations of Romans 11:26 in Pauline Scholarship." *JSNT* 30 (2008) 289–318.

6

How Then Shall We Live? (Romans 12:1—15:6)

L. L. Belleville

INTRODUCTION

Paul's letter to the Roman church is typically valued for its theological content. Many teachers and preachers, however, do not get beyond Rom 8, although some do make it to chapter 11. This is unfortunate, since Rom 12:1—15:6 contains some of the New Testament's most valuable ethical materials. In fact, virtually all of Paul's moral teaching spread out among his letters is found in very compact form in these chapters. One would therefore think that Rom 12:1—15:6 would receive significant attention in Pauline ethics volumes, theologies, and commentaries on Romans.

A quick perusal of three scholarly works on New Testament and Pauline ethics produces disappointing results. Richard Hays's 508-page *The Moral Vision of the New Testament* has 56 pages devoted to Paul (11 percent) with only a few scattered references to Rom 12:1—15:6.[1] Victor Furnish's *The Moral Teaching of Paul* references Rom 12:1–2,[2] and then focuses exclusively on Rom 13 and the Christian's relationship to Roman governing authorities.[3] Brian Rosner's collection of essays in *Understanding Paul's Ethics* has extended treatments of 1 Corinthians, Col 3 and 1 Thess 4 but no significant attention given to Rom 12–15 beyond a handful of scattered

---

1. Hays, *Moral Vision*, 16–72.
2. Furnish, *The Moral Teaching of Paul*, 23–24, 116, 123, 125–26.
3. Ibid., 115–39.

references.[4] Wayne Meeks in *The Moral World of the First Christians* allots a mere three lines of text to Rom 12:2, 13:7, and 14:1—15:6.[5]

Recent Pauline theologies do not fare much better. James Dunn's 808-page *The Theology of Paul the Apostle* devotes 42 pages to what he titles "Ethics in Practice" of which Rom 12:7—13:10 and 14:1—15:6 receive seventeen pages of attention.[6] In Tom Schreiner's 504-page *Paul Apostle of God's Glory in Christ: A Pauline Theology* scattered references to Rom 12:1—15:6 appear in chapters on "Spiritual Gifts" (21 pages), "Government" (5 pages) and "Unity and Food" (7 pages).[7] Donald Guthrie's revised 1,064-page *New Testament Theology* allots 60 pages to New Testament ethics of which only 13 are Pauline.[8]

As one would expect, commentaries do somewhat better. Equal treatment in a Romans commentary would be 18.75 percent. Among some major Romans commentaries published in the last twenty-five years, Colin Kruse devotes 66 of 627 pages (10.5 percent) to Rom 12:1—15:6,[9] Douglas Moo 140 of 1012 pages (13.8 percent),[10] Arland Hultgren 80 of 804 pages (10 percent),[11] Brendan Byrne 66 of 536 pages (13 percent),[12] Grant Osborne 63 of 448 pages (14 percent),[13] Ben Witherington 65 of 421 pages (15.5 percent),[14] Craig Keener 28 of 268 pages (10.4 percent),[15] Tom Schreiner 92 of 994 pages (9.25 percent),[16] Luke Timothy Johnson 36 of 239 pages (15 percent),[17] Robert Mounce 36 of 301 pages (11.8 percent),[18] Peter Stuhlmacher 50 of 269 pages (18.9 percent),[19] John Stott 58 of 432

---

4. Rosner, *Understanding Paul's Ethics*, 3, 19, 21, 41, 54, 61.
5. Meeks, *The Moral World of the First Christians*, 13, 37, 133.
6. Dunn, *The Theology of Paul*, 543–45, 554, 674–80, 680–89.
7. Schreiner, *A Pauline Theology*, 334–51, 351–70, 448–51.
8. Guthrie, *New Testament Theology*, 912–25.
9. Kruse, *Romans*, 460–531.
10. Moo, *Romans*, 744–884.
11. Hultgren, *Romans*, 435–528.
12. Byrne, *Romans*, 361–428.
13. Osborne, *Romans*, 319–65.
14. Witherington, *Romans*, 280–325.
15. Keener, *Romans*, 142–70.
16. Schreiner, *Romans*, 639–703.
17. Johnson, *Reading Romans*, 187–223.
18. Mounce, *Romans*, 229–65.
19. Stuhlmacher, *Romans*, 185–235.

pages (13.4 percent),[20] Joseph Fitzmyer 77 of 793 pages (8.4 percent),[21] and James Dunn 138 of 976 pages (13.2 percent).[22] Only German scholar Peter Stuhlmacher's Romans commentary gives proportionate attention to Rom 12:1—15:6. Otherwise, commentators fall short, with Catholic scholar Joseph Fitzmyer ranking as the lowest at 8.4 percent. Paul's ethical teachings in Romans do not appear to be a high priority in scholarly circles. Yet there is significant ethical material in Rom 12:1—15:6 that has much to say about how we ought to live as Christians in our global society.

THE CHALLENGES

Scholarly neglect can be attributed to several factors. There are some unique challenges. First, Romans is the only Pauline letter that addresses both Jews ("Now if you a Jew . . ." Rom 2:17) and Gentiles ("Now I am speaking to you Gentiles," Rom 11:13). As an apostle to the Gentiles, Paul's focus elsewhere is singularly non-Jewish.[23] Second, Paul's other letters are written to churches that he or a co-worker (Colossians) planted and he writes to address problems that have cropped up during his absence. Third, Paul had not planted or even visited the Roman church, although he had planned to do so without success several times (1:13a). Indeed, his explicit reason for writing is to announce an upcoming first visit (1:10–14; 15:23–28) with the intent to engage in evangelism among the Gentiles (1:13b) and to give and receive spiritual encouragement from the Roman Christians (1:12). Finally, a single chaptered letter such as Philemon would suffice to announce a visit. This leaves fifteen chapters for which to account, eleven of which consist of profound theologizing and four of weighty moralizing.

THE PURPOSE

Although the purpose of Romans has been extensively debated,[24] there is a reasonable construal that allows us to understand and judiciously apply Paul's theology and ethics. Romans can readily be seen as Paul's letter of self-introduction, providing the Roman church with a summary of his

---

20. Stott, *Romans*, 317–75.
21. Fitzmyer, *Romans*, 637–704.
22. Dunn, *Romans*, 705–843.
23. First and Second Corinthians, Galatians, Ephesians, Philippians, Colossians, 1–2 Thessalonians, and Philemon were written to Gentile congregations or parishioners.
24. See, for example, Donfried, ed., *The Romans Debate*; Das, *Solving the Romans Debate*; and Longenecker, *Introducing Romans*.

gospel message and an overview of his ministry as an apostle to the Gentiles (1:5; 15:15–18). Romans 1:16–17 is his mission statement:[25]

> For I am not ashamed of the gospel; it is the power of God for salvation to everyone who has faith, to the Jew first and also to the Greek. For in it the righteousness of God is revealed through faith for faith; as it is written, "The one who is righteous will live by faith."[26]

Romans 1:18—11:36 would then be the theological unpacking of this statement and 12:1—15:6 the ethical implications of the preceding chapters (Παρακαλῶ οὖν ὑμᾶς, "I urge you therefore").

Why Paul would be writing a letter of self-introduction can be surmised from statements in Rom 15. After his Roman visit, Paul states that he plans to engage in missionary work west of Rome and hopefully all the way to Spain (15:28). To fulfill this plan, Paul would need a supporting church that is closer to Spain than his home base of Syrian Antioch (Acts 13:1–3; 14:25–28; 18:22–23). Romans would thus be a propaedeutic letter, written with the hope that the Roman church would catch a vision of Paul's gospel and mission and want to support him as Paul moves west into unchartered territory (2 Cor 10:16; cf. Rom 15:24 "to have you assist me on my journey").

While propaedeutics may well explain Rom 1–11, the four chapters of moral sermonizing that follow require additional justification. On what authority does Paul give the Roman church moral imperatives regarding the Christian life and by extension us today? Structurally Romans fits Paul's other letters in moving from theology ("We know that . . .") to Christian life implications ("Since we know Christ died for our sins . . . let us live accordingly"). It helps that no other apostle could claim to be the church's founder. This is clear from Paul's statement in Rom 15:20: "I make it my ambition to proclaim the good news, not where Christ has already been named, so that I do not build on someone else's foundation"—Paul's circumspect way of referring to another apostle's church plant. The Roman church probably had its beginning with those "Jews from Rome" who heard Peter preach at the feast of Pentecost 27 years earlier and returned to Rome as converts (Acts 2:10), worshipping together as baptized Christian believers (Acts 2:38).

---

25. First put forward in 1982 by Robert Jewett ("Romans as an Ambassadorial Letter," 5–20).

26. Unless otherwise indicated, all English Scripture references are from the NRSV.

The Roman church is not a complete unknown to Paul. He greets numerous congregants in Rom 16 as co-workers (vv. 3, 4), co-laborers (vv. 6, 12), and even as co-apostles (v. 7). These connections were probably made after Emperor Claudius expelled the Jews from Rome in AD 49 due to what Roman historian Suetonius calls "disturbances by Jews at the instigation of Chrestus" (*Claud.* 25; cf. Acts 18:2).

There were also a significant number of Gentiles in the Roman church, which Paul claims to have authority over, stating: "Now I am speaking to you Gentiles. Inasmuch then as I am an apostle to the Gentiles" (Rom 11:13; cf. Eph 2:11; 3:1). As Paul reiterates his reason for writing (following epistolary custom), he states: "Nevertheless on some points I have written to you rather boldly by way of reminder, because of the grace given me by God to be a minister of Christ Jesus to the Gentiles." That the Roman Gentiles are his primary target audience is supported by several distinctives of the letter. First, Paul's explicit reason for visiting is "that I may reap some harvest among you as I have among the rest of the Gentiles" (Rom 1:13). Also, Paul cites Old Testament texts (drawn from the Law, the Prophets, and the Psalter) that specifically refer to God's inclusion of the Gentiles:

> Rom 15:9: and in order that the Gentiles might glorify God for his mercy. As it is written, "Therefore I will confess you among the Gentiles, and sing praises to your name" (Ps 18:49).
>
> Rom 15:10: "Rejoice, O Gentiles, with his people" (Deut 32:43).
>
> Rom 15:11: "Praise the Lord, all you Gentiles, and let all the peoples praise him" (Ps 117:1).
>
> Rom 15:12: and again Isaiah says, "The root of Jesse shall come, the one who rises to rule the Gentiles; in him the Gentiles shall hope" (Isa 11:10).

THE ISSUE OF RELEVANCE

Even though Paul tackles issues specific to first-century Roman Christians, the topics have transcultural import. The list of topics includes: (1) use of spiritual gifts (Rom 12:3–8); (2) congregational relationships (12:9–13); (3) social witness (12:14–18); (4) revenge (12:19–21); (5) dealing with governing authorities (13:1–5); (6) paying one's taxes (13:6–7); (7) avoiding debt (13:8); (8) Decalogue obedience (13:9–10); (9) not being caught unawares by Christ's return (13:11–14); and (10) dealing with less mature Christian brothers and sisters (14:1—15:3).

There are some cautions. The exhortations in Rom 12–15 do not have an immediate one-to-one correspondence. There are cultural differences to be considered. For example, ours is a democracy, while theirs was an absolute monarchy over an empire that encompassed the virtual known world at that time. Governing authorities included the emperor, whom Romans considered divine and worthy of worship, and those who governed the imperial provinces on his behalf. Also (as already noted), the Roman church was bi-ethnic, including both Jewish and non-Jewish converts and quite unlike most global churches today. This makes Romans an *occasional* letter that addresses concerns specific to Christians living in the imperial capital and instructs parishioners who have differing religious taboos such as Kosher food laws.

However, there is much in Rom 12–15 that is not only relevant but also essential for us today. Much of what is found in these chapters finds a parallel in the teachings of Jesus. For instance, Paul states, "the kingdom of God is righteousness, peace and joy in the Holy Spirit" (Rom 14:17). Although rare in Paul, "the kingdom of God" is central to Jesus' teachings, where the phrase is shorthand for God's rule over a people who are called to be righteous as God himself is righteous (Matt 5:48) and thus to be salt and light in our world (Matt 5:13–15). In turn, much of what is found in Jesus' teachings finds a parallel in Israel's law code:

> "Do not think that I have come to abolish the law or the prophets; . . . For truly I tell you, until heaven and earth pass away, not one letter, not one stroke of a letter, will pass from the law until all is accomplished. Therefore, whoever breaks one of the least of these commandments, and teaches others to do the same, will be called least in the kingdom of heaven; but whoever does them and teaches them will be called great in the kingdom of heaven" (Matt 5:17–19).

This indicates that there are fundamental moral imperatives irrespective of time, ethnicity, and location.

It is further to be noted that Paul's ethical teaching is plural versus singular: "I urge ($παρακαλῶ$)[27] you [plural $ὑμᾶς$] brothers and sisters to . . ." His is a "social" ethic. Paul is concerned with how we behave toward one another and toward society at-large; toward those inside the church as well as toward those outside. Also, Paul's instructions at Rom 12:1 begin with

---

27. All Greek text references are from the Nestle-Aland 27th edition.

"therefore" (οὖν). How Christians are obligated to live flows directly from the gospel presented in the preceding chapters.

Finally, Paul defines the goal of his mission "to be a minister of Christ Jesus to the Gentiles in the priestly service of the gospel of God, so that the offering of the Gentiles may be acceptable, sanctified by the Holy Spirit" and "to win obedience from the Gentiles in word and deed" (Rom 15:16, 18).

THE PRINCIPAL INJUNCTION: ROMANS 12:1–2

Paul begins at Rom 12:1 with a core ethical injunction: "Present yourselves (literally 'bodies') as a living-holy-pleasing sacrifice to God, which is your carefully thought out service" (τὴν λογικὴν λατρείαν ὑμῶν). To do this they must "stop being conformed to this age and be transformed by the renewing of your mind (negative plus present imperative) so that you can approve what is God's good-pleasing-perfect will" (one article plus three adjectives).

The mind is key. The mind is central to every decision that we make. In Greco-Roman anatomy, the heart is the seat of the human will, the intestines the seat of human emotions (cf. "gut" feelings), and the mind the seat of human knowledge and thinking. Our feelings and decisions flow from our thinking. Adultery doesn't happen in a vacuum ("You shall not commit adultery"; Rom 13:9). We look, we lust, we act on that lust (Matt 5:25–28). Murder doesn't happen in a vacuum ("You shall not murder"; Rom 13:9). We look, we feel angry, we act on that anger (Matt 5:21–22). Stealing doesn't happen in a vacuum ("You shall not steal"); nor does coveting what our neighbor possesses ("You shall not covet"; Rom 13:9). We look, we lust, we act on that lust.

Because like gives birth to like, to act spiritually requires that we think spiritually (1 Cor 3:6). This is what Paul means by the renewing of the mind (τῇ ἀνακαινώσει τοῦ νοός). This renewal is not a matter of mere human effort but of God's Spirit working in us. In short, we must experience spiritual birth to think spiritual thoughts. To think spiritual thoughts is not instantaneous. It is an ongoing process. However, as believers we have access to "the mind of Christ" (1 Cor 2:16) and "the power of the Holy Spirit" (2 Cor 6:6). As the mind undergoes renewal, so our decisions change. The Greek verb in Rom 12:2 is in the present tense. We are in the *process* of being mentally renewed and thus in the *process* of being transformed in our Christian walk (μεταμορφοῦσθε).

The centrality of the mind suggests that τὴν λογικὴν λατρείαν ὑμῶν has to do with our reasoning. The Greek λογικός refers to thoughts that take shape in the mind and then are worked out in life as action (LSJ s.v.). Τὴν λογικὴν λατρείαν ὑμῶν is difficult to translate into English. Commonly found are "our acceptable" (KJV, NKJV, DRA, ERV, Geneva, Bishops, NET, NJB), "intelligent" (DBY, ETH, MRD, YLT, NJB), "true" (NLT; TNIV), or "spiritual" (most modern translations) "worship" or "service." Serving and worshipping God in a carefully thought out fashion is the main idea. Yet, the "how" of the mind matters. The religious worship and sacrifice we offer to God that is "living-holy-pleasing" is one that flows from spiritual reasoning and godly thoughts.

What Paul's opening moral imperative of a renewed mind looks like in everyday life is spelled out in the verses that follow.

SPIRITUAL GIFTS AND CORPORATE CHARACTER IMPERATIVES: ROMANS 12:3–16

Paul's opening moral imperative is followed by instructions about congregational unity midst a diversity of spiritual gifts. At first glance the sequence is surprising. However, the ability of a bi-ethnic congregation in the imperial capital to pull together and present a united front is of first importance.

Romans 12:3–8 reads as a *Reader's Digest* condensed version of 1 Cor 12:4–31. Similar to 1 Corinthians the emphasis is on "many members but one body." "One" appears three times in Rom 12:4–5: "For as in *one* [human] body there are many members and not all the members have the same function, so we, who are many, are *one* [spiritual] body in Christ, and individually we are members *one* of another (τὸ δὲ καθ' εἷς ἀλλήλων μέλη)." Then in vv. 16 and 18 Paul commands the Roman church to "live in harmony with one another" (τὸ αὐτὸ εἰς ἀλλήλους φρονοῦντες; v. 16) and "peaceably with all as far as possible" (μετὰ πάντων ἀνθρώπων εἰρηνεύοντες; v. 18). This is also the way he concludes at Rom 15:5–6: "May the God of steadfastness and encouragement grant you to live in harmony with one another in accordance with Christ Jesus (τὸ αὐτὸ φρονεῖν ἐν ἀλλήλοις κατὰ Χριστὸν Ἰησοῦν), so that together you may with one voice glorify the God and Father of our Lord Jesus Christ." Presenting a united front is critical when facing social hostilities. Internal dissension is the last thing that the world needs to see. Paul's repeated commendation to live harmoniously and peaceably indicates that this was a difficult task for the church then and remains an equally difficult one for believers today.

Fortunately for us, unity is possible on a practical level because it is a theological reality. Paul states that the gifts (ἔχοντες δὲ χαρίσματα) and corresponding functions (πρᾶξιν) are "assigned to each as *God* has so determined" (ἑκάστῳ ὡς ὁ θεὸς ἐμέρισεν μέτρον πίστεως; Rom 12:3; cf. determined by the Holy Spirit in 1 Cor 12:11 and by Christ in Eph 4:11). This is by "God's grace" and not by human ability, training, or effort (κατὰ τὴν χάριν τὴν δοθεῖσαν ἡμῖν). So we should not be proud or boast as if this is our own doing. Nor should we be jealous of someone else's gift or feel unproductive because we do not have what some consider to be the more essential gifts or functions. For Christ's "body" to function as a well-oiled machine, we must literally "think the same thing" (τὸ αὐτὸ εἰς ἀλλήλους φρονοῦντες) and "not think too highly of ourselves" (μὴ τὰ ὑψηλὰ φρονοῦντες) or "think we are wiser than the other members" (γίνεσθε φρόνιμοι παρ' ἑαυτοῖς; Rom 12:3, 16) "Think," "think," and "think." It all comes back to the mind.

Unity is an issue at Corinth in part because of the elevation of certain spiritual gifts over others (1 Cor 12:15–17). Paul's emphasis on humility in Rom 12:3, 16 suggests a similar situation. It is interesting that Paul does not begin his spiritual gifts list with apostle as he does in 1 Cor 12:28 and Eph 4:11. Instead, he begins Rom 12:6 with gifts of prophecy, ministry (literally "serving"), and teaching: "We have gifts that differ according to the grace given to us: prophecy, in proportion to faith (εἴτε προφητείαν κατὰ τὴν ἀναλογίαν τῆς πίστεως); ministry, in ministering (εἴτε διακονίαν ἐν τῇ διακονίᾳ,); the teacher, in teaching (εἴτε ὁ διδάσκων ἐν τῇ διδασκαλίᾳ); the exhorter, in exhortation (εἴτε ὁ παρακαλῶν ἐν τῇ παρακλήσει); the giver, in generosity (ὁ μεταδιδοὺς ἐν ἁπλότητι); the leader, in diligence (ὁ προϊστάμενος ἐν σπουδῇ); the compassionate, in cheerfulness (ὁ ἐλεῶν ἐν ἱλαρότητι)" (Rom 12:6–8).

If apostles are understood as church planters and prophets along with teachers as those who grow the church plant, then the absence of apostle from the Romans list makes sense.[28] The Roman church was not the result of those gifted in church planting. Peter's Jewish converts at Pentecost re-

---

28. Paul's broader usage leads one to think that "apostle" is similar in function to a church planter. For one, the term appears in contexts that stress the person's role as a coworker in the church planting process (e.g., 1 Cor 9:1–6; 1 Thess 2:6–8). As "apostles of Christ," Paul, Silas, and Timothy could have been a financial burden on the newly founded Thessalonian church but waived this right (1 Thess 1:1; 2:6–7). It also fits with Paul's understanding of local churches as a house that is "built on the foundation of the apostles and prophets" (Eph 2:20). Moreover, Timothy, who had a Jewish mother and Gentile father, converted during Paul's first missionary visit, thereby excluding him from those who had seen the resurrected Christ—a commonly cited criterion for "apostle."

turned and formed a community of messianic Jews, so the startup of the Roman church was a group effort. The same could be said for the church in Syrian Antioch. It too was the result of messianic Jews, who fled Jerusalem after the stoning of Stephen and persecution by Jewish authorities. Luke records that those who scattered went as far as Syrian Antioch, some preaching to Jews and others to God-fearing Gentiles alike (Acts 11:10–21). Here too the leadership consisted of prophets (such as Barnabas) and teachers (such as Paul) and not apostles *per se* (Acts 13:1–3).[29]

The role of prophet in the early church was a complex one. Although it included at times a predictive element (e.g., Acts 21:10–11), the primary task is comparable to the forthtelling role of Israel's prophets in reminding God's people of their covenant obligations. Done in the context of public worship, prophecy served to convict of sin (1 Cor 14:24), instruct (14:31), exhort (14:31), encourage (Acts 15:32), and guide in the decision-making process (Acts 13:3–4; 16:6–7). How crucial this gift was can be gauged from the fact that it (along with apostle) is labeled as foundational in establishing and growing the church (Eph 2:20).

Teaching is found in all four Pauline lists of gifts. It is paired with "pastor" (literally "shepherd") in Eph 4:11 and is probably to be identified with "a word of knowledge" in 1 Cor 12:8. In the Paul-Silas pairing, Silas had the gift of prophecy and Paul that of teaching (Acts 13:1–3; 15:32). Luke states that Judas and Silas, who were themselves prophets, said much to encourage and strengthen the believers at Syrian Antioch (Acts 15:32).

Gifts of "serving" (διακονία), "exhorting" (ὁ παρακαλῶν), and "leading" (ὁ προϊστάμενος) are found outside of Romans. "Serving" is what all Christians are called to do in one capacity or another in the church. Yet there were some whom the church recognized for the leadership they provided in this area. The NRSV "minister" is a bit misleading, if understood as equivalent to "pastor." The title that the early church gave to διάκονος was "deacon." In the churches at Philippi and Ephesus, for instance, one of two primary leadership functions was that of deacon (Phil 1:1; 1 Tim 3:1–13) and Paul himself singles out Phoebe as a "deacon" (διάκονος) at the Cenchrean church and bearer of this letter to the Romans (Rom 16:1).

Just as the gift of teaching is probably to be identified with "a word of knowledge" in the Corinthian list, so the gift of exhortation is likely "a word

---

29. Barnabas was sent by the mother church to check out the church plant at Antioch (Acts 11:19–24). Barnabas, in turn, sent for Paul who came to encourage and teach an already existing congregation (vv. 25–26).

of wisdom" (1 Cor 12:8). Knowledge consists of facts or truths; wisdom is the right application of these facts. It is also probable that "leading" is to be equated with "pastor" (Eph 4:11). The NRSV "the person who leads" (Rom 12:8) is preferable to "the one who manages" or who is "in charge." All New Testament instances of the Greek ὁ προϊστάμενος point to "leading the way" or "guiding" versus making the decisions. In 1 Tim 3:4–5, a προϊστάμενος is someone who "cares for" the congregation. In Rom 16:1–2, Phoebe is described as a προστάτις or "patron" who helped both Paul and the broader Christian community.

Gifts of financial giving (ὁ μεταδιδοὺς) and compassion (literally "shows mercy" ὁ ἐλεῶν) are unique to Romans. Local churches depend on those who have such gifts. The Jerusalem church was known for its attitude of "having all things in common" so that when a need arose, someone would sell a piece of property and share the proceeds with persons in need (Acts 2:43–47; 4:32–37). "Merciful" is descriptive of those who are moved to compassion by another's ill fortune. It is a quality that God himself possesses and shows toward us as frail human beings (1 Cor 1:3), his people Israel (Rom 11:25–32), and the believers at Rome. At Rom 12:1, Paul states, "I urge you *through the mercies of God*" (διὰ τῶν οἰκτιρμῶν τοῦ θεοῦ). "Grace, mercy, and peace" was a standard New Testament greeting from and to Jewish believers (1 Tim 1:2; 2 John 1:3; cf. Jude 1:2). "It is the merciful," Jesus states, "to whom God will show mercy" (Matt 5:7).

The need for such gifts and gifted people in our churches today goes without saying. What Paul emphasizes both here and in the rest of Rom 13 is *how* one is to exercise these gifts and the kinds of attitudes necessary to be Christ's church in the imperial capital. The list is lengthy: (1) "generosity" (as a giver; Rom 12:8); (2) "diligence" (as a leader; v. 8); (3) "cheerfulness" (in showing compassion; v. 8); (4) "genuine" and "mutual" in love (vv. 9–10); (5) "hating evil and clinging to 'the good'" (v. 9); (6) "outdoing one another in showing honor" and "not lagging in zeal" (vv. 10–11); (7) "ardent in spirit" and "joyful in hope" (vv. 11–12); (8) "patient in suffering" and "persevering in prayer" (v. 12); (9) "contributing to the needs of the saints" and "extending hospitality to strangers" (v. 13); (10) "blessing versus cursing persecutors" (v. 14); and (11) "rejoicing/weeping with those who are rejoicing/weeping" (v. 15). Verses 16–18 form an *inclusio* with Rom 12:3, repeating the need for harmony and humility in both thinking and associating: "Live in harmony with one another; do not be haughty, but associate with the lowly; do not claim to be wiser than you are."

CHRISTIANS AND REVENGE: ROMANS 12:19-21

What follows in Rom 12:19-21 is unique to this letter:

> Beloved, never avenge yourselves, but leave room for the wrath of God; for it is written, "Vengeance is mine, I will repay, says the Lord." No, if your enemies are hungry, feed them; if they are thirsty, give them something to drink; for by doing this you will heap burning coals on their heads. Do not be overcome by evil, but overcome evil with good.

These verses can be explained in part by Claudius's expulsion of the Jews (including Jewish believers) from Rome eight years earlier and subsequent persecution of the Roman church.[30] We know from tracking Priscilla and Aquila's movements that by the time Paul writes Romans, they had returned to Rome: "Greet Prisca and Aquila ... and the church that meets in their home" (Rom 16:3-5). The fact that Paul commits five verses to prohibiting wrath and revenge for both past and present wrongs points to what is currently happening rather than what could transpire. The Greek negative plus present imperative would thus be translated as "stop it" (vv. 19-21). Sometimes we overlook how quickly news traveled in the Greco-Roman world, making it possible for Paul to be quite up-to-date on the readers' situation as he writes. Thoughts of revenge would have been a temptation for those facing persecution in Rome. Paul's response to the temptation to strike back at those who have injured us is to quote from Deut 32:35: "'Vengeance is mine; I will repay' says the Lord" (v. 19).

Rage and revenge are realities that we as Christians now face in the world. The popularity of the TV series *Revenge* is indicative of this reality in the United States. Recent campus, store, and movie theater shootings also confirm this reality. While writing this section, we received a call from my brother-in-law regarding a shooting at Seattle Pacific University, a Christian school of about 4000. My husband's niece was in the classroom building, at the time the shooting occurred. One person was killed and three hospitalized.

---

30. Emperor Claudius expelled the Jews from Rome in AD 49 due to what Roman historian Suetonius calls "disturbances by Jews at the instigation of Chrestus" (*Claud.* 25; cf. Acts 18:2).

CHRISTIANS AND GOVERNING AUTHORITIES: ROMANS 13:1–7

What follows in Rom 13:1–7 is distinctive. The fact that the church is located in the imperial capital poses some unique challenges and elicits theology that does not appear elsewhere in Paul.[31] Once again, we are confronted with the occasional nature of the letter.

Yet there are principles and elements that apply to believers regardless of their location and time. This is indicated by the fact that Peter treats the same issue regarding the Christian's relationship to governing authorities in his letter to the churches in Asia Minor (1 Pet 2:13–17). The situation is different: Peter aims to provide his Gentile readers with a survival kit for living in a hostile society. Paul is dealing with believers who are tempted to resist governing authorities (ὁ ἀντιτασσόμενος τῇ ἐξουσίᾳ; Rom 13:2). However, in both cases the response commanded is the same: submit to the emperor and his provincial governors (ἐξουσίαις ὑπερεχούσαις ὑποτασσέσθω; cf. 1 Pet 2:13–14: Ὑποτάγητε... εἴτε βασιλεῖ ὡς ὑπερέχοντι, εἴτε ἡγεμόσιν), whose job it is to praise those who do good and punish those who do wrong (θεοῦ γὰρ διάκονός ἐστιν ἔκδικος εἰς ὀργὴν τῷ τὸ κακὸν πράσσοντι τὸ ἀγαθὸν ποίει, καὶ ἕξεις ἔπαινον ἐξ αὐτῆς; Rom 13:3b–4; cf. 1 Pet 2:14 πεμπομένοις εἰς ἐκδίκησιν κακοποιῶν ἔπαινον δὲ ἀγαθοποιῶν).

That Roman believers are told to submit to imperial authority can hardly be questioned. The operative statement at Rom 13:1 is: "Let every person (literally ψυχὴ 'soul') submit themselves to the authorities in power (ἐξουσίαις ὑπερεχούσαις ὑποτασσέσθω)."[32] However, it is important to note that the Greek term is "submit" (ὑποτασσέσθω) and not "obey" (ὑπακούετε). The distinction is an important one. The Roman Emperor had absolute authority and his dictates called for unquestioned obedience from his subjects. Paul's term ὑποτασσέσθω, on the other hand, denotes a voluntary act of deferring to the wishes of an equal.[33] As such believers are addressed as free and responsible agents (Greek middle voice "to place oneself under").

---

31. Paul's only other mention of the Christian and the State is his one verse instruction that Titus remind the church plant at Crete to submit themselves to governing authorities (Titus 3:1: Ὑπομίμνῃσκε αὐτοὺς ἀρχαῖς ἐξουσίαις ὑποτάσσεσθαι). By comparison, Romans is seven verses in length and includes the theological rational that governing authorities are instituted by God (τῇ ἐξουσίᾳ τῇ τοῦ θεοῦ διαταγῇ) and function as his servants (θεοῦ γὰρ διάκονός ἐστιν σοὶ εἰς τὸ ἀγαθόν... λειτουργοὶ γὰρ θεοῦ εἰσιν; Rom 13:3–6).

32. Cf. 1 Pet 2:13: Ὑποτάγητε πάσῃ ἀνθρωπίνῃ κτίσει. While πάσῃ ἀνθρωπίνῃ κτίσει is often translated "every governing authority," the Greek is literally "every human creature."

33. *BDAG* 1bβ.

Paul uses the same term in Eph 5:21, where believers are instructed to "submit to one another out of reverence for Christ (Ὑποτασσόμενοι ἀλλήλοις ἐν φόβῳ Χριστοῦ)" and in Titus 3:1, where Cretan believers are commanded to submit to governing authority (Ὑπομίμνησκε αὐτοὺς ἀρχαῖς ἐξουσίαις ὑποτάσσεσθαι).

Paul and Peter give a similar reason for submission. Civil authorities are there to punish wrong behavior and reward right behavior: "Do what is good, and you will receive the government's approval . . . But if you do what is wrong, you should be afraid" (Rom 13:3-4; cf. 1 Pet 2:14). The assumption is that the imperial government is doing its duty. There is no hint that Roman or Asian believers are facing political persecution or that the Roman government was unjust or corrupt. If they were, the response would be different especially if obedience to God conflicted with obedience to governing authorities. In this case Peter tells the Sanhedrin: "We must obey God and not human beings" (Acts 5:27-29).

The source of local church persecution is typically unbelieving Jews (e.g., 1 Thess 2:14-16), Gentiles instigated by local Jews (Acts 16-18), or Gentile merchants whose trade in idols was threatened by the gospel (e.g., Acts 19). Paul himself was constantly hounded by Jewish agitators. His appeal to be tried by the emperor is a testimony to a just governing of Roman citizens such as Paul (Acts 26:32). Caesar is "God's servant for your good" (θεοῦ γὰρ διάκονός ἐστιν σοὶ εἰς τὸ ἀγαθόν; Rom 13:4) and "he who bears the sword" (τὴν μάχαιραν φορεῖ; v. 4) is the perspective of a Roman citizen.[34]

Paul gives a second reason for submission that Peter lacks, namely, that civil authorities are instituted by God: "For there is no authority except from God, and those authorities that exist have been instituted by God (οὐ γὰρ ἔστιν ἐξουσία εἰ μὴ ὑπὸ θεοῦ, αἱ δὲ οὖσαι ὑπὸ θεοῦ τεταγμέναι εἰσίν). Therefore whoever resists authority resists what God has appointed (ὁ ἀντιτασσόμενος τῇ ἐξουσίᾳ τῇ τοῦ θεοῦ διαταγῇ ἀνθέστηκεν), and those who resist will incur judgment (οἱ δὲ ἀνθεστηκότες ἑαυτοῖς κρίμα λήμψονται) . . . and wrath (εἰς ὀργὴν τῷ τὸ κακὸν πράσσοντι)" (Rom 13:2-4). It is difficult to determine whether the judgment and wrath are Roman, divine, or possibly both.

Paul concludes with commands for Roman believers to pay their taxes (ἀπόδοτε πᾶσιν τὰς ὀφειλάς), revenues (τῷ τὸν φόρον τὸν φόρον), and duties (τῷ τὸ τέλος τὸ τέλος) and to show respect where respect is due (τῷ τὸν

---

34. Beheading was considered a humane mode of execution to which only Roman citizens were entitled.

φόβον τὸν φόβον, τῷ τὴν τιμὴν τὴν τιμήν) so that one avoid indebtedness to non-believers (Μηδενὶ μηδὲν ὀφείλετε; Rom 13:6–8).

Paul's instruction is equally applicable to us today. Civil obedience to authorities, elected or otherwise, is what our laws call for. We are equally obligated to pay our taxes and to show respect. A situation where governing authorities do not fulfill their proscribed duties is something that neither Paul nor Peter addresses. Again, it is important to recognize that both letters are occasional and addressed to specific readers and situations.

LIFESTYLE IMPERATIVES: ROMANS 13:8–14

Paul goes on in Rom 13:8–14 to detail wrong behaviors that would attract the attention (and wrath) of Roman imperial authority. That he starts with the moral imperatives of the Decalogue is not surprising, since they apply to Jews and Gentiles alike. There is much debate regarding the relationship of Old Testament moral and civil law to the Christian life. However, the fact that Jesus reiterates their relevance for his disciples (e.g., Matt 5:21–28; Mark 10:19) and Paul for the Gentiles in virtually every letter (e.g., 1 Cor 6:9–10; 2 Cor 12:21; Gal 5:19; Eph 5:3; Col 3:5; 1 Thess 4:3; 1 Tim 1:9–10) indicates their transcultural application.

The list in Rom 13 is short: (1) "do not commit adultery" (οὐ μοιχεύσεις); (2) "do not murder" (οὐ φονεύσεις); (3) "do not steal" (οὐ κλέψεις); and (4) "do not covet" (οὐκ ἐπιθυμήσεις). And if there are any other commandments, they are summed up by "love your neighbor as yourself" (singular ἀγαπήσεις τὸν πλησίον σου), for the person who loves his/her neighbor does no wrongdoing (worthy of Roman imperial attention). "Honoring mother and father" is a surprising omission, given that it was a virtue highly esteemed in Greco-Roman society. One assumes that "do not bear false witness," which is missing, would be included in "any other commandment" and is included in loving one's neighbor. Indeed, Paul states that the person who loves one's neighbor has fulfilled the law (vv. 8, 10; πλήρωμα οὖν νόμου ἡ ἀγάπη). The term ἀγάπη denotes a waiving of self-interest for the sake of another.[35] It is not unlike the Greek term ὑποτασσέσθω, "submit." To love is to be willing to sacrifice even to death (John 10:11). This is often quite different from society's understanding of love both then and now. Ἀγάπη is not distinctive to Rom 13 but it is distinctive to the Judeo-Christian

---

35. *BDAG* s.v.

tradition. Love of God and love of neighbor sum up the Law for Old Testament and New Testament writers alike.

As an apostle to the Gentiles, it is not surprising that Paul goes on in Rom 13:11-14 to target typical Gentile vices: "Let us live" is literally "let us walk" (περιπατήσωμεν)—a favorite Pauline word to describe the Christian life. The question "walk how?" is answered by the adverb εὐσχημόνως translated in the NRSV as "honorably." It is a Greek word that means of good or pleasing external appearance. "Presentable" or "modest living" is what is in view. How not to "walk" is spelled out by means of three pairings. "Not in reveling and drunkenness" is the first pairing. The Greek terms κώμοις and μέθαις are used of drinking parties involving unrestrained indulgence in alcoholic beverages and accompanying immoral behavior. The second pairing is "not in debauchery and licentiousness." The Greek plurals κοίταις and ἀσελγείαις have to do with sexual excesses that know no moral restraints. Both pairings are descriptive of Gentile behavior that was particularly abhorrent to Jews. Sadly, it is no different today and such social behaviors have become increasingly acceptable even in some Christian circles. The final pairing is "not in quarreling and jealousy" (μὴ ἔριδι καὶ ζήλῳ). It is a pairing found elsewhere in Paul's vice lists (cf. 2 Cor 12:29; Gal 5:29). The basic idea is fighting over pride of place similar to Jesus' disciples arguing over who was the greatest (Mark 9:33-34) and who will sit at Jesus' right and left hand in God's kingdom (Mark 10:35-38). Human nature is such that jealousy often leads to quarreling. In this respect Jews were no better than Gentiles. Even Jewish believers are rebuked for jealousy and quarreling: "You want something but don't get it. You kill and covet, but you cannot have what you want. You quarrel and fight" (Jas 4:1-2).

Paul calls Christians to "put off" (ἀποθώμεθα) this kind of behavior and to "put on (ἐνδυσώμεθα) the armor of light (τὰ ὅπλα τοῦ φωτός) and the Lord Jesus Christ" (ἐνδύσασθε τὸν κύριον Ἰησοῦν Χριστόν; Rom 13:14). The same moral command of "putting off and on" is found in Eph 4:22-25 and Col 3:8-12. How one dresses matters.

The outfits are mutually exclusive. One cannot merely claim Christ as Lord but must behave (or 'dress') in a manner that shows he is Lord. Believers are called to "put off (NRSV 'lay aside') works of darkness" and "put on the armor of light" (Rom 13:12). The imagery of suiting up in Roman armor is found as well in Eph 6:11-14. The word "armor" (τὰ ὅπλα) indicates that the Christian life involves spiritual warfare and that victory lay in being properly "suited" to wage a successful war. The armor in Rom 6:13 and 2

Cor 6:7 is righteousness. The armor here is "light" (τὰ ὅπλα τοῦ φωτός; Rom 13:12) and the *Lord* Jesus Christ (τὸν κύριον Ἰησοῦν Χριστὸν)—τὸν κύριον placed first for emphasis.

For Christ to be Lord of our life, we must "put off" or divest ourselves of "works of darkness" (Rom 13:11) and "the desires of the flesh" (τῆς σαρκὸς πρόνοιαν μὴ ποιεῖσθε εἰς ἐπιθυμίας; v. 14). "Works of darkness" are worldly deeds (τῆς σαρκὸς) typically done under the cover of darkness and not in the light of day. There is an urgency about Paul's moral imperative. The "hour is already" (ὅτι ὥρα ἤδη), "our salvation is nearer than when we first believed" (νῦν γὰρ ἐγγύτερον ἡμῶν ἡ σωτηρία ἢ ὅτε ἐπιστεύσαμεν), and "the night is fast disappearing and the day is at hand" (ἡ νὺξ προέκοψεν, ἡ δὲ ἡμέρα ἤγγικεν). Some have concluded from Paul's language that he believed the *parousia* was imminent. Since Christ's return has not yet occurred, it is sometimes argued that Paul was wrong and hence his instruction not applicable. However, the perfect tense ἤγγικεν denotes that which "has drawn near and now arrived."[36] Jesus' proclamation is similarly phrased in the perfect tense: "The time is fulfilled, and the kingdom of God ἤγγικεν ('has come near'; 'arrived'); therefore repent, and believe in the good news" (Mark 1:14–15). Also, Paul uses the term τὸν καιρόν, which typically refers to a season, age, or era versus a precise chronological measurement.

According to Jewish thinking, salvation history can be divided into "this age" and "the age to come." With the incarnation, some aspects of the age to come have become a present reality. Jesus' presence means that God's kingdom has arrived and that Satan's turf is being invaded and reclaimed as the Lord's (Matt 12:28–29; Luke 11:20). This certainly applies to the church. We are part of God's kingdom albeit not yet fully realized. As such we have a choice to make. There is no grey area. We either choose to fulfill worldly desires or choose Christ as our Lord. It is not possible to serve two masters. There is both a corporate (our local and global church) and an individual decision.

INJUNCTIONS ABOUT TABLE FELLOWSHIP AND COMMUNITY UNITY: ROMANS 14:1—15:3

Romans is unique in treating the issue of Jewish kosher food laws and table fellowship. Yet this is not unexpected given the Roman church and its

---

36. *BDAG* s.v.

Jewish-Gentile constituency. Once again the occasional nature of Romans is evident.

The issue of what to eat and what not to eat surfaces as well in 1 Cor 8–10. However, at Corinth it is eating meat that had been sacrificed to an idol, while at Rome it is Jewish Christians keeping a kosher table. Jesus taught his disciples: "It is not what enters a person but what issues from the heart" that matters, thereby declaring all foods clean (Mark 7:19). However, this does not mean that Jewish Christians did (and do) not struggle with giving up a centuries-long tradition. The problem is that the Gentiles were looking down on those who kept a Kosher table as "weaker" brothers and sisters (Rom 14:1).

Paul treats this issue at great length. Scholars do as well. Yet the issue and Paul's response are fairly straightforward. Indeed, Paul's response in Rom 14–15 is strikingly similar to his response in 1 Cor 8–10. The Corinthian church consisted of Gentile believers who had come to understood that an idol had no real existence and those who wanted to but couldn't overcome their conscience (Ἀλλ' οὐκ ἐν πᾶσιν ἡ γνῶσις· τινὲς δὲ τῇ συνηθείᾳ ἕως ἄρτι τοῦ εἰδώλου ὡς εἰδωλόθυτον ἐσθίουσιν, καὶ ἡ συνείδησις αὐτῶν ἀσθενὴς οὖσα μολύνεται; 1 Cor 8:7). The concern at Corinth was meat that was leftover from temple sacrifices and sold at market or served while dining out. The temple priests took the first portion and the rest was sold to local vendors, who in turn sold it to the general public. Some Corinthians understood that because idols had no real existence, eating idol meat was of no moral consequence, but not all Corinthian believers thought this. Some believers saw Corinthian leaders eat sacrificed meat while out dining and were encouraged to do the same. However, they still thought the gods had power and that eating temple sacrifices gave the gods power over them. And they were looked down upon for their lack of theological conviction. To eat or not to eat resulted in a crisis of conscience that paralyzed the believer (ἐὰν γάρ τις ἴδῃ σὲ τὸν ἔχοντα γνῶσιν ἐν εἰδωλείῳ κατακείμενον, οὐχὶ ἡ συνείδησις αὐτοῦ ἀσθενοῦς ὄντος οἰκοδομηθήσεται εἰς τὸ τὰ εἰδωλόθυτα ἐσθίειν; ἀπόλλυται γὰρ ὁ ἀσθενῶν ἐν τῇ σῇ γνώσει; 1 Cor 8:10–11).

In the case of the Roman church, centuries of following Old Testament ceremonial laws persisted for some Jewish believers ("nothing is unclean in itself; but it is unclean for anyone who thinks it unclean"; Rom 14:14). They too saw the freedom of others to eat whatever they wished and faced belittlement for their Jewish scruples ("Why do you pass judgment on your brother or sister?" 14:10; cf. vv. 3, 4, 13) and a crisis of conscience about "unclean" foods ("those who have doubts are condemned if they eat, because they do not act from faith; for whatever does not proceed from faith is sin"; Rom 14:23). In both Rom 14 and 1 Cor 8 Paul responds in identical fashion. "Stop quarreling" (μὴ εἰς διακρίσεις διαλογισμῶν; Rom 14:1), "stop judging" (μὴ κρινέτω; v. 3; cf. v. 10), and especially "stop despising" your brother or sister in Christ (μὴ ἐξουθενείτω; v. 3; cf. v. 10). The Greek term ὀνειδισμοί is a very strong one and denotes making light of someone and treating them of no account.[37] Some Romans, like the Corinthians, were being encouraged to eat like the "more mature" believers, resulting in a crisis of conscience—their mind telling them: "Lord I have never eaten such foods per your Law" (Acts 10:14). If they are encouraged to eat either by word or action, Paul states that the encouragers cause that brother or sister to "stumble" (τὸ μὴ τιθέναι πρόσκομμα τῷ ἀδελφῷ ἢ σκάνδαλον; Rom 14:13; cf. vv. 20, 21), "be ruined" (ἀπόλλυε; v. 15), and "destroy God's work" in that person" (κατάλυε τὸ ἔργον τοῦ θεοῦ; v. 20). Similar again to 1 Cor 8–10, Paul states that, if eating such foods causes a brother or sister (who believes this is unlawful, wrong, or sin) to stumble and become morally paralyzed, one must abstain from doing so ("it is good not to eat meat or drink wine or do anything that makes your brother or sister stumble"; Rom 14:21).

In our pluralistic society and religiously diverse world, Rom 14–15 is even more relevant. Drinking in front of Muslims, eating beef in front of Hindus or pork in front Jews who have recently converted to Christianity can have the same effect. It can cause them to stumble. It shows disrespect for the young believer and total disregard for the ethical reality that spiritual mental renewal and lifestyle transformation is an ongoing *process* and not a done deal at conversion (Rom 12:1–2).

CONCLUSION

As we have observed above, Rom 12:1—15:6 contains some of the New Testament's most valuable ethical materials. Even though many New Testament scholars and commentators do not devote the same amount of space to this ethical material as they do to the theological sections of Romans, Paul conveys to the Romans many ideas regarding the church's behavior that resonate with other places in his letters and that continue to offer guidance to Christians today. In fact, virtually all of Paul's moral teaching spread out among his letters is found in very compact form in these chapters.

---

37. *BDAG* s.v.

BIBLIOGRAPHY

Byrne, Brendan. *Romans*. SP. Collegeville, MN: Liturgical Press, 1996.
Das, Andrew. *Solving the Romans Debate*. Minneapolis: Fortress, 2007.
Donfried, Karl, ed. *The Romans Debate*. Rev. ed. Grand Rapids: Baker, 1991.
Dunn, James D. G. *The Theology of Paul the Apostle*. Grand Rapids: Eerdmans, 1996.
———. *Romans*. 2 vols. WBC 38AB. Dallas: Word, 1988.
Fitzmyer, Joseph A. *Romans*. AB 33. New York: Doubleday, 1993.
Furnish, Victor. *The Moral Teaching of Paul*. 2nd ed. Nashville: Abingdon, 1985.
Guthrie, Donald. *New Testament Theology*. Downers Grove, IL: IVP, 1981.
Hays, Richard. *The Moral Vision of the New Testament*. New York: HarperCollins, 1996.
Hultgren, Arland J. *Paul's Letter to the Romans: A Commentary*. Grand Rapids: Eerdmans, 2011.
Jewett, Robert. "Romans as an Ambassadorial Letter." *Int* 36 (1982) 5–20.
Johnson, Luke Timothy. *Reading Romans: A Literary and Theological Commentary*. Macon, GA: Smyth & Helwys, 1997.
Longenecker, Richard. *Introducing Romans: Critical Issues in Paul's Most Famous Letter*. Grand Rapids: Eerdmans, 2011.
Keener, Craig. *Romans*. New Covenant Commentary Series. Eugene, OR: Cascade, 2009.
Kruse, Colin. *Paul's Letter to the Romans*. Pillar Commentary Series. Grand Rapids: Eerdmans, 2012.
Meeks, Wayne. *The Moral World of the First Christians*. Philadelphia: Westminster, 1986.
Moo, Douglas J. *The Epistle to the Romans*. NICNT. Grand Rapids: Eerdmans, 1996.
Mounce, Robert, *Romans*. NAC 2. Nashville: Broadman & Holman, 1995.
Osborne, Grant. *Romans*. IVPCS 6. Downers Grove, IL: IVP, 2004.
Rosner, Brian, ed. *Understanding Paul's Ethics*. Grand Rapids: Eerdmans, 1995.
Schreiner, Thomas. *Paul Apostle of God's Glory in Christ: A Pauline Theology*. Downers Grove, IL: IVP, 2001.
———. *Romans*. BECNT. Grand Rapids: Baker, 1998.
Stott, John. *Romans: God's Good News for the World*. Downers Grove, IL: IVP, 1994.
Stuhlmacher, Peter. *Paul's Letter to the Romans: A Commentary*. Translated by Scott Hafemann. Louisville: Westminster/John Knox: 1994.
Witherington, Ben. *Paul's Letter to the Romans: A Socio-Rhetorical Commentary*. Grand Rapids: Eerdmans, 2004.

7

The Old Testament and Romans
Interpreting the Scriptures Which Instruct and Encourage

Mark J. Boda

If the book of Romans is focused on anything it must be what it identifies as the "gospel." The very first description of this "gospel" within the book is found in Rom 1:2 where it is described as that which God promised beforehand "through his prophets in the holy Scriptures" (διὰ τῶν προφητῶν αὐτοῦ ἐν γραφαῖς ἁγίαις).[1] The closing pericope of the book (16:25–27) returns to the "gospel," now depicted as "my gospel," as "the preaching of Jesus Christ according to the revelation of the mystery which has been kept secret for long ages past, but now manifested, and" (now echoing his initial words in the book, but reversing the order) "by the Scriptures of the prophets (διά τε γραφῶν προφητικῶν), according to the commandment of the eternal God, has been made known to all the nations, for obedience of faith." The book as a whole moves from "through his prophets in the holy Scriptures" to "by the Scriptures of the prophets." It is clear from this letter that the gospel is based firmly upon the witness of the Old Testament.

In this chapter, I will explore the use of the Old Testament in the book of Romans and then reflect on its implications for our own reading of Romans and the Old Testament as Christian interpreters.[2]

---

1. Translations in this paper are drawn from the NASB.

2. This chapter is based on the hermeneutic for Biblical Theology that I laid out in Boda, "Appendix: Biblical Theology." I have expanded the model and here showcased the approach through engagement with a particular New Testament corpus.

DESCRIPTORS FOR THE OLD TESTAMENT

Before looking at the use of the Old Testament in the book of Romans, let us begin with how Romans refers to the Old Testament or Old Testament texts. At times the Old Testament is referred to as the holy Scriptures (Rom 1:2) or the Scripture (4:3) or the Scriptures of the prophets (16:26), at others as the law (e.g., 2:12), as the prophets (1:2), or the law and the prophets (3:21). In certain cases, the Old Testament is referred to as that which is written (e.g., 1:17) or whatever was written in earlier times (15:4) and in still others as the oracles of God (3:2), the commandment (7:12), the word of God (9:6), the divine response (11:4), this saying (12:9), and the promises to the ancestors (15:8). As can be seen, Romans uses a breadth of nomenclature to describe the Old Testament.

The reference to "the law and the prophets" may indicate the well-known Jewish canonical divisions or the more general term for the Old Testament Scriptures of that time, but even more interesting is that the words used for the Old Testament may indicate both written and spoken means of communication.

The majority of the terms reviewed above focus on the written character of the Old Testament, dominated especially by the use of the noun γραφή (Scripture) and the verb γράφω in the phrases καθὼς γέγραπται ("as it is written"; 1:17; 2:24; 3:4, 10; 4:17; 8:36; 9:13, 33; 10:15; 11:8, 26; 15:3, 9, 21) or γέγραπται γάρ ("for it is written"; 12:19; 14:11) and at one point with a reference to Moses writing (γράφω).

However, the oral character of the Old Testament emerges at times throughout the book as characters within the Old Testament are cited. At times, it is the deity who speaks, whether to Abraham (εἶπον, aor. of λέγω, 4:18),[3] Rebekah (εἶπον, aor. of λέγω, 9:12), Moses (λέγω, 9:15), Hosea (λέγω, 9:25), or Elijah (λέγω, 11:4). In other cases, revelatory human figures communicate, including David speaking (λέγω, 4:6; 11:9), Isaiah crying out (κράζω, 9:27), foretelling (προεῖπον, 9:29), speaking (λέγω, 10:16, 20, 21; 11:12), and Moses speaking (λέγω, 10:19; possibly 11:10). In these cases, we enter into the rhetorical world of the biblical text and hear the characters of the text, whether divine or human, as they speak authoritatively: Romans also refers to "the word of promise," emphasizing the oral character of this word which was God's promise to Abraham (9:9).

At times, however, the line between written and oral is fine, as we see in the association of the noun Scripture (γραφή) with the verb saying

---

3. Although passive, thus God is not identified as the speaker explicitly here.

(λέγω) in 4:3, 10:11, 11:2, and possibly 11:10. Similar is 7:7 where "the law said" (λέγω) and 10:6, 8 which refers to a theme like "the righteousness based on faith" as speaking (λέγω). It may be that these are just cases where λέγω is being used in its normal semantic range, that is, that what is expressed in written form can be described as "saying" something. However, this cannot be the case for a passage like Rom 9:17 where "The Scriptures speak to Pharaoh" (9:17).

Descriptors for the Old Testament throughout the book of Romans certainly highlight the Old Testament as a written phenomenon. But they also focus on the Old Testament as a dynamic authoritative word which spoke in the past and continues to speak to its present audience. The law and the prophets are key witnesses of the Old Testament, but as we will soon see Romans draws from beyond these as canonical units.

USE OF OLD TESTAMENT TEXTS IN ROMANS

Having established the general terms used in Romans for Old Testament texts, we now move to the core of the present study, a consideration of the ways in which Romans uses the Old Testament texts. There are many aspects to this topic. The dominant word we will soon see is diversity. Those who want to collapse the approach in Romans into a single model do injustice to the variety and creativity of the letter's hermeneutic.

To categorize the various aspects of the use of Old Testament texts in Romans, I want to employ the imagery of the ancient Roman road. The estimated 100,000 kilometer network of roads established within the massive Roman Empire was key to its economic, political, and military security.[4] It was what made possible the spread of the gospel in the decades and centuries which followed the death and resurrection of Christ. Such an image thus is well suited to a consideration of the book of Romans, this brilliant treatise on the gospel which draws regularly on the Old Testament for its foundational theology.

   4. Hitchner, "Roads, Integration, Connectivity."

As the Roman roads facilitated traffic throughout the empire (say from Rome to Jerusalem), so the hermeneutical roads seen in the book of Romans (Romans roads) take the reader on various journeys from the New Testament message found in the book of Romans to Old Testament texts. We will look at the diverse rock materials which comprise the road, then the diverse levels at which these materials are placed within the road structure, then the diverse routes taken from the New Testament to the Old Testament, and finally the singular intersection through which all routes pass.

Diversity of Materials: Rocks (Canonical Units, Text-Types, and Combinations)

Roman roads were typically 18–20 feet in width and comprised various types of rocks, ranging from the foundational layer of sand, upon which were built slabs of stone encased in cement, then crushed stone in cement, and finally dressed stone blocks. The road was bordered by a kern stone with openings into a stone drainage ditch. The Romans roads utilize a diversity of materials as well, that is, a variety of Old Testament texts and text-types, and brings them together in different combinations and formations.

Torah: Narrative
- Gen 3 (ch. 5)
- Gen 15–17 (ch. 4)
- Gen 15:5 OG (4:18)
- Gen 15:6 (4:3, 9, 22)
- Gen 17:4; OG 17:5 (4:17)
- Gen 18:10, 14 (9:9)
- Gen 21:12 OG (9:7)
- Gen 25:23 OG (9:12)
- Exod 9:16 (9:17)
- Exod 33:19 OG (9:15)

Torah: Legal
- Exod 20:17; Deut 5:21 OG (7:7)
- Lev 18:5 (10:5)
- Lev 19:18 (13:9)
- Deut 5:17–21 OG; cf. Exod 20:13–17 (13:9)

Torah: Parenetic
- Deut 9:4; 30:12, 13, 14 (10:6–8)
- Deut 29:3[ET 4] (11:8)
- Deut 32:21 OG (10:19)
- Deut 32:35 (12:19)
- Deut 32:43 OG (15:10)

Former Prophets: Narrative
- 1 Kgs 19:10, 14 (11:3)
- 1 Kgs 19:18 (11:4)

Latter Prophets: Prophecy
- Isa 1:9 OG (9:29)
- Isa 8:14; 28:16 (9:33)
- Isa 10:22–23 (9:27–28)
- Isa 11:10 OG (15:12)
- Isa 27:9 (11:27b)
- Isa 28:16 (10:11)
- Isa 29:10 (11:8)
- Isa 40:13 OG (11:34)
- Isa 45:23 OG (14:11)
- Isa 49:18 (cf. Jer 22:24; Ezek 5:11)
- Isa 52:5 (2:24)
- Isa 52:7 (cf. Nah 2:1[ET 1:15]) (10:15)
- Isa 52:15 OG (15:21)
- Isa 53:1 OG (10:16)
- Isa 59:7–8 (cf. Prov 1:16) (3:15–17)
- Isa 59:20–21 (11:26–27a)
- Isa 65:1–2 OG (10:20)
- Ezek 36:20–21 (2:24)
- Hos 2:1 OG (9:27–28)
- Hos 2:25[ET 23]; then Hos 1:9–2:1[ET 1:9–10] OG 1:9–2:1 (9:25–26)
- Joel 3:5[ET 2:32] OG (10:13)
- Hab 2:4 (1:17)
- Mal 1:2–3; OG Mal 1:2–3 (9:13)

Writings: Liturgical Poetry
- Ps 5:10[ET 9]; OG 5:10 (3:13a)
- Ps 10:7 (3:14)

- Ps 14:2–3 (cf. 53:3–4[ET2–3]) (3:10–12)
- Ps 18:49; OG 17:50//2 Sam 22:50 (15:9)
- Ps 19:4; OG 18:5 (10:18)
- Ps 32:1–2a; OG Ps 31:1 (4:6)
- Ps 36:2[ET 1]; OG 35:2 (3:18)
- Ps 44:23[ET 22]; OG 43:23 (8:36)
- Ps 51:6[ET4][OG 50:6] (3:4)
- Ps 69:9; OG 68:10 (15:3)
- Ps 69:23–24[ET 22–23]; OG 68:23–24 (11:9–10)
- Ps 107:26 (10:7)
- Ps 117:1 (15:11)
- Ps 140:4[ET 3]; OG 139:4 (3:13b)

Writings: Wisdom Poetry
- Job 41:3[ET11]; cf. 35:7 (11:35)
- Prov 24:12/Ps 62:13[ET 12]/Job 34:11 (2:6)
- Prov 25:21–22 OG (12:20)

The table above reveals, first, that Romans employs texts from all the various *canonical units* of the Jewish canon: Torah, Prophets (Former and Latter), and Writings. Among the Prophets, it is the Latter Prophets which is most commonly used, and among the Writings, the books of Psalms, Proverbs, and Job with possibly one or two allusions to Ecclesiastes (Romans 8) and no citations from Lamentations, Chronicles, Ezra–Nehemiah, Esther, Daniel, or Ruth.[5] Second, in terms of *canonical text-types*, the OG dominates, but is not always used. This reflects the multiplicity of canonical forms of text in the first century AD.[6] Third, the book of Romans uses these various types of materials (canonical units and text-types) in different *canonical combinations*. At times Romans utilizes a single distinct unit from an Old Testament source (e.g., Rom 3:4: Ps 51:6[ET4][OG 50:6]). In some cases Romans strings together a series of Old Testament citations, either without interruption (catena/chain: e.g., Rom 3:10–18: Ps 14:2–3, cf. Ps 53:3–4[ET2–3]; Ps 5:10[ET 9]; Ps 140:4[ET 3]; OG 139:4; Ps 10:7; Isa 59:7–8; Prov 1:16; Ps 36:2[ET 1]; OG 35:2), or with particles to distinguish them (e.g., Rom 10:6–8: Deut 9:4; 30:12–14). At other times Romans creatively interweaves fragments from Old Testament citations (Rom 9:33: Isa 8:14 fused with 28:16; Rom 14:11: Isa 49:18 fused with 45:23 OG).

These diverse uses of canonical materials (units, text-types) in a variety of combinations showcase a biblical theological impulse within Romans, that is, a hermeneutical approach that seeks to read the Old Testament as a canonical unity with authority for a Christian audience.

---

5. Interestingly the books of Psalms, Proverbs, and Job seem to be treated as a collection within the Massoretic scribal tradition as evidenced by the different cantillation system employed for these three books.

6. See further Ulrich, *Dead Sea Scrolls*; Tov, *Textual Criticism of the Hebrew Bible*. Also note the role of memory and textual traditions in Porter, "Paul and His Bible."

Diversity of Levels (Explicit to Implicit)

While there is diversity in terms of the materials used (canonical units, text-types, ways of combining these diverse materials), there is also diversity in terms of levels at which connections between canonical sections are made. These levels range from explicit to implicit.

As already noted above, rock was used at all levels in the construction of Roman roads, but some rock was employed at deeper levels, often in rough form, while other rock was utilized on the surface in dressed form. Similarly in the Romans roads, some rock is used on the surface, with explicit reference, while other rock is buried much deeper, reflecting more implicit reference.[7]

The most explicit method of employment of the Old Testament in Romans is seen in the citation of passages from the Old Testament. These citations are nearly always introduced by an explicit introductory formula (e.g., Rom 1:17), but not always, as the formula one time appears after the citation (Rom 2:24), and in several cases not at all (4:22; 9:20; 10:13, 18; 11:34, 35). There are also explicit references to characters or events (e.g., Rom 4: Gen 15–17, Abraham; Rom 5: Gen 3, Adam; Rom 9: Gen 18–25, Abraham, Rebekah; Rom 10:19, Israel), as well as explicit references to general promises (Rom 15:8) and textual units (2:12, the law; or 3:21, the law and the prophets) in the Old Testament.

At times, however, the connections are implicit, whether a paraphrase of an Old Testament text (10:5), articulation of more general themes in the Old Testament (e.g., 1:20; 8:20, "the creation"), a concept (e.g., 2:25, "circumcision"), legal tradition (e.g., chapter 14, food and festal laws), or metaphorical language (use of priestly language in 12:1–2 in reference to obedience; in 15:16 in reference to ministry).

There has been some reflection on the rhetorical significance of these various levels.[8] It is uncertain whether one can say with confidence that explicit citation signals greater rhetorical significance than implicit. In some cases, the implicit may even have a greater impact on meaning as Romans reads an explicitly cited text through the lens of a text that is only implicitly referenced. The various strategies, however, do highlight the ubiquity of the influence of the Old Testament on the book of Romans.

---

7. For this diversity see the articles by Moyise, Porter, and Ciampa in Porter and Stanley, eds., *As It Is Written*, 15–58.

8. See especially Moyise, "Quotations," 16.

The Letter to the Romans

Diversity of Routes (Continuity versus Discontinuity)

While there is diversity in terms of the materials used and the levels at which connections between canonical texts and sections are made, there is also diversity in the route used for such connections.[9] Within Romans, we find various routes that reflect a sliding scale from continuity to discontinuity.

The Old Testament Initiates What the New Testament Continues

The closest and most direct "route" between the Old and New Testaments in Romans is the one in which *the Old Testament initiates what the New Testament continues.* According to this route, a principle found in the Old Testament is carried over into the New Testament. This route represents the greatest continuity between the testaments. Very common in Romans is the introduction of a principle in the Old Testament whether theological (God is creator or God even reaches out to those who don't seek him), missiological (priestly values have enduring relevance, Rom 15), redemptive (faith of Abraham, Rom 4), ethical ("Love your neighbor as yourself"; Lev 19:18 in Rom 13:8–10; or how to treat one's enemy Deut 32:35; Prov 25:21, 22 in Rom 12:20). In Romans, these Old Testament principles had enduring relevance for the Christian community. Admittedly, there remains some element of discontinuity since the principle initiated in the Old Testament is always seen through the lens of the work of Christ in his death, resurrection, and ascension sending the Spirit (see below under Intersection). So although ethical principles from the law may be identical, the process by which it is fulfilled has shifted (precisely as indicated in Jer 31:31–34; Ezek 36:27; cf. 2 Cor 3:1–18; Heb 8:7–12).

The Old Testament Falls Short of the New Testament, Which Surpasses It

The longest and most indirect "route" between the Old and New Testament in Romans is the one in which *the Old Testament falls short of the New Testament, which surpasses it.* This route represents the greatest discontinuity between the testaments. Romans 10:5 cites Lev 18:5 in order to describe a righteousness that comes through the law, rather than through faith. The

---

9. This is a controversial area of study, especially concerning the relationship between the Pauline tradition and the broader use of authoritative traditions within the Greco-Roman and Second Temple Judaism contexts. For the purpose of this volume, I have chosen to use categories which are helpful to those who are preaching Romans.

treatment of the ceremonial law (food, festal, Leviticus–Deuteronomy) in Romans is related to this category (Rom 14). At the same time, it is important to note that such law was legitimate revelation that was operative for a time and thus does have theological significance as a revelatory witness as understood within its own phase of redemptive history (see Matt 23:23; Luke 11:37–42).

The Old Testament is Reactualized in the New Testament in order to Complete It

Between these two extremes of routes between the Old and New Testaments are a variety of routes with relatively similar directness and length, representing a balance between continuity and discontinuity. Some passages in Romans reveal that *the Old Testament is reactualized in the New Testament in order to complete it*. The most common name for this route is "typology," defined by Dockery as seeking "to discover a correspondence between people and events of the past and of the future or present."[10] In typology, the Old Testament is being relived in the New Testament. Patterns established through people, events, and institutions are connected to New Testament features. The most famous example of typology in the book of Romans is found in Rom 5 as Christ is identified as the Second Adam.[11]

The Old Testament Promises that which is Fulfilled in the New Testament

Other passages reveal that *the Old Testament promises someone who or something which is fulfilled in the New Testament*. Such promises can have multiple fulfillments in the New Testament. Showcasing this approach is Rom 1:2–3, which highlights the fulfillment of the Old Testament promise of a messianic royal figure in Jesus Christ, and Rom 10:19–20, which reveals the fulfilment of the expected salvation of the Gentiles.

---

10. Dockery, "Typological Exegesis," 166. Although sharing certain hermeneutical values in common, there is a distinction between typology and allegory, with typology retaining focus on the meaning of the Old Testament elements within their literary and biblical-theological context and allegory focusing on the meaning of the elements as symbols abstracted from their literary contexts; with thanks to Sid Sudiacal for further reflection: Bienert, *Allegoria und Anagoge*; Daniélou, "La typologie"; Young, *Biblical Exegesis and the Formation of Christian Culture*, 162; Martens, "Revisiting the Allegory/Typology Distinction."

11. See Schliesser, *Abraham's Faith in Romans 4*, 405 and debate over whether Abraham is a typological figure or exemplar figure.

The Letter to the Romans

The Old Testament Participates in the New Testament by Progressing the Redemptive Story

At times the road taken between Old and New Testaments highlights how *the Old Testament participates in the New Testament by progressing the redemptive story*.[12] On this road the Christian interpreter sees the ways in which the Old Testament story was essential for the realization of redemption in and through Christ and his community. Romans 9:4–5 affirms the experience of the Israelites (adoption, glory, covenants, law, temple, promises, patriarchs) as foundational for Christian salvation, while Rom 5:14 points to the progression of sin, death, and law as key components of the redemptive story that ultimately led to the revelation of Christ.

Summary

These routes which are showcased in Romans highlight continuity between the Old and New Testaments, but also the diversity of approaches that are taken. Of course, there is discontinuity and this should not be overlooked. The book of Romans sees in the revelatory and redemptive work of the Trinity a climax in the story of redemption, but this climax does not discard the Old Testament but affirms its enduring theological authority for Christian interpretation.

Unity of Intersection (Divine and Human)

While there is diversity in terms of the materials used (canonical units, text-types, even ways of combining these diverse materials), and diversity in terms of levels (explicit to implicit) at which connections between canonical sections are made, and diversity in the route (continuity to discontinuity) used for such connections, there is unity in a single intersection through which these various roads must pass. For Romans and the writings of the early church, there are certain core theological values that function as an intersection through which all connections on their various routes do run as they move between canonical witnesses. This intersection has a divine and human dimension.

Divine: Focus on Creator and Redeemer

The Old and New Testaments are *theocentric*, that is, these texts are focused on the revelation of the one true God. The God who is revealed in the

---

12. Cf. Bartholomew and Goheen, "Story," 144–71; Bartholomew and Goheen, *Drama*.

New Testament is the same God portrayed throughout the Old Testament, that is, the Triune God of the New Testament is the God of Israel, Yahweh. This God not only created and continues to sustain this world, but also redeemed and continues to transform this world. Romans identifies the triune character of God from the outset, identifying the God of the gospel as Father ("His Son"; 1:3), Son (Jesus Christ our Lord . . . the Son of God; v. 4), declared as such by the Holy Spirit ("with power by the resurrection from the dead according to the Spirit of holiness"; v. 4). As the book progresses it becomes clear that this same God is the God revealed in the Old Testament. For instance, the God in whom the Jews boast is the same God who will judge the secrets of humanity through Christ Jesus (Rom 2:16–17). This triune God is clearly the creator (Rom 1:20), but also the redeemer who empowers the gospel for salvation to everyone who believes (Rom 1:16).

The key to this theocentricity is the progressive revelation of the Trinity, in terms of both the Son and the Spirit and their role in redemption. The New Testament consistently emphasizes the key role played by the Son, Jesus the Christ, in the redemption of creation (Luke 24:44–45; 2 Tim 3:14–17), and this hermeneutical value is best described with the term Christotelic. As already noted, this plan to redeem creation is part of a plan which goes back to creation and finds its ultimate expression through Jesus facilitated by God's work in and through Israel. The book of Romans clearly reads the Old Testament through the lens of Christ's redemptive work, which is seen as the ultimate expression and final goal of God's redemption. The Christotelic nature of the gospel and use of the Old Testament is clear in the emphasis on Christ throughout Rom 1–8. He is the second Adam, he is the object of the kind of faith exemplified in Abraham.

But Christotelicity should not overshadow the key role played by the Spirit in the history of redemption, for the Spirit is revealed in the New Testament as the essential Trinitarian agent for the realization of the redemption and its associated ethic within individual, community, culture, and creation. Thus the Pneumamorphic character of the divine dimension of this intersection should not be missed. This is showcased in the book of Romans as Rom 1–8 ends climactically with a focus on the Holy Spirit in chapter 8. The Spirit not only sets us free "from the law of sin and of death" (8:2), but also fulfills in us "the requirement of the Law" as we "walk . . . according to the spirit" (8:4) and "testifies with our spirit that we are children of God," crying "Abba! Father!" (8:15–16).

The focus on the grace of God, made possible through the work of Father, Son, and the Holy Spirit in Rom 1–8, lays the foundation for the ethical guidance that Romans provides beginning in Rom 12, drawing regularly upon Old Testament instruction. It is thus not moralistic instruction, but rather ethical guidance founded upon the mercy of God in Christ made real in our lives by the Holy Spirit.

Thus, at the heart of this intersection which provides cohesion to the biblical witness as a whole is the assumption that all Scripture witnesses to one God who has revealed himself and enacted a plan of salvation in progressive ways throughout history.

Human: Focus on Created and Redeemed

While the divine dimension of this intersection should not be missed, it is important to not lose sight of the human dimension. The New Testament assumes continuity between the community which is created and redeemed in the Old and New Testaments. Not only is the same created world in view, but also the same community through whom the Triune God will bring redemption into the world. That community is identified as a single family identified with Abraham who are called by the name Israel in the Old Testament and by the name of the son of Israel, Jesus Christ, in the New Testament.[13] Thus, Old and New Testaments envision a single story of redemption that begins with creation and ends with new creation (Gen 1–2; Rev 21–22) and is realized through a single redemptive community.

Romans also not only assumes that the same God of the Old Testament is the one at work in and through the gospel, but also that this God is at work within the same family of humanity and the same cosmos first introduced in Gen 1–11 and for whom Abraham and his descendants were chosen to bring redemption. The plan of salvation and the community of faith are clearly one plan and one community, which begins with Israel (first the Jew, 1:16) that olive tree root into which Gentiles (11:17–26) are grafted as they receive the full Abrahamic blessing (Gen 12). Jesus Christ is the one who shows that this Jewish olive tree root is alive and as people are saved in and through him and enlivened by the Spirit to become the children of God they offer hope to an awaiting creation that it will be set free from corruption to freedom (Rom 8:19–23). This connection to the

---

13. On the relationship between the church and Israel, see Boda, *Haggai/Zechariah*, 51–57.

broader redemption of creation story found in the Old Testament makes possible the use of the Old Testament throughout the book of Romans.

Summary of Theological Themes: What is the Old Testament Used for in the Theology of Romans?

As Romans employs the Old Testament, drawn from diverse canonical units and text-types, in creative combinations, employed in explicit or implicit ways, and using a variety of hermeneutical strategies that range from continuity to discontinuity, what general theological themes are drawn from the Old Testament in Romans? First, Romans focuses considerable attention on the revelation of God, his character and his plan. The Old Testament is used as the foundation for expressing the key themes of salvation, judgment, sin, eschatology, redemptive history, and election, as well as for highlighting God's character of mercy and wisdom, and his sovereign election and gracious promise. Second, Romans also looks to the Old Testament to shape human response in terms of both faith and ethics. Thus, the Old Testament provides the theological foundation for human awareness of sin (the need for salvation), as well as for human response of faith rather than works for salvation. The Old Testament also shapes human behavior, whether that means living faithfully in the midst of suffering, eschewing revenge, adultery, murder, theft, covetousness, and criticism, while embracing love for one's neighbor and promoting unity within the Christian community. The Old Testament even provides ministry strategy for the church, whether that is reaching out to the Gentiles or extending the gospel to new regions.

RELEVANCE OF THE OLD TESTAMENT

It is obvious from this data above that the book of Romans considers the Old Testament as a key witness for Christian theology, clearly the foundation for the gospel that is proclaimed to the world. At a couple of points in the book this is expressed explicitly. Romans 4:23–24 declares: "Now not for his (Abraham's) sake only was it written that it was credited to him, but for our sakes also, to whom it will be credited . . ." This passage refers to the "written" scriptural dimension of this Old Testament statement, one that is not only for the sake of Abraham "but for our sakes also," that is, the Christian community that now reads the ancient Scriptures. The key role that the Old Testament Scriptures play in the life of Christians is clear as well from 15:4, which reads: "For whatever was written in earlier times was written for our instruction, so that through perseverance and the encouragement of the Scriptures we might have hope." That which is "written in earlier times" refers to the Old Testament Scriptures, and its purpose is identified as "our instruction," an instruction which is not identified in a negative way (that is, to condemn for instance) but rather positively, to encourage the readers to hope.

In Romans, the Old Testament is truly Christian Scripture, texts with enduring relevance for the Christian believer, understood of course through the lens of Christ's first and second advents and the work of the Holy Spirit in this new era of salvation.

ROMANS AS BIBLICAL THEOLOGY

Studying the use of the Old Testament in Romans is thus a helpful exercise for at least two reasons. First, it provides for us insight into the use of the Old Testament for our own exegesis of Romans. It is impossible to understand Romans without taking account of its use of Old Testament texts. Becoming familiar with Paul's interpretive strategies and especially understanding the diversity of the appropriations of the Old Testament in Romans saves us from making gross generalizations and ignoring the key witness of the Old Testament within the rhetoric of Romans. For instance, we can thus easily read the approach to the law in the first half of the book and assume the law is delegitimized, but then find in the second half of the book that Romans actually points to the law as the source for righteousness by faith and for ethical guidance for Christian ethics.

Second, the use of the Old Testament in Romans provides direction for our own biblical theological reflection on the Old Testament. Romans show us the indispensability of the Old Testament for Christian theology, ethics, and preaching, and this explains its continued use in the early church as a direct source for Christian reflection. The canon was not merely 27 books, but 66 (at least) and the first 39 were not merely strained through New Testament passages but seen as directly relevant to the development of Christian theology, understood within the broader drama of redemptive history which included Christ's sacrifice and the Spirit's indwelling. Romans is a model of biblical theological preaching, seen in the very structure of the book which founds present ethics (Rom 12–16) upon soteriology both past and future (Rom 1–11), a rhythm that can be discerned throughout the biblical witness as a whole, especially the Old Testament.[14]

With this let me add an important caveat: don't assume that the New Testament writers are "exegeting" the Old Testament passage, that is, providing a full exposition of the message of an Old Testament text. Rather they are often drawing on a certain aspect of the passage for use in a particular argument. So Christian preachers should not limit themselves to how a particular Old Testament passage is used in Romans (or in any New Testament passage). The examples in Romans show us that the Old Testament has enduring relevance and we need to preach and teach its message on its own terms, understood through the grand story of redemption, but not limited to the ways these passages were used in the New Testament.

ROMANS AND BIBLICAL THEOLOGY

Our study of Romans has shown very clearly the biblical theological orientation of this key New Testament writing: an awareness of the broader canonical witness as seen in Paul's use of all the majors sections of the Old Testament as well as of the broader scope of redemptive history that begins with Creation and will find its fulfillment in the New Creation. But Romans cannot be isolated as a canon within a canon, as a self-sufficient corpus within the biblical witness. The constant connections to the broader canonical witness remind us to resist such isolationism, to constantly consider Romans within the broader Drama of Scripture, those Redemptive and Revelatory Events that take us from the beginning of time until its denouement in the eschaton.

In this way, the book of Romans is appropriately situated in the canon, at the head of the epistolary literature which lies at the key transition between the witnesses to the redemptive drama that flows from Genesis to Acts and the eschatological perspective of the book of Revelation. This canonical position should be constantly recognized as the preacher or teacher unpacks the message of Romans, one that is difficult to ignore because it reflects the structure of Romans itself.

---

14. For example, Exod 19: Yahweh's demands of the Decalogue (ethics) are founded on the salvific event of the Exodus ("I am YHWH your God, who brought you out of the land of Egypt, out of the house of slavery").

BIBLIOGRAPHY

Bartholomew, Craig G., and Michael W. Goheen. *The Drama of Scripture: Finding Our Place in the Biblical Story*. Grand Rapids: Baker Academic, 2004.

———. "Story and Biblical Theology." In *Out of Egypt: Biblical Theology and Biblical Interpretation*, edited by Craig Bartholomew et al., 144–71. Scripture and Hermeneutics Series 5. Grand Rapids: Zondervan, 2004.

Bienert, Wolfgang A. *Allegoria und Anagoge bei Didymos dem Blinden von Alexandrien*. PTS. Berlin: De Gruyter, 1972.

Boda, Mark J. *Haggai/Zechariah*. NIVAC. Grand Rapids: Zondervan, 2004.

———. "Appendix: Biblical Theology and the Old Testament." In *The Heartbeat of Old Testament Theology: Three Creedal Expressions*, 151–82. Grand Rapids: Baker Academic, 2017.

Daniélou, Jean. "Qu'est-ce que la typologie?" In *L'ancien testament et les chrétiens*, edited by Paul Auvray, 199–205. Paris: Éditions du Cerf, 1951.

Dockery, David S. "Typological Exegesis: Moving beyond Abuse and Neglect." In *Reclaiming the Prophetic Mantle: Preaching the Old Testament Faithfully*, edited by George L. Klein, 161–78. Nashville: Broadman, 1992.

Hitchner, R. Bruce. "Roads, Integration, Connectivity, and Economic Performance in the Roman Empire." In *Highways, Byways, and Road Systems in the Pre-Modern World*, edited by Susan E. Alcock et al., 222–34. Ancient World: Comparative Histories. Chichester, West Sussex, UK: Wiley, 2012.

Martens, Peter. "Revisiting the Allegory/Typology Distinction: The Case of Origen." *JECS* 16 (2008) 283–317.

Moyise, Steve. "Quotations." In *As It Is Written: Studying Paul's Use of Scripture*, edited by Stanley E. Porter and Christopher D. Stanley, 15–28. SymS. Atlanta: SBL, 2008.

Porter, Stanley E. "Paul and His Bible: His Education and Access to the Scriptures of Israel." In *As It Is Written: Studying Paul's Use of Scripture*, edited by Stanley E. Porter and Christopher D. Stanley, 97–124. SymS. Atlanta: SBL, 2008.

Porter, Stanley E. and Christopher D. Stanley, eds. *As It Is Written: Studying Paul's Use of Scripture*. SymS. Atlanta: SBL, 2008.

Schliesser, Benjamin. *Abraham's Faith in Romans 4: Paul's Concept of Faith in Light of the History of Reception of Genesis 15:6*. WUNT 2.224. Tübingen: Mohr Siebeck, 2007.

Tov, Emanuel. *Textual Criticism of the Hebrew Bible*. 3rd ed. Minneapolis: Fortress, 2012.

Ulrich, Eugene Charles. *The Dead Sea Scrolls and the Origins of the Bible*. Studies in the Dead Sea Scrolls and Related Literature. Grand Rapids: Eerdmans, 1999.

Young, Frances M. *Biblical Exegesis and the Formation of Christian Culture*. Cambridge: Cambridge University Press, 1997.

Index of Modern Authors

Bakhtin, Mikhail, 59
Barclay, John M., 9, 33, 43
Bartholomew, Craig G., 156, 162
Baur, Ferdinand Christian, 2, 7, 8, 10–16, 28, 34, 37–40, 42–44
Bauspieß, Martin, 10, 43
Becker, Jürgen, 80, 113
Beeke, Joel, 68
Betz, Hans Dieter, 19, 43
Biber, Douglas, 46, 61–63
Bienert, Wolfgang A., 155, 162
Billings, J. Todd, 68, 78
Bird, Michael, 68, 86, 113
Blenkinsopp, Joseph, 124, 126
Blommerde, Acton C. M., 19, 44
Boda, Mark J., 5, 148, 158, 162
Bornkamm, G., 115, 117, 126
Bray, Gerald, 66, 67, 79
Bultmann, Rudolf, 116, 126
Burge, G. M., 111, 113
Burggraff, Philip D., 62, 63
Burns, J. Patout, Jr., 66, 67, 79
Byrne, Brendan, 72, 129, 147

Calvin, John, 69, 70
Campbell, Constantine R., 68–70, 79
Campbell, Douglas., 73, 74, 79
Carlson, Stephen C., 25, 27, 44
Carroll, Susanne, 46, 50, 63
Catford, James, 45, 63
Cohen, Ralph, 59
Colie, Rosalie, 59
Conrad, Susan, 46, 61-63
Cranfield, C. E. B., 67, 72, 79, 81, 95, 103, 113, 118, 125, 126

Daniélou, Jean, 155, 162
Das, A. Andrew, 55, 63, 130, 147
Dekar, Paul R., 125, 126
Deissmann, Adolf, 69
deSilva, D. A., 85, 87, 93, 113
Dockery, David S., 155, 162
Donfried, Karl, 65, 79, 130, 147
Duff, Paul Brooks, 34, 44
Dunn, James D. G., 69, 70, 72, 81, 96–98, 102, 109, 113, 129, 130, 147

Eisenbaum, Pamela, 8, 44
Elliott, Neil, 81, 113
Erickson, R. J., 101, 113
Esler, Philip Francis, 20, 44

Fairchild, Mary, 77, 79
Fanning, Buist M., 104, 113
Fitzmyer, Joseph A., 72, 81, 84, 90, 103, 113, 130, 147
Fitzpatrick, Elyse M., 68, 79
Fowler, Alastair, 59
Fredriksen, Paula, 37, 44
Frow, John, 58, 63
Furnish, Victor, 128, 147

Goheen, Michael W., 156, 162
Goppelt, Leonhard, 90, 113
Goulder, Michael D., 15, 44
Gregory, Michael, 46, 50, 63
Guillén, Claudio, 59
Gundry, Robert H., 103, 113
Gutbrod, Walter, 120, 126
Guthrie, Donald, 129, 147

Index of Modern Authors

Halliday, Michael A. K., 45, 63
Harrill, J. Albert, 94, 113
Harris, Horton, 10, 44
Hays, Richard B., 86, 113, 122, 128, 147
Hegel, Georg Wilhelm Friedrich, 11
Hitchner, R. Bruce, 150, 162
Holland, Tom, 65, 70–72, 79
Horton, Michael S., 68, 79
Hultgren, Arland J., 129, 147
Hunn, D., 17, 44

Instone-Brewer, David, 100, 113

Jewett, Robert, 20, 44, 72, 80–82, 85–89, 94, 95, 97, 101, 102, 105, 110, 113, 131, 147
Johnson, E. Elizabeth, 115, 118–20, 126
Johnson, Luke Timothy, 129, 147
Johnson, Marcus Peter, 68, 79

Käsemann, Ernst, 103, 113
Keener, Craig S., 107, 108, 113, 129, 147
Kruse, Colin G., 72, 73, 79, 129, 147
Kümmel, Werner Georg, 101, 103, 113

Land, Christopher D., 2, 15, 38, 44
Lee, Jae Hyun, 86, 113
Lee, Jae Won, 31, 44
Letham, Robert, 68, 79
Levinson, Stephen C., 54, 63
Lincicum, David, 11, 39, 44
Longenecker, Bruce W., 103, 113
Longenecker, Richard, 130, 147
Louw, Johannes P., 48, 49, 63, 100
Luther, Martin, 69, 70, 74, 79

Macaskill, Grant, 68, 79
Manson, T. W., 16, 44
Martin, J. R., 60, 63
Mathews, Alice, 78, 79
Meeks, Wayne, 129, 147
Metzger, Bruce, 82, 113
Miller, D. M., 8, 44
Moo, Douglas, 72, 80, 81, 84, 86, 94–97, 103, 109, 114, 129, 147
Mounce, Robert, 129, 147
Moyise, Steve, 153, 162

Murphy-O'Connor, Jerome, 8, 44

Nanos, Mark D., 20, 22, 44
Nida, Eugene A., 48, 49, 63, 100

O'Donnell, Matthew Brook, 48–50, 52, 55, 64, 114
Ong, Hughson T., 47, 48, 63
Osborne, Grant R., 79, 81, 104, 105, 107, 109, 114, 129, 147

Perkins, David, 59, 60, 63
Porter, Stanley E., 3, 44, 46, 48–50, 52–56, 61, 63, 64, 70, 79, 82, 90, 104, 113, 114, 152, 153, 162

Qimron, Elisha, 123, 126

Roberts, Maurice, 68, 79
Rose, David, 60, 63
Rosner, Brian, 128, 129, 147
Runesson, Anders, 12, 44

Sanders, E. P., 69
Schliesser, Benjamin, 155, 162
Schreiner, Thomas R., 81, 95, 103, 114, 129, 147
Segal, Alan, 103, 114
Siegert, Folker, 116, 126
Sloan, Robert, 103, 114
Smedes, Lewis B., 68, 79
Sprinkle, Preston M., 86, 113
Stott, John, 129, 130, 147
Strugnell, John, 123, 126
Stuhlmacher, Peter, 129, 130, 147

Tannehill, Robert C., 94, 114
Theissen, Gerd, 103, 114
Thompson, Geoff, 51, 64
Tilling, Chris, 69, 73, 79
Tomlin, Graham, 74, 79
Tov, Emanuel, 152, 162
Tuck, Tag, 77, 79
Tynyanov, Yury, 59, 60, 64

Ulrich, Eugene Charles, 152, 162

Verbrugge, Verlyn D., 82, 114

Index of Modern Authors

Westfall, Cynthia Long, 4, 103, 114
Wilckens, Ulrich, 81, 114
Wilken, Robert Louis, 66
Witherington, Ben, 129, 147
Wright, N. T., 69, 70, 72, 122, 123, 126

Young, Frances M. 155, 162

Zetterholm, Magnus, 13, 44
Zoccali, Christopher, 125, 127

Index of Ancient Sources

OLD TESTAMENT

Genesis

1	90
1–2	158
1–11	158
1:28	102
3	90, 151, 153
3:13	104
3:17–19	108
12	158
15–17	151, 153
15:5	151
15:6	151
17:4	151
18–25	153
18:10	151
18:14	151
21:12	151
25:23	151

Exodus

9:16	151
19	161
20:13–17	151
20:17	99, 151
33:19	151

Leviticus

9:5	86
18:5	151, 154
19:18	151, 154
23:10	110

Deuteronomy

5:17–21	151
5:21	99, 151
9:4	151, 152
28:4	102
29:3	151
29	122, 123
30	122
30:9	102
30:12–14	151
32:21	120, 123, 151
32:35	139, 151, 154
32:43	132, 151

2 Samuel

22:50	152

1 Kings

19:10	151
19:14	151
19:10–18	123
19:18	151

2 Chronicles

29:11	86

Job

34:11	152
41:3	152

Psalms

5:10	151, 152

10:7	151, 152	59:9–15a	124
14:2–3	152	59:19b–20	124
18:49	132, 152	59:20	124, 125
19:4	152	59:20–21	151
24:3–4	86	59:21	124
24:20	89	65:1–2	151
32:1–2a	152	65:2	120, 123
36:2	152		
44:23	152	\quad Jeremiah	
51:6	152	22:24	151
53:3–4	152	31:31–34	154
62:13	152		
69:9	152	\quad Ezekiel	
69:23–24	123, 152	5:11	151
85:8–11	83	36:20	151
107:26	152	36:27	109, 154
117:1	132, 152		
140:4	152	\quad Hosea	
		1:9—2:1	151
\quad Proverbs		2:1	122, 151
1:16	151	2:25	122, 151
24:12	152		
25:21–22	152, 154	\quad Joel	
		2:28	89
\quad Isaiah		3:5	152
1:9	120, 122, 151		
6:9–10	123	\quad Nahum	
8:14	151, 152	2:1	151
10:22	120, 122		
10:22–23	151	\quad Habakkuk	
11:10	132, 151	2:4	78, 151
27:9	125, 151		
28:16	151	\quad Malachi	
28:22	122	1:2–3	151
29:10	123, 151		
40:13	151	NEW TESTAMENT	
45:23	151, 152		
49:18	151, 152	\quad Matthew	
52:5	151	5:7	138
52:7	151	5:13–15	133
52:15	151	5:17–19	133
53	124	5:21–22	134
53:1	151	5:21–28	142
56–59	124	5:25–28	134
59	125	5:48	133
59:3	124		
59:7–8	151, 152		

Index of Ancient Sources

12:28–29	144
23:23	155

Mark

7:19	145
9:33–34	143
10:19	142
10:35–38	143

Luke

11:20	144
11:37–42	155
24:44–45	157

John

1:3	138
10:11	142
14:15–31	108
15:26—16:15	108

Acts

2:10	131
2:17–18	89
2:38	131
2:43–47	138
4:32–37	138
5:27–29	141
10:1—11:18	26
10:14	146
11:10–21	137
11:19–24	137
13:1–3	131, 137
13:3–4	137
14:25–28	131
15	19, 23, 26
15:1	26, 29, 30
15:24	30
15:32	137
16:6–7	137
16–18	141
18:2	132, 139
18:22–23	131
19	141
21:10–11	137
21:17–21	9
26:32	141

Romans

1	71, 110
1–4	3, 36, 65–78, 81, 84, 92, 94, 112
1–8	157, 158
1–11	161
1:1–6	73
1:1–15	65
1:2	148, 149
1:2–3	155
1:2–6	54
1:5	84, 131
1:7	54
1:8–16	55
1:10–14	130
1:12	130, 132
1:13	130, 132
1:14	89
1:15	84
1:16	157
1:16–17	74, 116, 131
1:16–21	66
1:17	73, 78, 149, 153
1:18	86
1:18—3:20	65, 90
1:18—4:25	84
1:18—11:36	131
1:19–32	71
1:20	157
1:30	86
2	71
2:1–16	55
2:5	86
2:6–8	87
2:7	88
2:9	117
2:10	117
2:12	90, 149
2:16–17	157
2:17	86, 87, 121, 130
2:17–29	55
2:23	86
2:24	153
3	50, 110
3:1–20	55
3:4	152
3:9–20	54
3:10–12	77

169

Romans (continued)

3:10–18	152
3:16	104
3:21	149
3:21–23	77
3:21—4:25	107
3:27	116
4	86, 153, 154
4:2	86
4:3	149
4:5	66
4:16–17	119
4:17	66, 149
4:21	66
5	75, 81, 82, 84, 92, 95, 105, 107, 110, 112, 153, 155
5–8	3, 4, 50, 80–84, 108, 112
5:1	77, 81, 83, 84, 87, 112
5:1–3	96
5:1–11	54, 83, 84, 86, 90, 91, 111
5:1–21	82–92
5:2	87, 89, 111
5:3	76, 83, 88, 89
5:3–5	81, 111
5:5–10	88, 89
5:6	66
5:8	77
5:11	89
5:11–22	109
5:12–14	90
5:12–21	83, 86, 90–92
5:14	91, 156
5:15–19	90
5:20	99, 102, 104
5:20–21	91, 95
6	82, 91–94, 98, 99, 104, 110
6–8	81, 84, 92
6:1–8	54
6:1–10	94
6:1–11	94
6:1–14	92, 95
6:1–23	92–99
6:4	102
6:5	95
6:6	110
6:7	100
6:10	95
6:11–14	94, 96
6:12	96
6:13	143
6:14	92
6:15	94
6:15–23	92, 97
6:17	97
6:18	92, 97, 105
6:20–22	97, 105
6:23	77, 97
7	91, 92, 99, 105, 110
7:1	99
7:1–6	92, 95, 101
7:1–25	107
7:5–8	99, 102, 104
7:6	102
7:7–12	104
7:7–25	54, 100–104
7:11	100
7:12	149
7:14	99
7:14–25	104
7:17–23	105
7:18	99
7:23	94
7:24	74, 103
8	89, 92, 100, 102, 104, 108, 112, 128
8:1	77
8:1–17	92
8:1–38	107–12
8:5–8	109, 123
8:9	100
8:9–11	110
8:12–17	110
8:15–28	54
8:16	111
8:17–18	76
8:18–22	108
8:18–39	111
8:19–23	158
8:23	110
8:26	111
8:27	111
8:28–30	105, 111
8:35	76, 81
8:38–39	108
9	54, 153

9–11	3–5, 12, 41, 55, 115–26	11:29	117
9–16	41	11:33	115
9:1–5	119	11:33–36	126
9:4–5	156	12	54, 158
9:5	117	12–15	3, 5, 55, 128, 133
9:6	149	12–16	160
9:6–29	121	12:1	133, 138
9:8	119	12:1–2	134–135, 146, 153
9:17	150	12:1—15:6	128–31, 146
9:24	119, 121	12:2	110, 128, 129, 134
9:24–26	122	12:3	136, 138
9:27–29	120, 122	12:3–8	132, 135
9:30–31	122	12:3–16	135
9:30—10:21	122	12:6–8	136
9:32—10:13	122	12:7—13:10	129
9:31	119	12:8	138
9:33	152	12:9	149
10	50	12:9–13	132, 138
10:1–3	119	12:9–21	54, 138
10:1–12	123	12:10–11	138
10:3	120, 122	12:14–18	132, 138
10:4	120, 122	12:19–21	132, 138, 139
10:5	123	12:20	154
10:6–11	122, 123, 153	13	128, 138, 142
10:8	116	13:1–5	132
10:9	77	13:1–7	140–142
10:10	77	13:2–4	141
10:12	121	13:6	129, 132, 142
10:13	77	13:7	129, 132, 142
10:14–21	122, 123	13:8	132, 154
10:19	120, 123, 153	13:8–14	142, 143
10:19–20	155	13:9	134
10:21	120, 123	13:9–10	132
11	9	13:11–14	132, 143, 144
11:1	120, 123	14	50, 146, 155
11:1–6	119, 123	14–15	9, 28, 39, 42, 145, 146
11:8–9	123	14:1	145, 146
11:11	124	14:1–2	9
11:11–16	124, 126	14:1—15:3	144–46
11:11–36	119	14:1—15:13	55, 129, 132
11:13	130, 132	14:2–4	56, 145
11:15	126	14:5–6	9, 56
11:17–24	124	14:10	145, 146
11:25	115	14:11	152
11:25–32	138	14:13	146
11:26	124, 125	14:13–15	56, 146
11:27	125	14:14	145, 146
11:28–32	115, 118	14:17	133

Index of Ancient Sources

Romans (continued)

14:20	146
14:21	9, 56, 146
14:23	146
15	131, 154
15:4	149
15:5–6	135
15:8	56, 149, 153
15:8–12	43
15:9–12	132
15:14—16:25	54
15:15	45–47
15:15–18	131, 133
15:17–22	9
15:20	131
15:23	8, 40
15:23–24	8
15:23–28	130
15:24	131
15:28	131
15:31	9
16	53, 55, 84, 132
16:1	53, 137
16:1–2	138
16:3–4	22, 109, 132
16:3–5	139
16:4–5	84
16:6	132
16:7	132
16:12	132
16:22	53
16:25–27	73, 148
16:26	149

1 Corinthians

1–4	36
1:3	138
1:12	36
1:27–30	89
2:15	105
2:16	134
3:1–3	105
3:6	134
3:21–22	37
3:22	36
5–6	37
5:5	97
5:11	38
6:9–10	142
8	146
8–10	37, 145, 146
8:7	145
8:10–11	145
9:1–6	136
9:27	110
11:17–34	35
12:4–31	135
12:8	137, 138
12:11	136
12:15–17	136
12:28	136
13:3	97
14:24	137
15:24	97
16:12	35

2 Corinthians

3:1–18	154
4:11	97
5:20	89
6:1—7:4	37
6:6	134
10:10	38
10:16	131
11	76
11:4–21	38
12	76
12:19—13:10	38
12:21	142
12:29	143

Galatians

1–2	16–32
1:6–10	16, 20
1:10—2:10	16
1:11–17	16–18, 117
1:13–14	32
1:18–24	16–18
1:23	116
2:1–10	15–26, 30
2:7	11, 17
2:7–9	11, 38
2:9	10, 35
2:11–14	15–28, 38

Index of Ancient Sources

2:12	22–29
2:13	24, 121
2:14	17, 28
2:14–21	29
3:1–14	32
3:2	116
3:5	116
3:15—4:11	32
3:27	95
4:12—5:12	32
5:19	142
5:29	143
6:6	33
6:12	32

Ephesians

2:11	132
2:18	85
2:20	136, 137
3:1	132
3:9	117
3:12	85
4:11	136–38
4:22–25	143
5:3	142
5:21	141
5:23	74
6:11–14	143

Philippians

1:1	137
3:20	74

Colossians

3	128
3:5	142
3:8–12	143

1 Thessalonians

1:1	136
2:6–8	136
2:14–16	141
4	128
4:3	142

2 Thessalonians

1:8–9	90

1 Timothy

1:2	138
1:9–10	142
1:13	103
2:3	74
3:1–13	137
3:4–5	138
4:10	74

2 Timothy

1:10	74
3:14–17	157

Titus

1:3	74
1:4	74
2:10	74
2:13	74
3:1	140, 141
3:4	74
3:6	74

Hebrews

8:7–12	154
10:18–25	85

1 Peter

2:13	140
2:13–17	140
2:14	140, 141
3:15	116

2 John

1:3	138

Jude

1:2	138

Revelation

21–22	158

Index of Ancient Sources

CLASSICAL WRITERS

Seutonius, *Claudius* 25   132

QUMRAN LITERATURE

4QMMT C 10–16   123

www.ingramcontent.com/pod-product-compliance
Lightning Source LLC
Chambersburg PA
CBHW062047220426
43662CB00010B/1688